Just a Little Somethin'

Inspirational Daily Meditations for the Searching Soul

Rich Melcher

iUniverse, Inc.
New York   Bloomington

Just a Little Somethin'
Inspirational Daily Meditations for the Searching Soul

iUniverse books may be ordered through booksellers or by contacting:

iUniverse
1663 Liberty Drive
Bloomington, IN 47403
www.iuniverse.com
1-800-Authors (1-800-288-4677)

ISBN: 978-1-4502-4406-0 (pbk)
ISBN: 978-1-4502-4407-7 (ebk)

Printed in the United States of America

iUniverse rev. date: 8/4/10

Dedication

Just a Little Somethin' is dedicated to my mother, Lorraine Melcher, who has been more than just a parent, but a friend and guide, helping me become aware of the teachable moments happening all around and within me.

I also dedicate the book to my wonderful wife, Sandra, who has thoughtfully listened to me, struggled with me and LOVED ME THROUGH every moment of this book's evolution, and beyond.

She also meticulously edited *Just a Little Somethin'* and made it possible for it to become fresh and alive with the richness that lives within its pages.

I LOVE you and thank you both!

Introduction

Just a Little Somethin' is an eclectic medley of daily affirmations/meditations, each inspired by a brief yet meaningful quotation. The book provides ideas, stories, prayers and poems that enlighten, encourage and inform readers on their daily walk.

Encompassing topics such as spirituality, interpersonal relations, mental health and motivation, *Just a Little Somethin'* offers a multi-faceted daily meditation experience that may just become a companion on your way.

This book is packed with many interesting stories from myriad sources that bring the readings to life. It also has some qualities of a memoir—employing personal stories and poetry that will give you a sense of who Rich is as an author, an educator, a poet, a regular person. The selected poetry is followed by Rich's pen name, "Corsair," in case you're wondering.

The hope is that you can find a moment each day to pick up *Just a Little Somethin'* and discover a gem or two as you read and think—and, possibly pray—opening yourself up to the moment, and to the wondrous gifts within you.

Rich Melcher: Biography

Rich graduated from Minnesota State University, Mankato, with a Mass Communications major and Speech Communications minor in 1984 and joined the Jesuit Volunteer Corps—a Peace Corps-type organization—right out of college. These experiences as a teacher's aide created a love for teaching that has been displayed in every profession for which he has worked—education, construction, printing, health care, janitorial and customer service.

He and his wife Sandra recently founded a communication consulting business, Authentic Journeys, that focuses on instruction for both youth and adults in the areas of creative writing, respect issues and mental health awareness.

~ January ~

The happiest people don't necessarily HAVE the best of everything . . .
they just MAKE the best of everything.

(unknown)

Have you ever met people who take every setback as temporary and move toward the positive outcomes relentlessly?

How does the song go? . . . "Accentuate the positive—eliminate the negative"? It's been said that it's not what happens to us but how we respond to what happens to us that matters. When we MAKE the best of a situation, we are deciding that circumstances do not rule our minds, hearts and souls . . . and that we have to make the ultimate decisions about what attitude we will take.

Helen Keller emerged outs of a world of silence and darkness to become a powerful communicator! Her perseverance and courage rose far beyond what most of us can imagine. She learned how to "make the BEST of everything" and to soar to great heights—intellectually, linguistically (she could "speak" French), socially and spiritually.

Helen proved that it's all up to us.
Which way will you move—toward the positive or the negative?

January 2

Beauty is in the eye of the beholder.

Unknown

...beauty is not a 'thing' but a special way of looking...

Fr. Anthony de Mello

In his book <u>One Minute Nonsense</u>, Fr. de Mello tells the story of an Eastern master discussing the spiritual world with his students. One asks:

"How shall we find God?"

"By looking at creation, not by analyzing it."

"And how is one to look?"

"A peasant sets out to find beauty in the sunset,
but all he finds is sun and cloud and sky and
earth's horizon—till he understands that beauty
is not a 'thing' but a special way of looking.
You will seek for God in vain till you
understand that God can't be seen as 'thing';
he needs a special way of looking—similar to
that of little children whose sight is undistorted
by prefabricated doctrines and beliefs."

And isn't this what we all need when our expectations are not met? Not to look at the 'thing' with our minimizing and scrutinizing eyes, but with clear vision of the greatness we see before us. I remember Grady, this 12-year-old boy I once worked with in an urban middle school. He was an angry young man who reminded me of a barracuda—silent but ready to strike at any moment. I worked with him for days in a small room that had only a table, two chairs and a drawing pad with huge paper sheets with light blue horizontal lines traveling across them—essentially, giant pieces of loose-leaf paper. We had spent a few hour-long periods there the past few days, with Grady refusing to do *anything*. He acted "dumb," but I knew he was actually quite smart. So I challenged him:

"You tell me a story and I'll write it down on this paper pad with a marker. You can tell me anything, as long as it is appropriate." He quietly agreed and began to tell me this hero story—with himself as the hero, of course. Grady went on and on, as I filled one sheet and flipped it behind to transcribe another! At the end of the hour we both kinda sat and looked at one another in amazement. Two pages of a wild and funny story were penned on the pad. He had broken through and come alive—in a constructive, nonviolent fashion!

It took a new way of looking at Grady to find a solution, and Grady suddenly had a new way of looking at himself. A little tweaking of the vision can make all the difference!

January 3

No trumpets sound when the important decisions of our lives
are made. Destiny is made known silently.

Agnes de Mille

If we had to wait for a fanfare of applause every time we made an important decision, we would be stuck with very few crucial decisions ever being made. The truth is that personal decision-making most often comes in moments of solitude and relative silence.

Many of my most life-altering decisions have been displayed in the world of my *journal*. These entries are not always written in a silenced atmosphere, but in a silenced mind. The words that come out of these moments of personal thought reflect the inner workings of a man who takes seriously the inner-life...and the spiritual movements that shift and sway in my heart and mind.

Quiet moments not only come in times of silence, but when we choose to shut out the noise and haste of daily life and focus on God and our relationship with God. Sometimes it occurs while waiting for the doctor, or driving to an appointment, choosing to shut the radio off...or on a walk through the neighborhood, breathing in the cool, fall air.

It's important to find God in the chosen moments of connection when we discover ourselves, making the important decisions of our lives.

January 4

*Sometimes you've gotta speak your words
and try to live into 'em.*

Corsair

Is it possible to live out every proclamation of virtue, every prospect of purity and every potential constructive contribution that we utter? I don't think so. What we CAN do though is to try.

Recently, I formulated a philosophy of life that I call *the Authenticity Code*. This credo promotes three universal maxims:

~to consistently show sincere respect
~to boldly live a life of integrity
~to courageously express your authenticity

Although I worked hundreds of hours distilling my ideas down to these three basic themes, I realize that living out these precepts will be one of the most difficult challenges I have ever encountered. Is it possible to show **respect** for someone who is in your face with anger or resentment, while you are just trying to find a little peace in your day? Is it possible to live a life of **integrity** with so many negative forces bombarding you each day? Is it possible to be **authentic** in a society that values conformity above most anything else?

YES...it is possible.

It is possible because the alternative is chaos. I believe we are all called to become our best selves—and this takes a lot of work. Character development is promoted throughout our "growing-up" years, so why should it not be a part of your "grown-up" years? There's a German saying that strikes me deep:

If money is lost, nothing is lost.
If health is lost, something is lost.
If character is lost, everything is lost.

So is it so outlandish that I have created and am emphasizing the basic ethical qualities of *the Authenticity Code*? No. And is it possible to reach toward attaining this standard? Yes. We always need a goal, a dream to reach toward—or would we ever get anything done if we did not have a dream or a goal?

Do you have a similar Authenticity Code that guides you on your way? Feel free to borrow mine.

January 5

"Happiness," according to rock star Sheryl Crow: ". . . is not having what you want—it's wanting what you've got!"

Explosive! It's all about *satisfaction* . . . and knowing yourself. These lyrics show a reverence for what we already **have**, not necessarily always getting what we *want*.

Years ago, I developed the helpful acronym...CLAM:

Choose

Less

As

More . . .

This implies being satisfied with what we have and who we are <u>right now</u>! We don't have to be acquiring things or skills or even relationships in order to be OK. We are OK now. We are just fine, as is. We are whole.

But this CAN BE turned inside out, too. Reaching toward what we want, and the time and effort it takes to get there, can be avoided if we're always just *"satisfied"* with what we have. Seems to be the easy way out. Sometimes *dissatisfaction* can help us rise to another level, by getting us motivated & moving toward positive change.

Isn't this how inventions are conceived? Someone is dissatisfied with a process or product and works feverishly to create a gadget that will solve the problem. Dissatisfaction is omnipresent, but only useful if one gets busy to find a solution.

It's helpful to learn the lesson of turning words inside out and looking at them from another perspective . . . but I really do relate to the concept implied in Sheryl Crow's quote (song) above the best. I believe we must make the best with what we've got, moving toward satisfaction with no envy or resentment.

Yet the paradox endures: Satisfaction AND dissatisfaction are both critical in the complicated human condition!

January 6

> *...the sort of person a prisoner became was*
> *a result of an inner decision and not the result*
> *of camp influences alone...it is this spiritual freedom—*
> *which cannot be taken away—that makes life*
> *meaningful and purposeful.*
>
> *Viktor Frankyl, Auschwitz survivor*

What is this "inner decision" that Frankyl was writing about? Some call it the will to live. Frankyl also wrote that the only prisoners who survived were the ones who had something to look forward to—someone to return to, a trade that they yearned to continue improving, or even the desperate need to tell the story of the horrors they were experiencing.

Hanging onto the will to live is one type of inner decision, but what do we use in our everyday lives, to guide us and send us on our way? Dr. Stephen R. Covey, in his book <u>The Seven Habits of Highly Effective People</u> writes that we need to "begin with the end in mind" by creating a *contribution statement* which defines what we can give to our world.

Fifteen years ago I created such a statement that, for years had lay buried under the thoughts and feelings and images of years of daily living—but the other day it arose once again in my consciousness:

I learn from and grow with <u>whatever</u> I've been given
and joyfully give it back.

When I rediscovered this proclamation, it occurred to me that this "inner decision" had been made many years ago. Having a purpose in our lives is probably the most important aspect of being successful—in every way in life. But, as I wrote in one of my first poems in 1982, *"Possession doesn't mean you own something—it means that you KNOW that you own it!"*

You see, just like Dorothy in the Wizard of Oz, I had the answer inside me all the time. Yet I had forgotten that I knew it! Strange, huh? But how many of you have done the same—at times lost your *spiritual freedom* by losing touch with your contribution—your special purpose in life?

Let me tell you, I will never again let mine slip away. Along with my faith in God, it is what will shine in and through me as I express my contribution in myriad ways. Thank you Viktor Frankyl and Stephen Covey for getting me on the path!

January 7

"I happen to believe you make your own destiny...
you have to do the best with what God gave you..."

Forrest's mama; movie, "Forrest Gump"

Although Forrest Gump grew up as a "special needs" child, he had a number of useful and admirable qualities: Loyalty, single-minded focus and perseverance, to name a few.

Forrest was fiercely *loyal* to his mother and to his "first best friend," Jenny—the girl who gave him a seat next to her on the bus on the first day of school. He named his fleet of shrimpin' boats after her—Jenny I,

Jenny II, Jenny III. Forrest also had supreme loyalty to Bubba, his very best Army friend. Forrest retrieved Bubba from an enemy-infested jungle, only to watch him die in his arms. He had risked gunfire and grenades to save his buddy's life, even though Bubba just couldn't hang on. *Loyalty* stands out on Forrest's list of gifts.

He also had a unique gift of *single-minded focus*, whether it was playing a ping pong game or re-assembling his gun in record time, his ability to focus on a single task was remarkable! Sure, he could only do one thing at a time—certainly not a multi-tasker—but his focus on a single task was unbreakable.

And Forrest had a huge amount of *perseverance*. He decided to go for a run and kept running from coast to coast for 3 years. This gift did him well when he started as shrimpin' boat captain, also. Pickins were mighty slim at first, but, with a stroke of luck (and a well-timed hurricane), he persevered into success, in time.

He "made his own destiny" simply by acting on immediate circumstances: ping pong champion, shrimpin' boat captain, (which he had promised Bubba he would seek out . . . and became a millionaire in the process), mega-long distance runner, and much more. This is a classic movie about an *unlikely man with a mission*—see it!

January 8

> *As we stand before any problem, any new task,*
> *any unfamiliar environment, dread may*
> *overwhelm us. We stand there alone.*
> *But the choice available to us, now and*
> *always, is to invite the spirit of God*
> *to share the space we're in.*
>
> *Each Day A New Beginning*

Tested By Fire

Lord, oh Lord, raise me higher
May I not be tested by fire

Tested by water—you keep me from drowning
Tested by wind--the trees sway surrounding
But give me the grace to live well in this place
And may I not be tested by fire!

Tested by fire—tested by fire, may I not be tested by fire!

When my vision's a blur and my mind confused
You see me and act before all my patience is used
If I'm suffering much you drive evil away
You bless me by night and protect me by day!

Tested by fire—tested by fire, may I not be tested by fire!

Give me a way to see Your Truth again
I give You my heart and gain a best friend
I know You will love me in all of my days
Please bless me with grace to follow Your ways!

Lord, give me the grace to live well in this place,
And *may I not be tested by fire!*

Corsair

January 9

Integrity is what you do when no one is looking.

(unknown)

Integrity is an inner quality that shows up on the outside.

In 7th grade, my hockey coach, Mr. Peterson, had a saying to keep us mindful of our status: "We're a class act!" he would say, especially between periods when we were playing a particularly rough & tough team (or, as we called 'em, a "dirty" team), and we felt like retaliating. There was NO FIGHTING in Bantam hockey.

In the first few minutes of one game, an opposing defenseman lifted his stick above his head with two hands and came down on my helmet as if splitting wood with an ax. The blow cracked my helmet and shook me up somethin' fierce! When I made it back to the bench, stunned and angered, my coach reminded me, "We're a class act, Melch!" With that, I let the anger go and focused on the game and my up-coming shift on the ice.

Coach Peterson gave us, handed u an appreciation of *integrity* . . . and I latched onto it with a full grip. Thank You, God, for coaches who teach more than the basics of a sport, but also teach LIFE!

January 10

Are you smart enough to know you do not know?

(unknown)

Working with a new co-worker, I could see myself in many of her blindly proactive, questionable actions. She would attempt to follow through on jobs she knew little or nothing about, and she didn't ask questions from more experienced co-workers before attempting the activity.

I admired her *proactivity* but not her inability to use the knowledge and wisdom of the more experienced workers. This used to be my preferred way of behaving, at times, with a mixture of burning pride and blind fear, trying to "do it myself"—which often brought failure and embarrassment.

But, in time and after many goofs and gaffes, I learned that if you don't know something—ASK! This gets me onto the right track, rather than fumbling and bumbling in my *improvisational ignorance!*

Knowing that *you do not know* can be very helpful. It forces you to reach out and risk asking <u>and</u> feeling a bit foolish. But if you don't know, *you don't know, right?* I have an acronym for this: "*NQDQ*"—<u>N</u>o <u>Q</u>uestion's a <u>D</u>umb <u>Q</u>uestion—this helpful hint works for me; maybe it can be helpful to you.

January 11

You perform exactly as you see yourself.

Dr. Alan Zimmerman

A dramatic scene in the movie Mr. Holland's Opus...Richard Dreyfuss plays a new high school music teacher who finds his lead clarinetist in tears because she feels she's a terrible clarinetist. Fact is, she IS struggling, so tense about her performance—especially since her mother and siblings seem to have great talent in other areas.

Mr. Holland asks her to pick up her clarinet and she ends up squeaking on the low note, instantly chastising herself. He, just as quickly, says, "Stop doing that." Then he asks her,

"When you look in the mirror, what do you like about yourself most?"

"...my hair," as she looks down, almost in embarrassment.

"Why?"

"Because my dad says it looks like the sunset," as she touches her long, auburn hair.

"Play the sunset."

When she looks at him questionably and pulls her clarinet up into position, Mr. Holland says, "Close your eyes..." The timid student submits to his request, relaxes and begins playing. She plays wonderfully then hits that difficult low note like never before! Stunned, she stops playing and looks at Mr. Holland in amazement! "Keep playing! Keep playing!"

And she did! As the song continues, the scene changes to graduation day and there she is, cap & gown, playing the solo she had struggled with many months earlier. She had envisioned herself as the sunset, and the sunset she became!

How do you envision yourself?
Is it a vision worth holding onto?

January 12

We shall continue to persist until we succeed.

Napoleon Hill

My brother was in a severe car accident three years ago that nearly killed him. He had to learn how to walk and talk again, and, since he had been on a respirator, he even had to learn how to *breathe* again. I hadn't had much contact with him for years, but the accident woke me up to see that I couldn't take this relationship for granted any longer!

As his speech developed, we began talking again, which was a blessing for both of us. This "have it all together" brother was now piecing his life back together and I offered my friendship in any way I could. Funny how, although *he* was the one in recovery, he was always there with an encouraging word when I told him of a struggle I was having! Ironic how those who are most in need often end up giving the most!

He came back from the edge of death a couple of times in his early recovery, yet with numerous hours of physical therapy, is walking—often without his cane. And his vocal chords have healed so well that his pre-accident, expressive voice has rebounded quite well. He has been **persistent** and **consistent**—leading him in the direction of a full recovery! God bless, bro!

January 13

(this poem sprung from my challenges with bipolar disorder):

what is it
this energy
this spark of life
which sometimes leaves us
and sometimes overwhelms us?
where is the balance between the glory light
and the pit of darkness?
this "illness" of manic-depression, bipolar disorder,
is really an oversensitivity
to the glory of life
and/or the cliff of despair ~
"in-between-ness"
is what we seek
to be in control, yet appropriately
vulnerable
to be insightful, but not
living in delusion,
to be happy
yet challenging life to
be more ~
balance is what we seek
(what we probably ALL seek)
yet walk that tightrope we will
steadied by the balancing bar
of good habits, healthy risking
and gratitude for the
opportunities to
live and learn

Corsair

January 14

*We herd sheep; we drive cattle; we **lead** people.*

Corsair

How many times have we been tactlessly herded like sheep, or forcefully driven like cattle? Leaders make a huge difference in our lives...let me describe two...one was *Razor*, the other, *Joe*.

The scene—my father's construction company, late 1970s. I was what they call a *"greenhorn"* (a beginner) in the construction field. I didn't know a blow torch from a welding rod! Razor, my boss, saw this vulnerability and embarrassed me—even ridiculed me—whenever he got the chance, especially when I goofed up (which was often).

Joe, the boss' assistant, on the other hand, didn't have ultimate power like Razor and never tried to lord over me. Joe was patient and kind, and when I did goof up, he explained how to do it better. He led with compassion and "good-naturedness." Joe taught me skills and common sense...Razor taught me nothing more than shame and self-degradation.

That summer job could have been a total catastrophe if Joe hadn't been there. It came out quite well in the end, actually, because Joe escorted me into friendship with the men in the welding, mechanics and pump shops. They all showed me the ropes, and, even though it was not a place where I received much approbation, it became an enjoyable place to work.

God bless good leaders!

January 15

"Victory Starts Here!!"

In the motion picture, "Renaissance Man," actor Danny De Vito plays a would-be teacher, Mr. Rago, trying to instill some intelligence and common sense into the minds of seven Army near-washouts. Somehow, the "students" become interested in the book Mr. Rago was reading—

Shakespeare's *Hamlet*—and he decided to teach his lessons on life using this as a text…this play…this masterpiece.

Mr. Rago tried his best to help them with their poor attitudes toward others and themselves. And with the amazing influence of *Hamlet*, he succeeded! At one moment, he points to his head, exclaiming, "**Victory Starts Here!**" This motto had been displayed on a banner at the boot camp, and his students finally <u>got</u> it! They changed their attitudes towards one another, towards themselves an towards life—passing the class with flying colors.

> they say
> "it's all in your attitude"
> and it's true, you ARE your attitudes
> your thoughts are your landscape
> and outlook the color of glass in your lenses
> distortions are seen as smudges capturing
> too much light
> or not letting enough light through
> making the glass an opaque brilliance,
> or a darkened cave
>
> if you want to "know thyself,"
> just run a print-out of your attitudes
> and your **self** will be hard-copy evidence

Corsair

January 16

Cocoon

wrap me up in silk
spin me a home
to comfort
me
I
want
a warm
dark, quiet
place that exists
only to serve my needs
a place where I feel safe
a place where I can grow and
change in my own space, silent
comfortable
alive

Corsair

Don't we all need this
at times? . . . the need to be pampered
and the need for solitude--to re-group and recuperate. . .
we need to build these times into our busy schedules
so the inner-self doesn't become neglected, brittle.

January 17

If you can just observe what you are and move with it,
then you will find that it is possible to go infinitely far.

Krishnumurti, Indian mystic

In the movie, *THE WIZ*, the African–American version of the Wizard of Oz, Glinda, the Good Witch of the South, tells Dorothy, "Home is knowing . . . if you know yourself, you're always home—anywhere!"

The word ***authentic*** comes to mind as I think about this quote, along with the prospect of *knowing-thy-self . . .* how could we ever be authentic, genuine, if we didn't invest time in contemplation and silence? We all probably know people we see as fake or phony—a curse that is pervasive in our world today!

My belief is that if we were ***authentic***—if we truly *knew* ourselves— we would have a base of self-honesty and self-acceptance that would make it impossible to kill another, to start a war or to abuse anyone—anywhere. We would value ourselves highly, seeing the glory of our uniqueness, which would enable us to see the beauty and uniqueness of all others.

Mother Teresa was a great example of an *authentic* individual. Working with the down and destitute in Calcutta, India, she led a group of sisters who took care of the dying, forgoing all comforts and freedom to serve these poor souls. Mother Teresa's spirit was one of pure giving. I've heard that all the women in her order spent the first hour of each day in prayer. This allowed them to go to the streets with a clean heart and a ready temperament. They knew who they were, and having lost Mother Teresa in 1997, they still know who they are.

Truly, as Krishnumurti wrote, *"If you can just observe what you are and move with it, then you will find that it is possible to go infinitely far . . ."!*

January 18

"Ain't no learnin' without being vulnerable!"

John Manz, counselor

We're all beginners at some time. The question is HOW are you a beginner? I've met some who act like they already *know*, seemingly in an attempt to avoid that vulnerable stage of *not knowing*. These folk seemingly get by merely by observation. They choose not to ask questions but skim by in a half-aware state, unable to learn the ropes because they refuse to gain the knowledge by asking questions in order to do the job well.

I'm talking about myself at times, here. So often, I don't ask clarifying questions but, until a few years ago, I had no clue I was doing (or not doing) this. A concerned supervisor once called me into her office and hit me with the truth that I was not functioning well at my job. The biggest reasons? I wasn't "engaged" and I wasn't asking questions. Engaged? Yes—paying attention, aware of my responsibilities and my environment…I wasn't "IN IT"!

This specter at haunted me at one time, at a teacher's assistant job. I sometimes felt in a fog when I didn't exactly know what I was supposed to be doing, not knowing how to ask the right question(s) that would have informed me properly.

But I did my best to be proactive and seek answers that would keep me involved and up-to-date. And I made extra efforts to stay engaged and active, even when it was questionable what my role was and with which students I should have been working.

Sometimes life calls us to take on that vulnerable state of *beginner*. Are you able to know when *you* do not know? When's the last time you found yourself as a beginner?

January 19

> *Optimism means seeking the opportunity*
> *in every difficulty, while pessimism means spotting*
> *the difficulty in every opportunity.*

(Dr. Alan Zimmerman/Richard Corsair Melcher)

Dr. Zimmerman, a world-wide public speaker, tells the story of 2 boys—Johnny & Jimmy who were polar opposites. Johnny was an unquenchable optimist, Jimmy a ravaging pessimist. Their parents were worried about them both, having such extremely opposite attitudes. So they hired a psychologist to see if he could somehow help bring both boys more toward the center, into more realistic outlooks. The psychologist surprised the parents with a peculiar—possibly even outrageous—technique.

He took Jimmy and put him in a room full the newest toys and games . . . with this test, the psychologist was sure Jimmy would see the good in life, breaking him of his *pessimistic* ways. Then he put Johnny in a room piled with nothing but horse manure, which would surely break him away from his *overly-optimistic* ways.

After 3 hours, they checked on Jimmy and he was sitting in the corner, sulking and complaining: "This game is so dumb, and I don't like these computer games! Why couldn't I have a decent board game? I'm not playing with those cards anymore!" The parents gasped— "Still the pessimist!"

So they hurried to Johnny's room, and, peaking in, saw Johnny running around and scooping up the manure with a shovel and throwing it in the air, laughing and jumping and tossing . . . .

"What are you doing, Johnny?" the psychologist exclaimed! Johnny stopped and to their surprise, cried out, "Mom—Dad . . . with all this manure, there **must be a pony in here somewhere!**"

Are you a pessimist or an optimist? Which side of the fence do you stand on?

January 20

Love every day as if it were your last,
because one of these days you're going to be right!

Leo Buscaglia

The story goes of a young man who was diagnosed with terminal cancer and reflected that he didn't really *start* living until he found out he was going to die. Ironic, isn't it.

We so often neglect to see life's preciousness until we encounter a crisis and are forced to look at our mortality. Why wait? If we choose—today, right now—to experience the greatness of "The Now," we can see the beauty and wonder of life . . . and we my just discover the key to happiness!

"Life is Beautiful" is the name of a movie in which the main character had an indomitable spirit and pursued the woman of his dreams with a creative and demonstrable passion. In the end, although he was not the most handsome man, he won her affection, and her hand in marriage. His approach was *to do little things in a **big** way!*

He even created a real-life fantasy for his son when they were sent to a Nazi prison camp. He had his son believing it was just a game in which his son was going to win a tank if he stayed quiet and out of sight. Ironically the prize tank picked the son up when the Allied Forces freed the camp. He got to ride in the first-prize tank!

This man lived every moment as if it were his last, and saved his son from the horrors of war. He died in the process, but his son lived on, unscarred because of the fantasy story his father had concocted. In the end, the boy was re-united with his mother and they went home together—joyfully!

How can YOU use your creativity to "Live every moment as if it were your last?"

January 21

You were born with wings. Why prefer to crawl through life?

philosopher, Rumi

Do you prefer to fly or crawl through life? *Assertiveness* is the proactive stance where we choose to extend our rights to the world, expecting our rights and choices to be observed and respected. Yet, assertiveness goes both ways—we need to respect others' legitimate human rights also.

When we stuff our emotions and opinions so others can't see what we think and feel, we have aborted your opportunity to *assert ourselves*. Oh yes, we must pick our battles, but hiding our true self—our preferences and opinions—can form a cautious buffer that may end in the squelching the innate powers that lie within.

I should know . . . I lived a *crawling life* in a relationship that was smothering me because I was unwilling—or unable—to share my preferences and opinions with my mate. I just didn't want to take the risk of conflict, or even friction, that would make for an uncomfortable atmosphere for us. This ended in my breaking out of my comfortable cocoon and ending the relationship.

I have now learned that I must **walk tall** and express who I am, in large matters <u>and</u> small! *Flying is much more fulfilling than crawling*! Don't you forget it! I won't!

January 22

If we had no winter, the spring wouldn't be so pleasant . . .
if we did not sometimes taste adversity,
prosperity would not be so welcome.

Anne Bradstreet

Coming through and out of depression may just be one of the most freeing experiences a person with bipolar disorder or major depression will <u>ever</u> have. It's the difference between stumbling aimlessly in a dark, dank cave, and discovering a sun-lit exit, walking out into the glorious spring sunlight!

The memories of pain and disillusionment may never fully dissipate, but can be overcome by fully enjoying life's little blessings: A cold glass of lemonade on a scorching summer day . . . a campfire to warm the bones on a chilly winter afternoon . . . or the warmth of your lover's arm around your waist on a crisp fall walk under the trees donning golden leaves!

I remember the feeling of freedom I experienced as my spirits rose out of the muck of depression in 1980, at age 18. I had started on medication to help balance my system—to bring me down from the ensuing manic state—and I prayed to Jesus that I may be freed from the memories of having been so depressed. As I walked across a parking lot at Minnesota State University, Mankato (where I was to begin school in two weeks as a freshman), I felt a warm hand upon my shoulder, as if to affirm that my prayer had been heard. Although there was "no one there," I knew whose hand was resting on my shoulder . . . my Savior's . . . I was a free man—finally!

From suffering there often comes clarity, perspective—a positive view—if we choose to hang on to the good & let go of the bad. The negative may sometimes still haunt us, at times...but in contrast, the positive happenings will often conquer the negative, as we focus on our blessings and *walk in the light.*

January 23

Being genuine is far more important than being great.

Touchstones

Ella May Miller, in her book <u>The Peacemakers</u>, wrote, "Too many of us go around with *masks* on our personalities. We lack self-knowledge . .

. no one can be at peace with (the) self unless he/she understands the self . . . 'who am I?'"

The problem is that, at times, we don't know when we're wearing a mask to disguise or hide ourselves. I was grateful to see progress in my own life recently when I went back to Minnesota to visit my family. I didn't even realize my *"mask-less"* progress until I discussed it with help from my future wife, upon returning to my home in Milwaukee.

She heard me say that I didn't feel the need to speak during a walk with my brother and sister. I had nothing to say, but enjoyed their company as I kicked through the leaves and soaked in the fall sunlight, "basking in my silence." And I didn't get too personal with another brother, later that day, who had been going through some tough times. I let him reach out, as far as he felt comfortable. Also, I didn't get flustered when my father and I came into conflict—I just let it roll off, "like water off a duck's back."

All these added up to 2 healthy components I have thankfully grown into: Not *personalizing*, (taking things too personally), and not feeling like I have to *PROVE* anything to anyone—to just enjoy being myself! I thank God for these growth-areas, <u>and</u> for my fiancée who extended a listening ear so I could discover/uncover and acknowledge them as qualities I had acquired.

I found out how *genuine* I had been on my trip to see my family. I found qualities that I hadn't seen in myself for a long time, such as how I value *authenticity*, and I realized, with a little help, that I *own* that quality! No need to *wear a mask* to hide my true self when I've got nothing to hide!

Do you have anyone with whom you can share your "inner stuff"? Are you willing to take the risks of open sharing—which may lead to crucial self-discovery? What positive attributes do you think you would find? You may just surprise yourself.

January 24

*Bipolar Disorder (manic-depression) is a hereditary,
chemical imbalance in the human brain that can
cause dramatic mood fluctuations and behavioral
complications. How do I know? I have bipolar.*

Rich Melcher

everything is poem
when mania creeps out of its
damp, dark mold-filled cave
so delighted to see its own reflection
in pen & purpose
purple passion
leaks out of old wineskins of depression
and captivity

yet poem is not as important as poet
the words in volley are mere
expression of self
not self
itself

manic trains of thought with no apparent track
wind among the smoky hills of a deeper mind
sometimes leaving engineer behind
in dust and gravel

hope lies in bending of rails
to bring the iron horse
back home again
to rest in the station of peace
awaiting freight of less weight
and passengers of promise

Corsair

January 25

Our deepest fear is not that we are inadequate.
Our deepest fear is that we are powerful beyond measure.
It is our light, not our darkness, that most frightens us.

Marianne Williamson

Fear of success . . . fear of freedom . . .
Two of the most frightening aspects of life? Really?

Fear of success: *"What if I do well, and they come to expect it from me...then I'll have to do better, and better and better—until I just can't do it anymore, and hit the wall!"* Sure, this is one way to look at it. But success is *naturally progressive*...the more you do, the more you **CAN** do. YOU have to take the responsibility to tell others when you are saturated and can handle no more.

Fear of freedom . . . *"All these choices, all these decisions...it's all so confusing . . . I don't want to have all this responsibility and pressure to always make the right decision, at the right time, in the right way!"* This is better than having all your decisions made for you, isn't it? That would be a form of slavery.

Both of these fears need to be countered with common sense and optimism. Sure we need to shoot for success—what else are you going to do? Shoot for failure? Oh yes, losing is so much *easier*, but often carries "rewards" of self-pity and desperation. You can always shoot for incarceration rather than use your freedom properly! Kinda dumb, huh! But enjoying your freedom, no matter the pressures and rules and effort expended, is **always** better than giving up your freedom.

When we *believe in ourselves*, we minimize these fears and maximize our potential. Do you see YOUR goodness? Are you truly free? Are you moving toward or running from freedom?

January 26

We are more planters of seeds than reapers of harvest.

Lorraine Melcher (author's mother)

These wise words expose important aspects of my mom's philosophy of life. As mother of nine, one way she kept her sanity was through her steadfast belief in God. As a Catholic, she reared us to respect all others and to *find out who we were*, . . . and to discover our gifts so we could share them with the world.

My mom has been one of my best and favorite teachers as she "planted seeds" of optimism and hope in my heart, mind and soul! She was there when I had my first depression, and there when my bipolar illness led me into mania. She knew better than to expect immediate results and, many times, it took years for her wisdom to sink in—but it did!

She lives life couching a sense of humor that never runs dry. One time she "accidentally" stole the principal's car. Not to be outdone, one Christmas she surprised Dad with a statue of a boy holding a puppy which is licking his chin, with a note attached reading "from one who understands <u>to</u> one who understands." Mom must have been trying to appeal to Dad's cuddly, sensitive side but being that Mom and Dad are polar opposites in temperament and communication style, *Dad didn't "understand"* and the whole family laughed uproariously at the irony! Dad laughed so hard that he couldn't breathe!

She is a classic! Mom's memoir, written a few years ago, is appropriately entitled "Life with a Twist"…chronicling this lively woman's life and times. I am ever-grateful for being blessed with a mother who shows me the way, never gives up on me, and still makes me laugh! Thanks, Mom!

January 27

*You can have all the desire and the technique you could wish
for, and still sound flat and dull because your topic is external
to your experience—to your life. The most eloquent speakers
employ what Cardinal Newman described as
"cour ad cour loquitar"—heart speaking to heart.*

Joseph Brown, SJ

What are you passionate about? Me, I'm passionate about teaching, and the quote above reflects exactly how I want to teach. Whether it be by face-to-face instruction or through writing books and articles—*teaching is my thing!* I want to reach people—mind/body/spirit—so they can learn to love themselves more *and* expand their educational horizons.

It is this heart-to-heart that people remember and can replicate the most. When a student feels heard and is encouraged to be creative and constructive, the outcomes can be fantastic—no matter what age the student may be.

One 5th grader I once worked with had to spend the whole afternoon with me—a one-on-one "time out" I performed as teacher's aide, when a student had been particularly disruptive. She complained and groaned for about 45 minutes, then began to show interest in a folder I carried with me especially for these one-on-ones—a folder that had some interesting and engaging projects in it.

She started working on one of these projects and became very creative and involved! I saw the child return from being an angry, out-of-control quasi-adult, as she drew pictures of three "good" animals, and three "bad" animals, correlating each to a mood or behavior she had been experiencing. She took on the project with fervor, and she performed exquisitely! I gave her an A+ for the afternoon's efforts!

Sometimes a teacher is surprised by what works. This student has been special in my heart ever since that afternoon. My materials had been a catalyst for her discovery, and she gained in confidence and creative skills in the process…and she learned that success WAS in her repertoire.

January 28

If you can walk, you can dance! If you can talk, you can sing!

Zimbabwean proverb

"*JOY*" is what this proverb seems to be
talking about. Joy is a wellspring of the love for
life that God offers us...the joy to dance, the joy
to sing, the joy to live life with a natural
exuberance.

There is a Gospel song that grabs me.
In fact, I used to sing the solo
in my church choir. It's called
"*The Joy of the Lord Is My Strength*"
("JOLIMS")...it went like this:

Troubled, not distressed
But I don't get despaired, for the "JOLIMS"!!

Persecuted, but not forsaken,
Cast down, but not destroyed, for the "JOLIMS"!!

I've been tempted, I've been tried
But I don't worry, I don't cry, for the "JOLIMS"!!

I've been abused and pushed aside
But I've got the victory! For the "JOLIMS"!!

Joy of the Lord...Joy of the Lord...Joy of the Lord
is my strength!!

(composer unknown)

This joy is available to all of us because
it's *inside all of us*, just itchin' to come out. A
carefree perspective and a loving stance may
just usher in this joy—so just let it come out...
and feel free to *dance and sing!*

January 29

I was going through the hardest thing,
also the greatest thing, for any human being to do...
to accept that which is already within you, and around you...

Malcolm X

It's been said that "what you see is what you get"...well, there is so much inside of each of us that is not visible, which nullifyies this statement.

We don't know what is inside us until we have sat still enough to ponder who we are and what we're about. Yet many of us never take this time much less know how important it is. Many people keep so busy with outer activities that their inner-worlds never see daylight.

Journaling is one way to discover that inner-self. Taking 5-10 minutes a day to record our thoughts and feelings about our lives can bring heightened dividends as we begin to see our inner-selves.

Try it for a week. Take any old notebook and write a half page a day... what you find when you re-read each day may surprise you! Journaling can become a valuable tool in self-discovery—a way to help uncover what Malcolm X referred to as *"the greatest thing."*

January 30

My satisfaction with myself and my satisfaction
with other people are directly proportional.

Sue Atchley Ebaugh

Self-acceptance is not only important to the individual but to those who encounter the individual. If you are unhappy with yourself, it easily washes off onto those around you.

"Misery loves company" is a real phenomenon! In the 2006 motion picture "The Devil Wears Prada," Meryl Streep plays a New York fashion magazine editor who is clearly an unhappy person. And she does her best at keeping others under her shoe by debasing, embarrassing and even abusing them…all because she is unhappy with herself.

The opposite is also true, such as with George Bailey, played by Jimmy Stewart, in the classic movie, "It's a Wonderful Life." Bailey is the eternal optimist who changed the world around him with his positive, resilient attitudes. His courage and generosity were contagious. He was a huge influence in his small town of Bedford Falls because he believed in the good—and LIVED it!

Never forget that you and your small deeds of goodness and kindness are never forgotten, and you *are* making the world a better place.

January 31

*If you don't know what you really love, your
only alternative is to settle for something less.*

Dr. Alan Zimmerman

I grew up without opinions. Well, not totally, but it seemed that way. Youngest of nine in a Catholic family, most things were just chosen *for* me. I was told what classes to take, where to go to church and what to wear. My birthday was the only day I got to choose what I wanted to eat, what I would do and where I would go. Oh, sure I could go to the ball park, or over to a friend's house—I wasn't a slave to my parents' wishes or constantly grounded—but I just didn't have much ambition to make decisions for myself—it was never encouraged, as the "baby of the family."

So, as an adult, it has been a struggle, at times, trying to figure out what I really love, and love to do. But it has been a process of emancipation and unification to make my own decisions and discover (uncover) "what I truly love."

As adults, we're constantly making decisions and need to be aware of what we truly love. Or, we can do no better than settle for something less.

~ February ~

February 1

"You gotta get busy livin', or get busy dyin'!"

Andy Duphresne (actor Timothy Robbins),
movie, Shawshank Redemption

Quite a philosophy, huh? Off or on! Yes or no! Existence or non-existence! Sounds kinda radical? Maybe. Didn't Shakespeare's Hamlet say it too?

"To be or not to be? That is the question."

But actually, it's a very motivating stance to take because to "get busy livin" sets the sails for productivity and optimism, while turning its back on the opposite.

Do you know people who live like this? My father's late business partner, Wayne, was a *"yes-to-life* man." At age 89 he was still golfing, riding bike, fishing and loving life. He still *had his foot in the door* at the family business...while being a devoted husband, dad and grandfather. He was always up to something—always active and alive!

My hope is to be active like Wayne in my...sixties, seventies, eighties... it's a blessing to live long, yet an extra blessing to be "ON" like Wayne was...a man of character in motion.

February 2 (Groundhog Day)

Our behavior is a function of our decisions, not our conditions.

Stephen R. Covey

If you get a chance, view the movie *Groundhog Day*, with Bill Murray. In it he plays Phil Connors, a Pittsburgh TV weatherman who always seems to get picked to cover the Groundhog Day festival in Punxsutawney, Pennsylvania—an annual event he detests and even ridicules.

But this year after Phil covers *the glorious event*, he wakes up the next day, and it's Groundhog Day—again. . . and again . . . and again! His initial state of mind moves from repulsion to amazement when he realizes he can do anything he wants—and wake up the next day with no repercussions! Then, as he gets turned down for a date, over and over, by his co-worker (played by Andie McDowell), he becomes deeply depressed and wakes up and quickly ends his life—for the day.

Finally, Phil realizes that he must be some kind of god—invincible—and he reaches a place of peace with himself. Phil realizes that the only person who can change—truly change, at all—is himself! Everyone else in the world will relive this day as they may, but HE gets the opportunity to create his day! Phil begins to study and learn many things . . . piano, French poetry, ice sculpting,...and finds comfort in assisting a down & out old man—finding ways to make a difference, day upon day (although it's the same say over and over).

It's truly inspirational to watch someone make the best of life—to make wonderful and life-changing choices—in a stuck-situation when he could have easily wasted every day, and no one would have noticed. Instead he finds a life of dignity, meaning, passion—even mission, right there in little Punxsutawney, PA.

February 3

*Think positively and you create an atmosphere that nurtures
the development of positive outcomes.*

Norman Vincent Peale

In 1952, author/speaker Norman Vincent Peale coined the phrase
"Positive Thinking" and it has been used countless times since. Peale
believed *it is our attitude toward life that makes all the difference between
success and failure.*

How often in your life has a positive attitude made all the difference?
It surely has made a difference in mine! Formerly, at a retail job, I just
made up my mind that I was going to smile more often, and extend a
warm, friendly welcome to my customers. Not only was I more successful
and happy at my work, but I received many compliments for my friendly
ways of reaching out. This encouraged me to give even better service in
any way I could, and it was an ascending spiral of success.

One author put it, "If you want to change *everything*, just change your
attitude." And author Harvey McKay wrote, "Little things don't mean a
lot—they mean EVERYTHING!"

Attaining <u>and</u> maintaining a positive attitude will make life more
interesting and enjoyable—not to mention successful!

Where is your attitude these days?

February 4

Nothing is either good or bad (but) thinking makes it so.

William Shakespeare

Have you ever had one of those days that just seemed crummy?!
Maybe—just maybe—you were doing your best work on that day!

I have a friend who recently had a let-down day like this. She felt like every issue she thought she had solved turned into two issues she couldn't solve, or delegate. I gave this situation a term we now call *"sand duning"* . . . like trying to crawl up the side of a steep sand dune, and only becoming frustrated and fatigued by the sand shifting and sliding down beneath your feet and hands, as you struggle to move upward. She talked of feeling overstressed and under deadline!

But I saw this as one of her BEST days. She got many things accomplished and she faced issues instead of procrastinating. Maybe she didn't get as much done as she had planned, but she accomplished a ton, with confidence, integrity and poise!

This friend of mine just needed someone to point this out to her—& I just happened to be that person for her that day. Sometimes a fresh new perspective is the best prescription for what we may have considered a "hard day."

February 5

If you love something, you will not be afraid to set it free...if it comes back, it's yours; if it doesn't, it never was.

(unknown)

Rock star *Sting* sings **"If you love someone—set them free!"** Healthy relationships call for a sense of freedom. I once had a female friend lambast me for 10 minutes on the phone about how I wasn't spending time with her. We weren't dating, so I couldn't understand her abrasive complaints. This friendship was suddenly on the rocks. So I wrote her a note a day later, after I had cooled down, telling her I felt put down and that I felt almost *owned* by her, but that I was a slave to no one!

My letter was never answered, and she never called again. Too bad a relationship had to end on such a sour note, but *c'est la vie*...that's life! I had set this bird free, and it never came back to me. I guess I didn't own *her* either.

Rock star Sting wrote and sang this song in 1984..."If you love someone—set them free!" Sounds like a good policy—and "if it comes back, it's yours; if it doesn't, it never was!"

February 6

> *It's a funny thing about life—if you refuse to accept anything but the best, you often get it.*
>
> *Somerset Maugham*

Expectations are closely related to goals. Denis Waitley, an international motivational speaker for 30+ years, encourages us to set forth goals and seek earnestly to fulfill them.

Waitley tells the story of one Father's Day when his daughter coyly used HIS OWN techniques of the *expectation and goal-setting* processes to get a new dog. When she first talked about it, Waitley cringed and told her she was absolutely <u>not</u> getting a dog! But she persisted, even walking down the sidewalk dragging a leash, talking to her "doggie-to-be." She approached her dad using HIS language of setting a goal to get a dog, and telling him how she would take care of it and walk it and bathe it and . . . .

Then he was shown the picture in the paper of the cute malamute puppies for sale, and she convinced him to go for a leisurely Father's Day drive, in order to—eventually—stop off and see the puppies. He roared something like "*we're just looking!*", but when the only puppy left rolled over in front of his legs and looked into his eyes with its baby blue eyes—the deal was clinched! They brought the puppy home!

Goals which are followed through on CAN become our *reality*. And expecting only the best in ourselves creates a goal-stance that is unbeatable! Waitley's daughter had *his own* skill-set down pat—and SHE GOT HER DOG!

February 7

*Mystery means you don't know all the answers, but you're
continuing the journey anyhow.*

Corsair

In the movie, *The Majestic*, actor Jim Carrey plays an uncharacteristically *straight-man* role of a young Hollywood writer who gets in a car accident and loses his memory. He ends up in a small, close-knit northern California town of Lawson, whose residents come to believe he's a hometown boy, Luke, who went missing in action on D-Day, 1944—during WWII. Although it was 9 years later, they were convinced he was LUKE, the movie-house owner's boy.

The new "Luke" had no idea who HE was, but followed the lead of "his father" and the community to fit *Luke's* role...even the real Luke's old girlfriend was confused, ending up "sorta" convinced—and very attached. Carrey's role as *the new Luke* became the inspiration and driving force for getting the old run-down theatre—**The Majestic**—up and rolling again. He was still "in the movies," only now on the other end—*showing* the movies rather than writing them. Although Carrey's character was lost in a world of doubt and certainty, he continued the journey anyway.

When the movie that HE himself wrote comes to Lawson, to The Majestic, his viewing it suddenly brought back his memory that he was not Luke, but Peter Appleton, the writer. When the FBI catches up with him, accusing him of running away and that he must be a communist, he ends up in a Red Scare McCarthy court hearing. Awakened to the fact that he was indeed NOT Luke Trumble, the missing soldier, he defends himself with the right to free speech, and to peacefully assemble...the Bill of Rights. He so shocks the accusers that he walks out of court a free man!. (Continuing the journey).

Risking rejection, Carrey then wrote a note to his "girlfriend" expressing how he needed to tell her something important. Little did he know that as he entered Lawson on the train, there would be a hero's welcome waiting. The once lost Luke was found as Peter and was welcomed home to the relationships he had built up in his stay there.

You've got to see this movie of integrity & mystery & *finding the self,* & how love conquers all! This movie brings a sense of innocent romance and fierce loyalty into play like no other show I know. This man had followed his heart, even in the mystery of the loss of his own identity, but he carried on and found success and happiness in the end!

February 8

You can sit and agonize until your agony's the heaviest load!

Indigo Girls, musical artists

When the inner turmoil becomes greater than the actual problem, this <u>may be</u> called *depression.* In my experience, depression is one of the most painful and distressing experiences I've ever encountered. It's a type of torture one can't get away from, although some people try to muffle it with drugs or alcohol. I thank God that I did not choose these options! But in the end, it doesn't often fade with these distractions—and may even get worse.

Depression creates feelings of being continually unsettled and upset, full of non-confidence and self-doubt—anxiety ruling life with an iron fist! In fact the "feeling" part gets exaggerated and over-exposed, and the pain of emotional disruption can be intense—even overwhelming!

This is where **"the agony's the heaviest load"** (lyrics above) come into play...first it's thought that one's problems were causing the depression, but depression is sometimes actually caused by a chemical imbalance in the human brain that creates distorted thoughts, and eventually these bad feelings appear. They can be experienced in "major depression" or even on the depressive side of "bipolar disorder."

Life situations, no matter how sunny, can become cloudy and stormy in the depth of depression. But depression can be overturned with medication, therapy (such as "REBT": Rational Emotive Behavioral Therapy) and healthy attitudes and responses. We must NEVER give up, even when full of doubts and confusion! Depression CAN BE overcome! If you are experiencing depression, hang in there . . . you <u>will</u> find help!!

God <u>WILL</u> <u>NOT</u> leave you stranded!

February 9

(below is an untitled poem I wrote about a semi-depressive bout I had with my bipolar disorder) . . .

and so
once again
the hurricane hit the beach
(never thought I'd see another)
after all those I've lived through –
the forecast had shown only partly sunny
and yet the gale-force winds of my mind began to swirl
waves of my heart came crashing in
on the beach, my soul, my personhood

lost

once again
but with a better shelter
than past storms –
do I fight the storm
or ride it out?
knowing that storms "don't last always"
(kind of a combination this time)

trying to straighten out
my trade-wind thoughts
while feeling the heat of depression

don't run away!

face the demons!

but do I face them by trying to change them?
or understand through waiting?
or just let 'em be?
(I really don't know!)

Corsair

February 10

The Canvas of my Heart

be my canvas, oh Spirit of Truth
to guide me ever on my way
there to enlighten and to soothe
my journey throughout the day

a canvas of Hope, a canvas of Peace
You guide me at every turn
my pain and sorrow to release
my memories to no longer burn

be my canvas, oh Lord, in every way
readying a place for paint to rest
in a multi-colored majesty
as I give You & the world my best

letting go of outcomes and selfish desires
You bless me with a fresh place to paint
Your canvas, clean & white, inspires
the blessings fit for a saint

be my canvas, oh Spirit of Love
to guide this shepherd's path
send me gracious blessings from above
and bless my weathered shepherd's staff

39

help me mold this staff into a brush
to paint Your *Will* in colors wide & free
and adorn Your canvas in a silent hush
as I become the painter **You** want me to be!

Corsair

February 11

*There is a purpose for our lives far grander and more
significant than perhaps we might have ever considered.*

David McNally

Purpose. Purpose. What is your purpose? Why are we here? What is your mission? How can you best serve your community?

Huge questions that need to be answered sometime in the life of a spiritual person—a person searching for meaning in an often-broken world. The late Fr. Anthony de Mello, an East Indian Catholic (Jesuit) priest, once stated:

"Spirituality means never being at the mercy
of any person, thing or event."

Oh, how this statement challenged me, years ago, in my job as a paraprofessional (teacher's aide) in an urban Milwaukee grade/middle school. In my first 4 days I saw more disrespectful and undisciplined behavior than I had seen in *my entire* grade/middle school years in rural Minnesota, in the 1970s! It was much more challenging than I had imagined, going in!

But the challenge was mine—attempting to find ways to reach kids in need of structure, discipline and love...a pat on the back, not just "a kick in the pants!" — I had found a purpose: *To be an effective force for good in all areas of this school environment.* It turned out to be an extremely stressful seven months, as I struggled to find my place. But I learned a ton and came out a better teacher—and a better person.

I learned that no matter the circumstances, we don't have to be at the mercy of others or the situation at hand. Sometimes it's a rough road to travel but worth it in the end.

February 12

> *We no longer seek some big moment when we finally*
> *get the outcome or a "cure" for life's experiences…*
> *the experience along the way is all we need.*
>
> *Touchstones (meditation book)*

This is a true act of faith—to live life from one moment to the next, knowing that God will provide—that's where "Providence" comes from (do you see the word "provide" there?)—God's faith in us that WE will make the right choices and fulfill God's will.

There have been so many times in my life when I was praying for and expecting a BIG BANG…an immediate and permanent lifting of my spirits and positive change in my behavior. The big bang has never come… only the daily uplifting moments and slight changes in my behavior and viewpoint that have led me to be the man I am today—seeking integrity, promoting dignity and living happily!

There IS NO CURE for life's experiences, only the incremental shifts and sways toward being the best person you can be. It will not happen all at once, and *many times you will not even see or feel a change.* But like a rose bud slowly opening, you can find success in each moment as you decide to meet it with courage, hard work and a grateful heart.

February 13

> *The soul is a God-centered, God-nurtured,*
> *unique, developable, immortal human spirit.*

> *M. Scott Peck, The Road Less Traveled*

The most interesting word, to me, in this definition of "soul" is ***developable***. I think of Martin Luther King, Jr., or Mother Teresa, or St. Francis of Assisi . . . spiritual giants who had to come from *somewhere*! Their **souls**, their *"one unit of God,"* (as I like to put it), were not fully formed at birth and, as I see it, must have ***developed*** along with their social, moral, physical, and emotional components.

The soul...*developing*?   Yes! The conscience must be formed—the moral self must be formed. Why wouldn't the soul—the eternal part of us—need to be transformed? I definitely believe that the most precious part of us, our soul, is ***developable!*** But I suppose that if it can be developed, it can also be ignored, beat up and/or trashed—like anything else can be!

So, we need to be aware of our soul-roots and *prune the branches* when needed.   By nurturing our souls with the arts, silence, beauty, pleasing music, nature,...we will be gifting ourselves (and our God) with life beyond Life!

February 14

> *An error gracefully acknowledged is a victory won.*

> *Carloyn G.*

"My fault!" the African-American youth said to me after committing a minor offense in my classroom. It was 1984 at St. Leo's, a predominantly African-American grade school in Milwaukee, and I had rarely heard a youth at the school speak in an apologetic way before.

But the youth man's respectful tone and tune began to reoccur with others quite often as I served as a teacher's aide in the school. With all the push-&-shove, and rude behavior, it was refreshing to hear *"my fault"* once in a while.

At other jobs since then, I have learned to offer a "my-fault-attitude" and just admit my mistakes if/when they occur. This levels the playing field and makes it clear to those I'm working with (or for) that I realize I'd made a mistake and I (we) could go about correcting it. Truly, "an error gracefully acknowledged IS a victory won." No shame in saying "my fault"!

February 15

> *You don't really know how much you can do*
> *until you stand up and decide to try.*
>
> movie, *DAVE*, with Kevin Kline

"Dave" is a presidential look-alike who ends up BEING president due to the real president's untimely stroke...and he makes the presidential seat a better place than the actual president did. He realizes his power and decides to start an extensive jobs program to help willing (and unwilling) people find jobs.

I believe that the key word above is DECIDE . . . to make *a definitive decision* to follow through on a particular action. Deciding to TRY is one of our biggest decisions—ever!

Dave makes friends with the First Lady who finds out he's a fake, yet affirms him that he wasn't just **faking it**—he wasn't just acting, and that he was making a positive difference.

What positive difference can you make today? How can you be your best *you*? When will you *"standup and decide to try"*?

February 16

> *Everything can be taken from a man but one thing—*
> *the last of human freedoms…the freedom to choose one's attitude*
> *in any given set of circumstances—to choose one's own way!*
>
> *Viktor Frankyl*

Every person has **dignity**—and we all have a choice as to who we are going to be and who we are becoming.

Frankyl's quote comes from <u>Man's Search For Meaning</u>, a book he wrote about what it was like to live in Auschwitz, a Nazi death camp during World War II. Frankyl came to realize that they could do whatever they wanted with his body, but they could not harm HIM, the person inside! He suddenly saw that the Nazis could not take away his will to live or act in the way he wanted to. To live (or die) was HIS decision—not theirs!

It was his attitude, his chosen state of mind that the Nazis could not get to. Even though his environment was miserable and ugly, Frankyl realized he had a choice—and no death camp could take that away from him.

We also have that choice—every day—to live a life of gratitude or complaining, hope or despondency, joy or sadness . . . it is all in the palm of our hands. What will *you* choose? And who will you end up affecting by your choices?

February 17

> *It's easier to act your way into a new way*
> *of thinking than to think your way into a new way of acting.*
>
> *KTIS Radio, Minneapolis, Minnesota*

Who would have known that my friend Jerry was experiencing depression? He always seemed so positive and happy. But Jerry's secret was he had bipolar disorder, which, at times, nearly incapacitated him—in the depressive state.

Jerry taught me a good lesson . . . his trick was to act, even when he didn't FEEL like doing anything. When the bed loudly called his name, he would pick anything—go for a walk, read a book, watch TV—rather than succumb to the temptation of the pillow.

"Act first—feel later" was his motto, and it encouraged me to do the same when I felt a bit down. Of course, depression is much deeper than simply "feeling a bit down"—sometimes one needs medication and counseling to assist in coming out of it. But attitude is all-important and acting your way into thinking/feeling can be very beneficial. Jerry overcame his bipolar struggles and lives a very happy and productive life . . . more power to him!

February 18

We're

All

In   "WAITT"

  This

    Together

Dick Rice

Twenty years ago, in one of his spiritual talks, my friend Dick once stated that "We're all in this together." It stuck with me after all these years. WAITT is one of the *acronyms* I use to make sense out of my life. It is a mindset of openness and camaraderie that focuses on the cooperation and energy of getting together with others in social and work environments, surmounting problems that couldn't be solved by a singular effort.

WAITT can "open a lot of doors." There's the story of a woman on her way to a job interview who, in the lobby, opened the door for a man whose hands were full, giving him a big smile as he passed. It was just her *way*. When she got to the interview, the same man was one of the interviewers and recognized her immediately. Never doubt it, the interview went very well!

There are so many ways to encourage a WAITT attitude in everyday life—courtesy, humor, friendliness, showing genuine interest in another… WAITTing on one another can be very beneficial. *We're in the same boat traveling the same sea.*

February 19

> *For us, there is only the trying . . . the rest is not our business.*
>
> *T.S. Eliot*

I once heard a description of our relationship with God as riding on the back seat of a bicycle built for two—God steering and pedaling, while we pedal too. It's a faith thing, I guess.

But I see it another way—with us in the front steering and God the navigator in back telling us which way to go. We don't SEE this *phantom rider*, only hear His voice, barely audible in the wind created by riding, and Presence felt in the pressure and strength added to *our* pedaling efforts.

I believe we are called to have faith . . . faith that God will be with us in all we do, and faith that this "still, small voice" we hear is indeed God's, no matter the whoosh of wind created by riding that "bi-bicycle."

Also, faith that God is IN us, a holy Presence that, as children of God, we encounter Him from the depths of our being . . . pedaling along with us as we struggle to keep the bicycle wheels on His narrow path.

February 20

*Failure is, in a sense, the highway to success, inasmuch as
every discovery of what is false leads us to
seek earnestly after what is true.*

John Keats

There's the story of a farmer whose prize horse ran away, and the townspeople exclaimed, "What a stroke of bad luck!" The farmer responded, "Maybe so, maybe not." A few days later, the prize horse returned with a herd of mustangs following it. The townspeople remarked, "What great fortune!" The farmer said, "Maybe so, maybe not."

Then the farmer's son fell off one of the mustangs while attempting to break it and broke his leg. The townspeople cried out, "What a pity!" The farmer came back, "Maybe so, maybe not." The next day, the army came through the area taking every able-bodied young man for use in their campaign. The farmer's son, with his broken leg, was spared. The townspeople remarked, "What good fortune for you!" The farmer again replied, once again, "Maybe so, maybe not" . . . .

We can learn from any fortunate or misfortune event that it's all in our attitude and how we see an event that makes it good or bad. And that, often, it is the unfortunate events that teach us the most! It's our challenge to learn our lessons as they come along. Will you take the active role in learning your lessons? (Maybe so, maybe not)...

February 21

Obstacles are what you see when you take your eyes off the goal.

unknown

Below is a school house "rap" I wrote in 1985 when the students in

the urban Milwaukee school (St. Leo's) where I was
serving as teacher's aide--a 5th grade class--had been
actin' up, and so I wrote this to counter their
behavior...was it effective? I don't know—
but it was fun!

Turn Around

If you come in class & you fool around
I'm tellin' you now what be comin' down
You're headin' for trouble & you're headin' there quick
And the consequences might jus' make you sick!

So what do you do? You're feelin' in a trap-
We're wantin' you to change here—in a snap!

You better sit down & think sister / brother
Better change your tune--& soon you will discover
That the energy & effort spent foolin' around
Can be put to better uses than playin' the clown!

I said TURN . . .
TURN AROUND!!

Corsair

February 22

*Don't mistake motion for action,
and certainly not for progress.*

Unknown

Any Minnesotan, like myself, who has driven on a snowy afternoon,
knows that when the speedometer kicks up to 30 or 40 miles per hour,
it doesn't mean that the vehicle is actually accelerating at that speed. Icy

roads create slippery conditions, and the wheels often spin with little vehicle movement.

I bet you've had those days when you feel like you're "spinning your wheels." We all have. The trick is to get in motion for the right cause at the right time. When you're in gear with a worthy goal and have the time and energy to follow through, action readily turns into progress, follow-through into success.

Yesterday, I edited 60 entries of this book—more than I have ever done before, or even thought I could do in one day. It was an extremely productive day, partly brought on because it was snowy & windy, which kept me inside and toasty warm...and I wasn't in my car spinning my wheels! It was a day of action.

February 23

The best way to destroy your enemy is to make him your friend.

Abraham Lincoln

This is a reality our world needs dearly. We would have such a better world if *this* were the policy. But we must start with the children. When Jesus said, 'Let the little children come unto Me,' He was well aware of the power children have to shape attitudes in all of us. Jesus also said, 'You must become like a child to enter the Kingdom of Heaven,'...I believe He was talking about a return to innocence that comes through forgiving those who harm us and making friends with those who are our "enemies."

I believe it starts from the bottom up, not the top down; children showing us how to love, how to cooperate and how to serve. One of the most joyful moments in my life occurred last summer when I was privileged to spend the day with my step-granddaughter—whom I just call *my granddaughter*. There we were, hand in hand—a 10-year-old black girl with her 47-year-old Caucasian grandpa, walking through the streets of downtown Chicago. The joy this brought me was nearly indescribable— enjoying myself intently with this jovial, beautiful girl, full of curiosity and spunk! Children are our greatest gifts!

Yes, it must start with the children . . . they have the answers! I once tutored a 5th grader named Everett who had showed little potential and put in very little effort. Then, I took an oversized tablet and put 8 words at the top, telling him our challenge today was to create a paragraph using these 8 words.

Everett started out slow, but as I wrote his responses on the tablet, he came up with an interesting and uniquely involved story. The next day we did the same and he included dialogue in his story. Then he continued the previous story on 2 full sheets of the giant tablet paper! He went from a do-nothing stance to being an excited young man, all because he got into it and saw his potential laid out in front of him! It was exhilarating for him <u>and</u> for me! He had made friends with himself!

Yes, *it <u>does</u> start with the children!*

February 24

> we lock eyes . . .
> I share with you
> the ME
> I'm unable
> to see
> or maybe
> the ME
> I have trouble
> showing myself–
> or even
> the ME
> full of passion &
> playfulness–
> or maybe *even*
> the ME
> searching for
> significance
> acceptance
> connectedness–

but then
you free
inside of me
joy
and *wonder*
as you
give my selves
back to me
touched
loved
heard

Corsair

February 25

We can learn to soar only in direct proportion to our
determination to rise above the doubt
and transcend the limitations.

David McNally

Doubt is a double-edged sword. In one sense, it slows our progress and is the opposite of belief. It can bring us to a screeching halt by challenging what we had thought to be true.

I once froze up during the introduction to a speech for a *humorous speech* contest. I had been doubting my abilities, and it showed when I got up to speak. I lost all comprehension about what I was speaking about—and couldn't speak at all! Funny thing was that my speech was about—of all things—forgetting! I was trying to tell the story of when I forgot a hockey skate at home, and the antics that followed! Oops!

But doubt can also be very helpful, too. When we are about to do something foolish, it is doubt that can kill our pride and stop us from doing damage. When we are about to "tell someone off," it is doubt that would have us question whether it would be a proper thing to do and jolt us into keeping our mouths shut.

It was "healthy doubt" that brought to light deep questions about my becoming a grade school teacher, years ago. The most influential doubting thought was "Can I really DO this job?" Imagine. The multi-faceted attention-grabbers..."Mr. Melcher, I need to use the restroom!... Mr. Melcher, he hit me!...Mr. Melcher, do you have a pencil?!" All the mini-picky-puny interactions all day long! Don't get me wrong—I love kids, but I don't think my mind could handle it. This doubt worked for my *good*. I chose NOT to pursue becoming a grade school teacher—and I still have my sanity!

To transcend limitations we must let go of the doubt that causes us to second-guess our goodness, and fuel the doubt that keeps us from acting in unhealthy ways.

And from there we can SOAR!

February 26

*I would imagine what You (God) really desire from us
is a kind word in our impatience, a good deed
in our busy-ness, or an act of Love
in a moment of intolerance.*

Corsair

Integrity—spiritual integrity—comes at a high price. I believe it only comes through meeting our demons face-to-face and not backing down, defeating them with our pure Presence. How many times have you come up to a brick wall of fear or pain and not known how to climb it, dig under it, or go around it?

Funny how often it is merely a matter of reaching out with your hand, tapping a single brick and watching the entire wall crumble onto itself. Illusions need only be touched for their "unrealness" and pushed over with a tap of concentrated imagery, reaching a new freedom by releasing the tension and seeing beyond it.

I like to describe this <u>touch</u> as a matter of "FOG": Focusing On the Good, also known as *optimism*. We have a choice as to how we will react to the events that we encounter. Will you choose to love or run? To bless another with your presence or isolate yourself in ambivalent uncertainty? To hope you will not be discovered as different or odd? It's ALL an illusion. We are ALL different, and this is what brings the spice to life.

We can bring the world our blessings—our talents, skills, gifts and personality—or choose to withhold them. Which will you do?

February 27

"Acceptance," from As Bread That Is Broken,

by Van Breeman

Acceptance means that people with whom I live give me a feeling of self-respect, a feeling that I am worthwhile. They are happy that I am who I am.

Acceptance means that though there is need for growth, I am not forced. I do not have to be the person I am not! Neither am I locked in by my past or present. Rather, I am given room to unfold, to outgrow the mistakes of the past.

In a way, I can see that acceptance is an unveiling. Every one of us is born with new potentialities. But unless they are drawn out by the warm touch of another's acceptance, they will remain dormant.

Acceptance liberates everything that is in me. Only when I am loved in that deep sense of complete acceptance can I become myself.

Upon reading this passage, my wife remarked that, sure, we need others' acceptance, but WE play a part in this milieu also…we need to accept ourselves—it's not just acceptance from another but an active self-acceptance that plays a vital role in healthy living. I agree. How about you?

Rich Melcher

February 28

*Of all the judgments we pass in our life, none are more
important than the judgments we pass on ourselves . . .
(those judgments) have an impact on every moment
and every aspect of our existence.*

Nathaniel Brandon

Self-esteem is a recent (past 40 years) term that has come to be very important in our world. It has been used and overused so much that it has nearly become a cliché. Yet it is still a term to describe how we see ourselves, and it can play an important role in increasing our psychological and emotional health.

Think about it: Isn't it true that if you are "in a bad mood," it affects *everything* that happens to you and around you? If you don't feel good about yourself, every thought and emotion is affected! Brandon continues, "Our self-evaluations are the foundation for which we act & react, choose our values, set our goals & meet the challenges that confront us...."

Paraphrasing a Newsweek article on the importance of self-esteem a few years ago, the writer contributes that "self-esteem is the basic building block of success." How right he was. It is this healthy sense of self that guides our inner world and leads us towards happiness and fulfillment. Don't downplay the role of self-esteem, no matter how corny it may sound. It IS the foundation of personal success and hope-filled living. Believe in yourself and you're on the road to winning, no matter what your field of endeavor!

February 29

You don't pay the price for success—you enjoy the benefits!

Zig Ziglar

A little change of focus can go a loooooooooong way. When I first heard the above quote, I downplayed it and even denied its significance. It sounded like an avoidance of the effort it takes to succeed.

But I have come to believe in the optimism of this statement because it states a simple truth: *The attitude you choose makes ALL the difference!* Ziglar encourages us to focus on the outcome and possibilities rather than the struggles we may encounter in getting there. The quote lays the prize out before us so we can see what goal we're heading toward.

Ziglar's "enjoy the benefits" helps us decide what we want the outcomes to be—we can *keep the eyes on the prize* in these multi-distracting days and reach success in due time.

~ March ~

March 1

*The choice to survive, knowing we never have
to do it alone, gets easier with time.*

Each Day A New Beginning

This quote points out a spiritual truth that *we have a God who will always
be there for us...most often in the form of people—people who understand and
support us.* Yes, God is present in everyone around us, and we have lessons
to learn from each person we meet.

But most people will not know us enough to even know how to
support us. This is why we depend upon those few close ones, *chosen
ones*—friends, significant-others, co-workers, and family—the people who
get the opportunity to see us in action and get to know us, choosing to
love us for who we really are.

We must, consciously or unconsciously, choose to *survive* every day.
"Life is difficult" were the first 3 words of M. Scott Peck's book The
Road Less Traveled, and it's possible that no other three words (although
somewhat pessimistic-sounding) could better summarize our existence
on this planet.

We can move on through difficult circumstances when we keep in
mind that **we are not alone.** We will always have an understanding
and compassionate God living within our being, and we will need to keep
our eyes and ears open for the people who will support us. In the end,
the choice to survive *does* get easier with time. We will need to stay close
to those who truly SEE us and SUPPORT us. They are there, no matter
HOW hidden. Find them, and *find who you really are*—in the mirrors of their
eyes, hearts and voices!

March 2

What is "I-sensitivity"?

While rummaging around at a garage sale in northern Minnesota a few summers ago, I came across a green, glass object, about the size of a fist. It was an *insulator*, which was used on old transmission lines to keep the electrical current from zapping the pole. Insulators made it possible for the electrical current to travel unencumbered.

At first I didn't know what to do with my one-dollar find, but 6 months later I got an idea: To use the insulator as a representation of how I needed to "insulate" myself from negative influences. In my job as a special education teacher's aide, there were numerous times when I was confronted with unpleasant, and even destructive, language and behavior. The insulator came to my defense each time.

So I invented *"I-sensitivity"*—not *insensitivity* or *oversensitivity*, but "insulated"—**I-sensitivity.** This little connection has helped me many times when the going has gotten rough, and I felt misused or violated. I-sensitivity allows negativity "to travel unencumbered" over the top of me. I imagine the "negative current" in a caustic situation traveling through the insulator as it's held high like the Statue of Liberty's torch—as if I were one of those old transmission poles holding up the electrical lines. The double meaning is not only that I'm *insulating* myself from negativity but also achieving freedom from destructive situations. Then I can act without the disrupted emotions and tangled thoughts—acting with a clear head & a *clean heart*.

I challenge you to try this in a future destructive situation—this imagery may just allow you to show your best side in an uncomfortable situation and keep you from experiencing painful emotions and unneeded conflict.

March 3

*The most powerful thing you can do to change the world
is to change your own beliefs about the nature of life,
people, reality, to something more positive.*

Shakti Gawain

My first two years out of college, 1984-86, were invested in volunteering in urban Milwaukee, Wisconsin, at two predominantly African American schools. Then I returned to my home state of Minnesota, (1987-2005) and for years I was cut off from urban communities.

On a visit back to Milwaukee in 1993, I wondered how the racial tension was in this city—considered by some to be the most segregated city in America! When I took a right turn onto a side street, on Milwaukee's predominantly black north side, car windows down, I was startled by groups of black people on the sidewalk who were yelling & waving at me—one group here, a couple of other people there…and I thought, "Gee, it really HAS gotten bad!" It seemed like all these black people giving me—a white guy—such a hard time!

Then I looked ahead and suddenly noticed that the parked cars on the right **and** the left were facing me. *I had been driving down a one-way the WRONG way,* and my "prejudiced" black sidewalk-goers were merely trying to wake me up to my error! There went the assumption!! I laughed heartily upon this discovery, enlivened and relieved—<u>and</u> *"feeling a fool"* for having *my own* prejudiced thoughts. Just goes to show how we must let go of our assumptions and **try to think positively first!**

March 4

Your Life Is Now!

John Mellencamp, rock star

Former UCLA basketball coach, John Wooden's teams valiantly won 10 NCAA Championships in 12 years. This unprecedented explosive movement has never been, and may never BE, matched in college ball—or in ANY sporting event!

Wooden's father used to tell him, "Make each day your masterpiece!"---and so, from early on, young Wooden saw that *life is now!* This played out in his coaching style where he made it clear that every practice was as important as a championship game. This attitude encouraged the players to give their all at every moment on the court. And when it came to "important" games, they performed as they had in practice—like champions! They became champions because of this attitude—this discipline—and living it out, day after day, year after year.

There is a little acronym I came up with in my freshman year in college that has been very useful: NIATI...*Now Is All There Is.* It helps me realize that **this is it!** This is Life, and we only get one chance at it, so make it your best!! Sounds like something Coach Wooden may have told his teams as they rolled on to victory, *on and off the court.*

March 5

"2 X 10" = *if it is to be, it is up to me!*

The above is so true and so *untrue.* True—we need to be independent and proactive in seeking our goals and desires. We need to see what we want and move toward it!

Yet we have help—much help, not only from those we love but from a loving God who is always present to us. This makes "2 X 10" somewhat *untrue.* If it were ALL up to me, I would be quite lonely and anxious lest I fail to make it happen—whatever "it" is.

It's a thin and mysterious line that separates what we think we can do for ourselves and that with which we need assistance. Sometimes important people or other resources are there for us to help with questions, problems or negative feelings. "That's what friends are for" is an apt phrase that can be helpful to remember in times of need.

Also, God—who rests within us, always—is a mighty force for goodness and clarity when confusion and discouragement make their rounds. I believe the "12-Step" Serenity Prayer fits in here well:

"God, grant me the serenity
to accept the things I cannot change,
the courage to change the things I can,
and the wisdom to know the difference."

Will you do it all yourself, or drop your pride and ask for a bit of help?

March 6

No man is an island, entire of himself . . . any man's death
diminishes me because I am involved in Mankind; and therefore,
never send for whom the bell tolls—it tolls for thee.

John Donne

This is a *secular* message that can easily be brought into the spiritual realm. Where would we be in this world if we followed this precept? We probably wouldn't have war, starvation or hatred—to name a few ills.

Jesus Christ spoke of loving everyone, and may He have even been the inspiration for Donne's statement. If we were to value people as brothers and sisters, we would naturally move toward taking care of these torments that plague our world.

My church, All Saints Catholic Parish, in central city Milwaukee, serves the poor in the neighborhood by providing a food pantry where people can get basic grocery items. The church also provides hot meals three times a week for anyone who walks through the door. No proselytizing or indoctrinating—no questions asked. Only a friendly welcome offered. I've enjoyed serving in both capacities and feel a closeness to needy people not previously possible...realizing that, in heart, mind and spirit, I am as "needy" too!

Donne's "I am involved in Mankind" reminds me of how Jesus moved freely among the people, valuing each person as He walked His path of Righteousness and loving service. When Jesus was crucified, the bell tolled (a medieval sign that someone had died) for each of us also. If we come to believe that "any man's death diminishes me"—this is a *clarion call* for respecting all human life!

March 7

Tolerance is the greatest gift of the mind.

Helen Keller

When you have a wicked cold, with the runny nose and stuffed-up head, tolerance can bring you through. When you have interpersonal problems with a co-worker—and you're forced to work with this person for a spell, tolerance can bring you through. And when you have a woman-friend who insists on pushing her "religion" on you, tolerance can be the thing that pulls you through. It IS a gift to be able to tolerate minor annoyances.

But when violence occurs in our schools, do we tolerate that? And when your basic human rights are violated, do you tolerate that? It seems tolerance has "morphed" into complacency in America, with the Iraq war into its 5th year. Is this where *tolerance* has brought us?

In a song by Phil Collins, he sings these words over and over: "I don't mind...I don't mind...." Sometimes an "I don't mind" of tolerance becomes an "I don't mind" of inner-slavery...and we may need to set tolerance aside and stand up for what we believe! This is a very fine line, and we may reach it often.

Do you know when you should be *tolerant* and when to stand up for your Truth? This is a crucial balancing act. How will you bend & sway with the winds of resistance? And when will you let a branch break to save the tree in a tornado's path?

March 8

> *If you don't actively fulfill the job you're given to do,*
> *no one is going to ask you to do anything else.*

> *Mary Jo Palaranta, communications consultant*

What do you think about that? Is that fair? Well, actually it's a good notion to keep in mind, no matter what job you do. My father's late business partner once told me, "There's ALWAYS something to do!" Great advice in helping me be observant and "in it," on the job!

Being **observant** is one of the most crucial skills any person can carry with them into any job: The doctor who notices a latent symptom to an on-coming illness, the service station worker who notices a frayed belt that could cause trouble down the road for an unaware customer, the grade school teacher who notices a child's "incorrect" way of clutching a pencil, and moves to correct the possible deficiency . . . .

I remember, when I was in junior high, a blind boy named John, from the other side of town, came to visit. I couldn't get over how he "noticed" *everything...* the smell of coffee coming from the kitchen, the roughness of a couch we had recently reupholstered, the soft music being playing on the phonograph...things I had never really thought about or noticed myself. I was amazed by John's perceptive skills!

Observation is a front-line skill that allows us to "actively fulfill the job we've been given." What perceptive skills do you bring to a job to make it a success? How keen are *your* observation skills? Is it possible to develop John's perceptive abilities? I urge you to begin paying more attention to your 5 senses—something called "mindfulness."

Mindfulness means being *aware*—aware of what is going inside and around you each moment. It's a movement from the inner to the outer. I call it "CAIS": Connectedness with my Authentic Inner Self. It is from this connectedness that I move out into the world. Some call it being "centered." I call it *essential*—and tricky to maintain. I struggle to live out CAIS each day. It is a challenging stance, but I try to move toward it. Sometimes I even succeed. You need to be able to let go of daily pressures and find the peaceful place inside.

Do you meet the world this way? It is a beautiful way to live a life of Presence with others.

March 9

Keep on keepin' on ("KOKO") the road that you choose.

Scarecrow, the movie, THE WIZ

There is actually no yellow brick road. Sometimes it gets confusing, even if we have set goals and have worked hard to reach them. The heat of the moment and pressing issues can steer us away from our goals, rolling them over into the next day, week, month.

But there is the inner-journey, the spiritual path that leads us to meaning, awareness, God. I was just telling my loving wife, Sandra, that it is our *spiritual connection* that is most meaningful aspect of our relationship! I have been blessed with the gift of writing prayers. Actually, this is something I told Sandra the night we met). Let me write one now:

Dear loving God,
we come to you with our
goals and dreams, hoping to find
meaning and fulfillment in our daily activities.
But, deep down, we know we can only find these
precious jewels in You. Bless us this day to
discover You in all we do, and may we
"keep on keepin' on" the road
that YOU choose!

Amen

Corsair

March 10

If we meet our challenges with a zest for adventure,
we will gain even from our losses.

Dynamics of Personal Motivation

This quote seems to fit Lance Armstrong perfectly—an American who won the Tour de France bicycle race seven times. Did you know that in 1996, Armstrong was diagnosed with testicular cancer and he was given a 40% chance of recovery? But he beat the cancer and was considered cancer-free in February of 1997. He took the rigorous training he established during recovery and parlayed it into his training for the Tour de France, which he first captured in 1998.

Armstrong *met his challenges with a zest for adventure* and became the top bike racer in the world! He gained strength, ironically, from his cancer bout, and blasted back onto the bicycling scene after recovering—winning 7 times! Don't we all wish we could have this ZEST?

We can! It's called into being by *healthy risk-taking* and persistence, and we can all participate! One author wrote, "You must go out on a limb—that's where the fruit is!"

What healthy risk will you take today?

March 11

Let us look for the good (in others and ourselves) and,
in time, it is all that will catch our attention.

Each Day A New Beginning

Dr. Alan Zimmerman speaks of an 11th grade classroom of all boys had run off 6 teachers in 7 weeks, and the principal frantically searched the district for another replacement. He found a 70-year-old woman who had retired a few years earlier. She was shocked to hear he would put an armed guard in the back of the classroom if she would agree to teach.

"How silly!" she touted; "I don't need that—I've always gotten along well with boys—let me see their data."

She looked at the class list for a few moments and then stood, pronouncing, "This is a tremendous opportunity—let me at 'em!" The principal didn't understand her enthusiasm but sent her into the classroom. Soon the boys stopped skipping school, and the behavior in the classroom turned from futility to formation of healthy young men...they changed so much that they became the model citizens of the school, and all went on to the 12th grade!

At the end of the year they had a banquet to honor this *successful* teacher, and, after 3 speakers had praised her, she stood up and called out, "Thank you, but no one's praising the principal—it was his idea to get all those nice boys into the same room." At this proclamation, there was a hush, people thinking she was a bit strange—knowing the reputation of those (previously) naughty boys.

"When I looked at the data at the beginning of the year," she said, "and saw Dave Wyant 134, Troy Daniels, 142, Steve Frander, 141—when I saw the boys' names and their IQs, I <u>KNEW</u> I had never had a more gifted class!" The principal, totally flabbergasted, stood up and called out, "When you looked at the data, those were NOT their IQ's, *those were their locker numbers!!*"

This teacher believed the boys were intelligent and cooperative and that's how they responded. The power of positive expectation! Is it working in your life?

Rich Melcher

March 12

<u>what does it mean</u>

in these days of hurry and often-glaring rudeness
what does it mean
to have family
to share LIFE with?

it means that no one goes hungry in the heart
no one goes thirsty from an unfed mind
no roofless tenants shiver in the soul
and no one abides in broken down shacks of withered personality

I love being loved by the ones I love
and I love loving those I treasure so dearly
it's as though God has matched us all up
to be there for each other in ever-special ways

I see it as a poignant and fruitful notion
that it was all supposed to be this way somehow
that family is meant to be something special
and even when separated we're only a heartbeat away

isn't it amazing the feelings realigned
the time melted away
and the hope renewed like a running stream
when we get together and see eye to eye once again?

God bless the family that never forgets
the gift given in a smile, a hug, a kiss
the Presence offered and received
whenever we as family come around the bend once more

Corsair

March 13

Everything has its wonders, even darkness and silence,
and I learn, whatever state I may be in,
therein to be content.

Helen Keller

Wow! What an attitude exuding from this woman who *knew* trial and suffering very well. To take in each moment with an attitude of *wonder*—THIS is a challenging and inspiring stance!

Helen shows us that contentment is a choice, an option, a possibility, rather than a far-off dream. The choice to be content, no matter what's going on, is new for many of us who may have struggled to climb out of a depressing state in which we may have found ourselves.

Even in Helen's state of blindness and deafness, her *joy* is palpable. She CHOSE her psychological state, not allowing life to settle in on or smother her. As you see that our state of mind is a choice, what will YOU do next time the depressing and/or mundane grips you? Can you reach for a higher level? Can you reach for Helen Keller "vision"?

Everything has its wonders. Where can you discover wonder in *your* life?

March 14

Many are strong in all the broken places.

Earnest Hemingway

Bent metal is stronger than straight—at least in many cases. Take the hood of a car. It is contoured not merely to look sleek, but to give it strength and durability. So too are we. It is the struggles, the tough times, the bumps in the road endured that produce character.

There is a German saying that fits this well:

> *To lose money is nothing.*
> *To lose health is something.*
> *To lose character is everything!*

Have you ever gone through a deep personal struggle and, after overcoming it, looked back and seen the various areas of growth the struggle has promoted? I bet we all have. A couple I know from church has encountered cancer many times. The husband has had four bouts over the past several years and survived each quite well. Yet this last round took his vision. Still, they are faithful to God's promise that there is a purpose to all things.

Their greatest gift is their example of faith. They praise God that life has not been snatched from them and that overall health is very good. This couple is a blessing to all who encounter them, for their optimism, their cheerfulness, their confidence, and their belief that everything will turn out right. This gift of inspiring others is testament that we can be strong—even in our broken places!

March 15

> *Friendship of a kind that cannot easily be reversed tomorrow*
> *must have its roots in common interests and shared values.*
>
> *Barbara W. Tuchman*

Friendship, to me, is one of the most important things in life. Not that we have to be friends with everyone—this is impractical and impossible. But it is our friendships that pull us through and give life to Life.

A shocking discovery I encountered over a year ago was that I had all kinds of what I call *False Fantasy Friends* (FFFs). These are people I had IMAGINED were my friends but really weren't—an old high school friend who never reciprocated when I contacted him; a guy I met on a retreat years ago and had *one* real conversation with; a woman who worked for an old employer who helped me start a support group...and many more people with whom I really had NO relationship for many years.

So I bought a new address book and purged the old one of all FFFs only keeping people and organizations in which I actually have a connection! It was a *lightening force* for good and an enlightening moment of reason to get rid of the FFFs and reaffirm and recommit to the people I <u>really</u> know and love.

Do YOU have any FFFs in your life? Whatchya gunna do about it?

March 16

Marianne Williamson wrote these fine words
about fear and reality:

OUR GREATEST FEAR

*Our greatest fear is not that we are inadequate,
but that we are powerful beyond measure.*

*It is our light, not our darkness, that frightens us.
We ask ourselves, Who am I to be brilliant,
gorgeous, handsome, talented, fabulous?*

*Actually, who are you not to be?
You are a child of God.*

*Your playing small does not serve the world.
There is nothing enlightened about shrinking
so that other people won't feel insecure
around you.*

*We were born to make manifest the glory of God
within us. It's not just in some; it is in everyone.*

And as we let our own light shine, we consciously
give other people permission to do the same.
As we are liberated from our fear,
our presence automatically liberates others.

Do you relate to this reading? Do you ever
encounter a "fear of success?" How can you find
liberation in your inhibition?

March 17

When you walk away from the light
you only dance with your shadow.
Walk toward the light and your shadow can only follow.

Corsair

I was walking on my local park path the other night and a long shadow stretched over the top of my head as the bright security light shone on my back. Suddenly, taken by the dark specter pushing its way in front of me, I decided to do a 180 and walk *toward* the light. The shadow instantly disappeared as I walked with the light on my face and this same shadow dragging behind me.

This was a huge lesson for me...that I could *choose to* walk toward the light—the goodness, the spiritually-profitable, the hopeful and consistent, rather than the unknown, the pessimistic, the lost-in-unawareness that can swallow us up at times.

Have you ever come to the point of needing to make the decision if you would walk away from the light or toward it? Sure. It happens often. When our integrity is challenged by an unexpected temptation to slip by with a tad of dishonesty. When we are challenged by the tendency to shy away from an opportunity to better ourselves with exercise or better eating habits. I fall in these areas often.

But we need to pick our battles—we are not perfect and cannot do it all. Yet, in the end—in the BIG things—we need to walk toward the light or be cursed with watching our shadow creep over our shoulders at all times. My brother calls it "facing the music," taking the risk and having the faith to put in the effort to be successful.

Will you walk toward the light or live in the shadows?

March 18

Love is . . . clarity of perception and accuracy of response.

Fr. Anthony de Mello

De Mello tells the story of an old couple resting after their 50th anniversary party. They were tired, lounging on the porch…when grandpa turns to grandma and said, "Lena, I'm proud of you."

She retorted, *"Speak up Grandpa—you know I can't hear well without my hearing aids!"*

He said once again, but louder, "I'm *proud* of you!" She shot back, "Oh, that's OK—I'm tired of you too."

Sometimes we don't have all the facts and have other than a clear perception. But the aim is to see and understand others clearly, and then respond accurately to who we know the other to be. We may not always be right, but our attempts to understand and love others are what make relationships click.

Leaving the house yesterday, I got upset with my wife when she started to close the front door as I was trying to exit. Then I realized my car was in the garage, requiring me to exit through the other door, to the left. I felt a fool! This was the first time I had parked my car in the garage all winter and I was definitely heading in the wrong direction. Upon realizing my error, I began to laugh at my silly quick-temperedness. I apologized, and we laughed together. Then, I giggled all the way out of the neighborhood, driving slow and sure in my humored state!

My perception had been temporarily skewed and I had had an "inaccurate" response. I learned a good lesson about taking it easy and not getting so huffy when things don't go my way.

Perception, like attitude, is everything!

March 19

If you aren't making errors, you aren't trying a lot of things.

Rich R. (Beyond War)

Oh, this statement has helped me! In times of feeling a fool, where the *faux pas* seems to rule—in times of apparent failing, over and over, I have found comfort in these words. Have you ever had those days—or weeks—when nothing seems to turn out right?

In 1989, I had three fender-benders in a two month period! I was wondering if I was competent to even *drive* a car! But I realized that, in each instance, I was on the move toward fulfilling a positive goal. I wasn't watching where I was going, but I was trying to do something positive. One learns when and where to do things (preferably not taking down a quotation from the radio while traveling 40 miles per hour on a busy highway)!

The saying goes, "God doesn't steer parked cars!" Well, maybe a parked car is good sometimes, but the quote has relevance. If we never DO anything, out of fear, confusion or laziness, we will be stuck with a life full of lost opportunities and regrets. Yet, how can you have a regret for something we never knew would have been a good experience because we didn't try? I don't know.

But I do know that it has been in taking the risk that I have gained the most fulfillment. Even when I have made errors, my intentions were good, and that's what counts. Upon first meeting Milwaukee Mayor Tom Barrett, I said, "Hi Tom"— when "Great to meet you <u>Mayor</u> <u>Barrett</u>" would have been more appropriate. I felt like a goof but laughed it off later, having never met the mayor of our fine city before. At least I had the courage to extend my hand in greeting.

Mistakes are a part of the territory if you are going to be a socially-active person, and the ability to *take yourself lightly* is crucial. Gaffs have happened to me so many times that I, at times, feel like a pair of muddy old army boots. But I get over it, with a giggle and a confident stride toward my next worthy goal.

Indeed, *if we are not making errors, we probably aren't trying a lot of things!*

March 20

The greatest gift we can bring to any relationship, wherever we go, is being who we are.

Melody Beattie

Recovery author Earnie Larsen tells a true story of a Minnesota Twins open baseball try-out where *anyone* could try out for the team. One participant was a 17-year-old boy who had...no legs! This young man was no new-comer to sports. He was a varsity wrestling letter winner and played nose-tackle on the football team.

He was seen chasing down fly balls, batting, and running faster in the 40-yard dash than some other able-bodied participants. When asked by reporters why he would come and try out, he returned with a marvelous answer—"I wasn't doing anything until 3 o'clock!"

Larsen remarks, "Imagine the inner-map this young man had in his head!" Now if I've *ever* heard of optimism, this is it! Does this motivate you to reach toward your potential? In my head I can hear the old "If HE can do it—I can do it!"

Do we really have any excuse not to put forth our best effort in every situation? I hope we all can emulate the example of this boy with no legs... and a huge heart.

How can you take healthy risks like this young man and make a difference? When will you start? Today is a good day!

March 21 (the questioning soul of one who has bipolar disorder)

Bruised Fruit

what does it mean to see the self
  less than and lower than others around?
   a square peg in a world of round holes
    but could this not just be
     a perceptive mis-view
      caused by inner sense that
       I am different?

    somehow I've run-aground on the notion
    that I'm the only one with a history
   a history of struggles and failures that
   now seem to grip me tightly ~
   does a grocery shopper choose
     the bruised fruit, or is it rolled and tumbled
   up and across the slanted shelf so shoppers can
       get the pick of the litter?

reminds me of the movie The Horse Whisperer
        where a girl who lost her leg in a horse riding accident
        cries in her mother's arms,
   "Who will ever want me this way?!"
        upon hearing the story of a young man who ended up
        in a wheelchair after diving off a bridge (who was "just
   not there" when she looked in his eyes) she says,
          "I know where he goes,"
            making a connection
            with the hopelessness, the "lost-ness"...
      I too know where he goes, having struggled with
        bipolar disorder for over 30 years—way over ½ my life
      yet I claim my dignity and wear solid integrity for
      "I have come this far by faith"
and will travel on despite the troubles and discrimination
        and hatred that seem to surround me at times

    Bruised Fruit? Maybe...but we're all bruised fruit in some area ~
    no avoidin' that reality . . . and on we go—hopefully together

                    Corsair

March 22

*Connect to what gives you a sense of excitement,
happiness and gratitude for being alive – and you will
spread "positiveness" wherever you go.*

unknown

Do you know people who bring sunshine with them wherever they go? Such people seem to reflect an inner joy that radiates goodness and content, calm hope. This presence is *contagious*. When one person brings this to the scene, positive influences are not merely possible, but inevitable.

This fits our church choir director quite well. When she steps into the room, it seems to light up with enthusiasm and possibilities. This powerful woman radiates a joy that, indeed, is contagious!

I remember—when our church choir traveled to Rome in 2006—the exuberant look on her face as we prepared to sing for the pope in St. Peter's Square! She was beaming with excitement as the opportunity of a lifetime approached. You could touch her fervor as we began to pound out a gospel tune in this Orthodox environment—you could sense the rebel in her and her delight with our performance for the mass audience.

This presence is not merely a social but also a spiritual happening. It's as if the light of Christ flows through certain people, or, at least, it's more visible in some. This is true **enthusiasm**, which means "full of God,"..."in – theos" (God). This perspective is attainable, it is reachable, if we choose the positive and avoid the negative, and ride with the moment with joy.

Who will YOU choose to be today?

March 23

*The movement from loneliness to solitude is not
a movement of growing withdrawn, but it is instead
a movement toward a deeper engagement in
the burning issues of our time.*

Henry Nouwen

Solitude does not mean loneliness, but simply *being alone.* Quieting the self. Often, the spiritual life calls us to be alone, to "figure ourselves out," to recharge our inner batteries and to understand our place in the world.

Aloneness, also, does not mean loneliness, which is *a desperate need* for people. Aloneness can happen ANY time—even when you are with others. Sounds strange, huh? It entails being content with who we are and what we're about. Even when we may be upset or discontent, aloneness allows us to experience who we are and not be distracted by an often-turbulent world.

Being our own selves, coming from our own personal perspectives, and being aware of our presence with others allows aloneness to be a positive force—either in solitude or when we're around others.

You can only be you…aloneness and solitude help you figure out who this YOU is, so that you can present this SELF to your world…alive, rejuvenated, free.

March 24

*Above all these things, put on love, which binds
everything together in perfect harmony. And let the
peace of Christ rule in your hearts, to which
indeed you were called in one body.*

St. Paul to the Colossians (3: 1-17)

<u>One Family</u> (a modern-day spiritual)

I am Christ to you
you are Christ to me
in this body of Christ
we are all one family

we've all had our struggles
we've all been led astray
but in our dear Lord Jesus
we truly find the way

we are all one family
in the body of Christ we find
that He has set us free
and gives us peace of mind

you are Christ to me
and I am Christ to you
as a family we know
that He will see us through

Chorus: we are all one family
with Jesus' spirituality
we are here for one another
we are one family

Corsair

March 25

The only REAL mistake is the one from which we learn nothing.

John Powell, SJ

Do you realize that it is under *your* control <u>and</u> it is responsibility to learn your lessons—crucial lessons—**at any place and time**? Just because something "bad" may have happened to you does not write the outcome in stone. You are not a gravestone, but a Michelangelo's David, to be *released from imprisoning stone*. At any time you can choose to recall a negative incident and learn your lesson, capture its rejuvenating force, make it a positive NOW transformative event!

These are golden opportunities to unleash the power of forgiveness and hope. I learned an important lesson recently, 29 years after a dangerous and embarrassing action I took at a construction site. It could have cost me my leg, or <u>my</u> <u>life</u>! I relived the incident in my heart and mind for many years before I recently corrected my folly in my imagination, learning the lesson that had lay dormant for the past 29 years. Lesson learned! And on I go, strengthened, enlivened—knowing I can do the same with ANY past mistake.

The lessons are just waiting, for *you* too, to be approached, imagined, corrected and freed—to build a new you! What are you waiting for?

March 26

There is a variety of gifts, but always the
same spirit…it is the same God working…the particular
way in which the Spirit is given to each person is for a good purpose.

1 Corinthians 12: 4-7

Isn't it fantastic that we are all unique? Our gifts, temperaments, perspectives, motivations, beliefs, hopes, dreams…yet often we may feel the weight of our uniqueness, the heaviness, in an American culture that thrives on conformity, beauty and youth. If you aren't driving the right car, wearing the right cologne, or drinking the right soda, you just don't fit in. Bunk!

Smash the molds, I say! And be who you are and who you want to be! One quote reads, "You were born an original—don't die a copy!" What a refreshing insight in this often-form-fit world we live in.

I'm reminded of the variety of hair styles I have seen in the African-American community in Milwaukee…braids, "corn rows," "dread locks"… so many ways to express themselves in coif creativity! I love it!

Celebrate your uniqueness through your actions, words and choices. **"Be who you be"** and happiness will find its way to you.

March 27

If a man does not keep pace with his companions, perhaps it is because he hears the beat of a different drummer…let him step to the music he hears, however measured or far away.

Henry David Thoreau

David was in a special 1st grade class. They labeled him "retarded." One day, David was playing with a fist full of play dough, and the teacher came up and asked, "What do you have in your hands, David?" He remarked, *"It's a lump of cow dung."* "And what are you making with it?" *"I'm making a teacher!"*

The teacher thought, "David has regressed. I need to tell the principal." So the principal, now informed, came up to David and asked, "What have you got in your hands, David?" *"A lump of cow dung."* "And what are you making with it?" *"I'm making a principal!"*

The principal thought, "Oh, this needs the expertise of our school counselor." The coy psychologist approached David and said, "I bet I know what you've got in your hands…" *"What?"* "It's a lump of cow dung." *"Right."* "And I bet I know what you're making with it." *"What?"* "You're making a psychologist." *"No!* ***NOT ENOUGH COW DUNG!"***

David sure had a lot of "intelligence" for being put in a slower class. Do you keep people boxed in with the labels you put on them? I sure do sometimes! Do you keep *yourself* in a box with labels others have imposed on you?

Rich Melcher

March 28

<u>*Walk In Beauty*</u>

(a Native American prayer)

*O, Great Spirit
whose voice I hear in the winds,
and whose breath gives life to all the world ~*

*Hear me!
I am small and weak, I need Your
strength and wisdom . . .*

*Let me **walk in beauty** . . . make my eyes
ever behold the red and purple sunset ~*

*Make my hands respect the things You have
made--and my ears sharp to hear Your voice ~*

*Make me wise so that I may understand
the things You have taught my people ~*

*Let me learn the lessons You have hidden
in every leaf and rock ~*

*I seek strength, not to be greater than my brother,
but to fight my biggest enemy—myself!*

*Make me always ready to come to You
with clean hands and straight eyes ~*

*So when life fades, as the fading sunset,
my spirit may come to You without shame . . .*

March 29

> *Life is now. Yesterday is past and gone, and*
> *therefore unreal – only real in its affect on the moment.*
> *The future is not real, and possibly it will never be more*
> *than simply a dream. This leaves us the NOW, the moment, as reality.*

> *Leo Buscaglia*

Oh, how true! Here, Buscaglia speaks one of the most life-changing truths..."THIS IS IT! There is no practice session.

We are in this life now and only now!"

This may sound a little harsh—what are novels, movies and vacations for but escape? We all need that, no doubt.

But it's so tempting to put off our challenges and wait until another day. "There's always tomorrow," it's said, but tomorrow never comes—only turning into another *today.*

In the movie <u>Annie</u>, the young orphan sings,
"Tomorrow, tomorrow—
I love ya, tomorrow—you're
always a day away!"

To me, this song makes procrastination sound romantic and worthy. But it's a travesty to believe tomorrow's more important than today.

Could the song be rewritten as:
"Today, today, I love ya today,
you make for a better way". . .?

Nike's got the idea too, with its slogan,
"Just Do It!"—and singer John Mellencamp proclaims
"Your life <u>IS</u> now!"...another great idea. I would be
honored for you to try out my acronym "LETM"...
<u>L</u>ive & <u>E</u>njoy *This* <u>M</u>oment. *LETM* has led me in
the right direction many-a-time.

Are YOU living fully in the moment?

March 30

"I think I can, I think I can . . . I know I can! I know I can!"

(Children's book, The Little Engine That Could)

Growing up, I distinctly remember reading these words of The Little Engine...I had no idea that this type of affirmation was more than just talking to myself, but creating a pathway for my mind, heart and soul to follow.

An affirmation is . . . stating a desired goal as a present-time fact. Affirmations can shape the topography of our unconscious mind and lead the conscious mind toward successful activities and eventual positive outcomes.

The gentler we are with ourselves, the gentler we will be with others. And when we feel our life is heading in a positive direction, it will most likely promote the affirmation of our goodness. What's stopping you from affirming yourself? There's certainly nothing wrong with "being your own best friend." And, what you give to yourself you will naturally give to others.

One author wrote, "Look for the good (in others and yourself) and, in time, that's all that will catch your attention."

I was taught the power of personal affirmation back in the 1980s and have written down myriad detailed affirmations over the years. This has helped me focus on my positive points and perform more consciously and effectively. This has focused my attention on possibilities, while decreasing potential "non-thinking" ways.

Look for the good—**affirm** the good—**do** the good—**be** the good. It's a natural progression. See if you can discover it for yourself, if you haven't already!

March 31

*Aloneness means being right in the middle
of people, but they no longer have the power
to make you happy or miserable.*

Fr. Anthony de Mello

Do you see the value in solitude? Do you see how being alone, doing your own thing, can be beneficial? Or is it always the rush-rush, the coffee house conversations and bar scenes?

I can remember many times in my life when I couldn't stand being alone. My freshman year in college was such a time. Loud music, the night life, classrooms filled with energy, sitting in the student union with friends. It was as if I couldn't stand myself unless I was with others

A couple of years later, in March of 1982, I decided to pick up a notebook and begin writing a journal. I remember writing on that first page that I was making no commitments to write every day—or every week—but, at <u>that</u> moment, writing it was.

I had no idea that this simple act of picking up a ballpoint pen would lead to 10,000 pages of journal entries in the following 27 years, along with hundreds of poems and three books (with more on the way). I had made an investment in getting to know myself that day, and it has paid off a thousand-fold.

What simple connection can you make with yourself that may bring you to a greater place? Are you willing to risk it?

~ April ~

April 1

It takes courage for a person to listen to
his own goodness and act on it.

Pablo Casals

Imagine, for a moment, who you will be 20 years from now...where you will be living, what you will be thinking and feeling, who you will be in relationship with, what you will be doing; this can be called your *future self.* As you picture this *future self,* what one word or phrase does he/she want to say to you? Can you hear it?

When I did this exercise a few years ago, I saw myself:

-living with my wife in a big rustic house built into
a hillside, by a lake in northern Minnesota;

-thinking constructive thoughts and feeling fulfilled;

-piloting a single-engine airplane with my own personal
landing strip on a nearby plateau...

My 65-year-old *future self* climbed down from my airplane and called out one word to me:

"COURAGE!"

The message was instantaneously clear. It's as if the word had been hanging on my lips for years, just waiting to come out. *I needed to have courage and confidence in what I was doing and where my life was heading. Courage was to be my calling.*

I remember, in the movie *Braveheart*, Mel Gibson, as William Wallace, exclaims, "Men don't follow titles—they follow courage!" We can tell who the courageous ones are—the ones following their hearts, and, yes—the ones we ultimately follow. And in the *Wizard of Oz*, the lion couldn't find his courage. He had to look inside to discover it was right there all along.

The above quote speaks of *listening to our goodness*...do you know what your goodness is? Many of us never focus on what's good inside of us and can lose the ability to find it within. Think of your toughest struggles in the past...have YOU found YOUR courage?

One of my biggest challenges occurred when I was a teacher's aide in urban Milwaukee. On a fateful day, one of the 5th grade teachers was absent, and the principal didn't get a substitute teacher—which meant it was my duty to RUN THE CLASS for the day! I had no teaching degree, nor had I ever had the experience of actually *running a class*. I had no knowledge of previous assignments, no schedule for the day—and no idea what the students' names were! Forced into a corner, I had to ruffle up all my courage to meet the challenge head on.

These were busy, somewhat aggravating hours—but *successful* ones— and my heart was still beating when I left the building at the end of the day. That was a plus! This was my toughest struggle as a teacher's aide, and I achieved many notches in my belt that reflected my successes! And, therein, I discovered much *courage* from this experience.

How do you meet YOUR toughest struggles? Do you muster up the courage or back away in fear? We all have probably done both. I promote that if we seek courage, our fears will fall away behind.

What word is your *future self* speaking to you today?

April 2

We are unique in our gifts and united in our struggles.

Corsair

It was my turn to speak in the support group, and I chose one of my favorite topics...***uniqueness.*** I went on for 3,4,5 minutes, jabbering on how glorious it is that we all share one quality—uniqueness.

I must have thought I was being quite profound and eloquent, when a woman in the group raised her hand and stated, "I don't want to be considered *terminally unique!*" The words cut deep to my bone; I was shocked and stymied.

"*Terminally Unique.*" You mean that uniqueness can be a negative thing? "Yes", she said, "if your uniqueness separates you from others... if you are the only one with a problem...if you are looked at as weird or strange because of your 'uniqueness' . . . that is painful!"

It was in many hours of pondering this occurrence that I realized, "*We are unique in our gifts and united in our struggles*"...a realization I never would have come to if this wise, honest woman hadn't awakened me to a blindness. It is in this unique/united realization that an awkward moment has brought me to an inner truth...an extremely important moment hidden in an uncomfortable situation. What's new?

Do you *celebrate* your uniqueness, or *guard* it? Both actions are necessary at different moments in life. Which do you do the most?

April 3

An easy life teaches nothing.

(fortune cookie wisdom)

Who would have known that a simple fortune cookie could be so wise—and helpful. Wise, in that it is so often our difficult situations that help us grow. These situations are important learning experiences if we believe that our struggles indeed <u>can</u> help us grow, especially when we *take the time* to learn our lessons.

A man came across the site of a monarch butterfly just beginning to burst from its cocoon. So he took out a tweezers and carefully assisted the butterfly in escaping from its "prison" by pulling numerous times on the edges of the cocoon. When the butterfly made it out, it was warped and deformed, and died within a few minutes. The man discovered that it was the struggle of getting out—the effort and stress and wriggling—that the butterfly must endure to make the transition.

Only if the defeats, the failures, the wrong moves are analyzed can we learn our lessons. It's true that "the only REAL mistake is the one from which we learn nothing" (John Powell, SJ), but it is in the pondering and evaluating that life teaches us.

The man who "helped" the butterfly could have gone away thinking he had nothing to cause its deformity. But he kept observing and saw his error, regretted it—traveled on a wiser and more sensitive man because of it.

April 4

It is only with the heart that one can see rightly—
what is essential is invisible to the eye.

Antoine de St. Exupery
(The Little Prince)

An open heart means self-honesty. When the above says "only with the heart," this refers to our emotional intelligence—our ability to "see" who another is by observing (with the senses) and "observing" with our emotions.

St. Exupery's quote is priceless because it goes light years beyond our society's judgments of the physical person. He had the insight to know that true love, love for the whole person, values the INNER person more than the outer.

"What is essential" is indeed the *inner beauty* in each of us. Have you ever been valued for such inner qualities? It feels wonderful when someone notices your patience or brilliance or hopefulness or gratitude—and reflects this back in a kind and gentle way. It goes far beyond "your hair looks *nice*" or "you have a *nice* smile"—physical compliments that do not go very deep. We are **all** precious—sometimes we just need someone to notice our inner goodness and express it to us.

Can you find a way to compliment another for a positive *inner* quality? You may just make their day—or week—or year!

April 5

*The trouble with most of us is that we would rather
be ruined by praise rather than be saved by criticism.*

Norman Vincent Peale

We all need praise—yes—this is not questioned. It is doing well and KNOWING, inside, that we did well, that can be a powerful plus in our lives.

Yet, criticism from an appropriate source—such as a tutor, teacher or parent—is also essential in our growth process. I received two crucial pieces of criticism from a former principal that not only changed my life as a teacher's aide, but as a person.

She told me that (1) I was "not engaged" (not paying close attention nor being "with it") enough, <u>and</u> (2) I was not asking enough questions. These two criticisms changed my work life by helping me focus more on doing a "heads up" job. And they changed <u>my</u> <u>LIFE</u>, in that I "began paying more attention" to everything around me and inside me—and I becoming a *new man* because of it!

I'll never forget the morning, in 9th grade, when my history teacher took me out in the hallway and severely scolded me for (subtly) making fun of a disabled kid in the school—who happened to be his neighbor. It was very embarrassing—even shaming. But I never did so again, and, ironically, this has been the population—special education—that I have often worked with as a teacher's aide. Funny how it goes. What do they say—*what goes around comes around*?!

Yes, we can be *SAVED by constructive criticism* (such as my crucial transformation above) or *ruined by praise*, if we just sit around waiting to be affirmed. It takes a "big man" (or woman) to rise above criticism, but if we can see the gifts it offers—the lessons to be learned—it can lead to golden opportunities and fruitful, personal advances in character and skill.

April 6

He who knows others is wise;
he who knows himself is enlightened.

unknown

sometimes it seems
the harder I struggle
to be independent
the more I end up
in dependence

so I stop

and at times
I choose to find out
more about myself
(concentrated effort)
and discover how little
I really know myself

that scares me

oh how I long for
my thought to
give birth to
global significance
and for my feelings
to learn the definition
of serenity

I cling to fragments
of hope
often

Corsair

April 7

You must claim your own worth before you can help others.

unknown

The old pop song goes, "Nothin' from nothin' leaves nothin' . . . you gotta have somethin' if you wanna be with me!" It's true. We must have something if we're going to give anything of value.

It's also been written that "the more I love myself, the more I'll be attracted to people who will love and respect me." This love of self only comes with *knowledge of self.* We must seek self-awareness in order to learn who we are, and from there learn how to love ourselves, leading to self-love.

My struggle for self-love is on-going and pervasive! I first discovered this quality of self-esteem at age eight, yet have had it battered by the buffets of daily life and the misadventures of my bipolar illness. It's difficult to see your goodness if your moods and behaviors coarsely converge with reality that is altered by an illness as cunning and baffling as bipolar. When I look back on—and am forced to live with—the poor decisions, the impulsivity, the gyrations in emotional stability that are a part of living with this illness, I see that self-love can be illusive and, at times, invisible.

But I have had the advantages and blessings of having a wife, a family and friends who always bring me back to my goodness—to my excellence! Without them, I would be what I once heard a co-worker referred to as "a lost pup"!

It is crucial, this self-love, because without its presence, it is very difficult to love others—if not impossible! When we know ourselves, we can conquer any massive mountain, ford any strident stream. Like good witch Glinda proclaimed in the movie *The Wiz*, "When we know ourselves, we're always home—anywhere!"

Find your home.

April 8

Being genuine is far more important than being great.

Touchstones

Recently, I met a young African American gentleman who showed interest in what I was writing about in this book. He seemed very genuine, especially when he moved over to my table at the coffee house and began to tell me his story.

He stated that he wants to write a book using quotes and poetry. (Sound familiar?) He also said he wants to go into elementary classrooms and talk to kids about making right decisions—a man who had a tough up-bringing, who had been to prison, had made it through his struggles and recently started a small business. He finds himself succeeding in the community and reaching toward his dreams!

This young man fits the above quote—a *genuine* individual who has a burning desire to give back to others in productive and inspirational ways.

The circumstances and hopes of my new acquaintance are not uncommon. There are plenty of people who choose to truly learn from their mistakes and live a genuine life. I remember a classmate of mine in high school whom I envied because he was such a "free spirit" and had a mind of his own—something I had not yet developed, in my acquiescence to power and my need to please others. It took me <u>many</u> years to develop this genuine sense of self—which only came through much soul-searching and inner struggle. But develop it, I did!

Where do <u>you</u> weigh in on the "genuine scale?"

April 9

Shared joy is double joy ~ shared sorrow is half sorrow.

Swedish proverb

Such is the nature of companionship. Do you know where the word **"companion"** comes from? *"Com"* = <u>with</u>; *"pan"* meaning <u>bread</u>...*one we eat bread with.*

Meals are often times filled with the joy of sharing more than just food. Growing up in a family of nine kids, I so fondly remember the up-beat meal-times that we once had—and still have—at larger family occasions, these days. There was (and is) always a flurry of conversation, laughter and story-telling, and—God bless us—*puns* and word-play to moan about.

Over 30 years ago, we taped a family dinner for some reason, and in the background you could hear my older brother Steve repeating over and over, "These beans are sour! These beans are sour!" It was a classic Melcher dinner, captured on tape for posterity.

Companionship is one of our greatest needs, as humans...someone with whom we share *the bread of life*—our stories, our "days," our hopes and our dreams. Yet, building relationships must *not*, in my opinion, be built solely on companionship—this "simply being together." There must be mutual expressing, hopefully a spiritual connection, and an intellectual component. All of this builds trust and strengthens relationships.

I was once in an intimate relationship that had plenty of companionship, but little else...not much bonding, emotionally nor spiritually. This led to an eventual break up because, as we found out, it was like building a house with plenty of mortar, but few bricks! Companionship is essential but not the sole building material for growing healthy, vibrant relationships.

Do you have enough *companionship* in your life? Is it balanced with mutual sharing of emotional, intellectual and/or spiritual ideas and life experiences?

April 10

Our greatest glory consists not in never falling,
but in rising every time we fall.

Ralph Waldo Emerson

"It's not what happens to you," international speaker W Mitchell once stated, *"but what you do about it!"* Some people have all the advantages, and do very little with them. Others are the opposite...like W Mitchell.

As a younger man, Mitchell was involved in a motorcycle/gas tanker accident which burned over 75% of his body—including his face! He kept his optimistic ways, surviving many skin grafts and surgeries, showing the courage of 10 men. Years after Mitchell had recovered from his burns, he was involved in a small aircraft accident and became paralyzed from the waist down!

Undaunted, Mitchell—soon after recovering from the plane accident—decided to run for mayor in his small Colorado town, running on the slogan, *"Not Just Another Pretty Face"*...seemingly referring to a face that had been completely redone with skin grafts. And HE WON!

More of Mitchell's wisdom comes out in his statement, **"I could choose to see this as a setback or a starting point!"** Wow! This applies directly to me as I have struggled with bipolar disorder. It gives me hope, purpose and direction, as I think of all the challenges W Mitchell must have gone through. He is a true inspiration to me? How about you?

If you can relate to either of his above quotes and <u>NOT</u> be moved, at least a little, I believe you may be missing some life-changing wisdom.

Who are those who inspire <u>you</u> to greatness?

April 11

*The kind of person we become is just as important
as what we accomplish in the world around us.*

Each Day A New Beginning

Generally, our deeds will flow from who we are and who we are becoming. But some "good" actions come from an <u>in</u>authentic self—not from who we really are but from how others wish us to be.

When I was growing up in rural Minnesota, our parish priest would sing the "Our Father" gloriously, even though he was secretive about how parish funds were being spent, and he was trying to conceal that he was an alcoholic. Here was a case when words & deeds were not matching character.

It was confusing to me, as a youth, yet I believe there are ample people living with this type of inconsistency. If "the kind of person we become" <u>IS</u> important, what are we doing today to match our words & actions with a wholesome character? Do we value BEING as well as doing?

Writing this book has been a "doing *and being*" process. It has called out my best thinking, storytelling and writing skills. Plus, I am trying to LIVE what I'm writing about---easier said than done . . . but possible.

God bless you in YOUR journey, as you read this book. May it be helpful and encouraging! My hope is that it assists you on a healthy path of "becoming"!

April 12

There is no sweeter prayer than a grateful heart.

Fr. Anthony de Mello

What do you consider to be "prayer"? I believe it is much more rich and diverse than simply asking God to meet our needs—this is "petition." There is also the prayer of *gratitude*, simply saying "thank You, God"... and the prayer of *desperation*, when we seem lost in our problems and ask God for comfort and guidance. Communicating with God through these wonderful forms of prayer is very fulfilling and empowering.

I like the *"Clean Heart"* prayer—when we ask God to clean up and organize our lives as we are doing the same in our personal, interpersonal and outer environments. Having a *clean heart theology* means connecting how we clean up our inner lives with cleaning up our environment—while cleaning the bathroom, kitchen, garage—organizing, putting the good stuff on a shelf to be used and throwing out the garbage. The connection between simultaneous inner and outer "cleaning" can be very real, and very powerful!

Letting go and expressing *"I give it to You, God,"* is a fantastic way to pray also—acknowledging that God has the answers, and we do not. By surrendering to God, we often find peace and even, at times, the hidden answers to our problems.

Yes, prayer is multi-dimensional and can come in many forms. What type(s) of prayer do you bring to the table that differ from the forms above? My bet is that God sees them all as legitimate and welcomed!

April 13

There is nothing so bad, so ugly, so horrible,
so heavy, so deep, that you can't work through it,
move around it, step over it—but you have to believe.
If you don't believe it, you can't do it.

Unknown

I remember the darkest, ugliest days of my first depression, in the spring of 1980, my senior year in high school. I quite nearly lost all hope when my emotions took a nose dive because of the onset of bipolar disorder. I had no idea I had bipolar—a hereditary chemical imbalance in the human brain that can cause dramatic mood fluctuations and thought malfunctions. I didn't even know what it was!

Many times I came close to losing the will to live, living life neither from day-to-day nor even minute-to-minute, but second-to-second. It was as if a large brick wall had fallen on me and there I lay, stranded in the rubble, covered, bleeding, barely conscious (figuratively).

Summer brought a gladly-distracting job and a break from "the eyes" of high school life—other students always watching, evaluating. The depression waned and soon the excited mania kicked in. It took a few months of living in the kaleidoscope world of mania for me to get diagnosed with bipolar, but when I started taking medications to control the ups and downs, my life got back on track. Because I had a mother who never gave up on me and a God who orchestrated a way out, I survived with my swaggering hope and my near-sunken soul intact.

Believing in myself and my power to overcome difficult circumstances has developed as my sense of hope has increased. Hope is a powerful thing, something we must hold close and protect with all our might. As Dostoyevski said, "*Those who cease to hope cease to live.*" And I've touched the edge of that. Have you?

What is the state of your hope?

April 14

CAIS

Connectedness with the
Authentic
Inner-
Self

Corsair

There is this place, inside all of us, where the **authentic self** thrives. Often, in this busy world in which we live, this place—this essence of *peacefulness*—goes undetected... unrecognized.

Maybe some of us have never heard of—or even imagined—this spiritual and motivational place---this *CAIS*---that connects our psycho-social life to the inner-life.

It is so beneficial to know that *CAIS* can give voice to the soul, the inner-guide who is always there for us to call on. When we are stressed or upset, we <u>can</u> connect with the inner-self to ease the strife and calm us down. One way is simply to take a few deep breaths while whispering the word "relax" over and over.

Our *CAIS* can become a place to go <u>not</u> <u>only</u> in times of stress but at any moment in our day when we yearn for a spiritual connection and a better grip on the awareness of our unconscious, resilient goodness.

When do *you* feel this connectedness? If you don't, are you willing to look within and locate it? It's definitely worth the time and effort.

April 15

*We are inbred with a certain amount of resiliency.
It's not until tested that we recognize inner-strength.*

Kweisi Mfume (former head of NAACP)

Working as a special education paraprofessional (teacher's aide) over the years, I've been blessed to witness a great amount of courage and resiliency in my students.

Case in point: Mandy...a 14-year-old girl in a wheel chair, who seemed inattentive and only occasionally made guttural sounds, not words. She could only walk a few steps—aided by a paraprofessional—and was one student of whom I had quite low expectations.

One winter day in 2002, while I was wheeling Mandy by the empty cafeteria, I heard humming: "Nah nah nah nah, nah nah nah nah (hey hey, goodbye)...." I recognized the nostalgic tune immediately but looked all around trying to detect its origin. Suddenly, I realized it was coming from Mandy! I was shocked and delighted! She kept humming it—in tune—all the way down the hallway!

My impression of Mandy was immediately transformed and forever altered by her humming...she was "with it" and "in it," and she did have intelligence and creativity! I felt a bit ashamed for having judged her as a not being very intelligent, but I suddenly had a new camaraderie with her. Mandy went on to hum a number of tunes as I worked with her. With my altered attitude, I often found myself reading to her by a sunny window and talking to her, knowing she could understand. It may sound silly and even prejudiced (based on my previous impressions), but she "became a person" to me, rather than just an uncommunicative "handicapped" young girl.

God bless Mandy for breaking out of her shell and allowing me to see her *good stuff—and breaking me out of MY shell*...an encasement of prejudice toward her disabilities. I will never forget the *hope* Mandy brought me that day—a hope I will always carry within! My hope is that I can present *creative surprises* to those I encounter, just as Mandy did for me...offering the gift of awakening to the power of the human spirit & the unceasing resiliency that lies within all of us!

April 16

Learn to be intense without being tense . . . pressure is NOT tension.

Joe Torre, pro baseball manager

Do you know how you react to anxiety? Do you tap your feet, twiddle your thumbs, or does your neck stiffen up? Most everyone has *some* physical reaction when times get tense. Half the battle on the road to curtailing these physical reactions is won when you recognize how you react to stress. If you bite your nails but are not aware of it, how could you ever expect to stop the bad habit?

After giving a speech at my Toastmasters International (public speaking) club a few years ago, my evaluator told me that I play with my wedding ring at times when I am speaking, and that it was quite distracting. I thought it over, looking at my hands, and realized her critique was inaccurate. I *do not* play with my wedding ring (left hand), but with the ring on my right hand. Whatever. But I did finally see that this bad habit was detracting from my speeches and was unneeded. So I changed. I stopped playing with my ring and have become a better speaker because of the change.

Professional baseball players, at bat, spend so much time and energy spitting and chewing on their Skoal, kicking around the dirt, stepping in and out of the batter's box, and gripping & re-gripping their bats that I sometimes wonder how they ever get around to watching the pitch and swinging the bat! What if they put their full attention on batting instead of fumbling with these seemingly nervous habits? Would they get *more hits* and less spits?

Yes, it is good to be intense, but not tense. It's best to focus all of our attention on the project or event at hand, without creating visible nervous habits. One way I've heard it put is "We may have the butterflies—the goal is to get them *flying in formation!*"

Rich Melcher

April 17

> *Seeing is the most arduous thing that a human being*
> *can undertake . . . for it calls for a disciplined, alert mind.*

> *Fr. Anthony de Mello*

"What does it mean 'to love'? It means to **see**—a person, a thing, a situation—as it REALLY is, and not as you imagine it to be—to give it the response that it deserves. "You can hardly be said to love what you do not even see!" exclaimed de Mello.

He continued, "And what prevents us from seeing? Our conditioning, our concepts, our categories, our prejudices, our projections—the labels we have drawn from our culture and from our past experiences. 'Am I really seeing this person, or am I coming from my conditioning or from my prejudiced view?' It calls for an alert mind. But most people would much rather lapse into mental laziness than to take the trouble to *see* each person, each thing, in **present moment freshness**."

Seeing means awareness, and de Mello—a Catholic priest from India who wrote books and led retreats on the topic—was a breath of fresh air (from my view point) in an often-stale and regimented Catholic spirituality. He brought this freshness—promoting awareness and living in the now— to Catholics and non-Catholics alike.

"To see—that is the least we could demand of love...see ME...as someone said once, 'I'll always love the false image that I had of you!' Am I loving the image or am I loving this person? Am I projecting something from the past onto this person?"

De Mello's view is a powerful reminder of how we so often glaze over and "un-notice" the people and events around us. We live with the daily grind, the busy-ness, the structures and side-bars that keep us from delighting in the now moment. Oh what a world it would be if we could wake up and see the world for what it really is—beautiful, wondrous, unique!

De Mello ends with, "Very well, to drop your conditioning in order *to see* is arduous enough." Can you see a bit of your conditioning dropping into reality in the near future? Are you willing to SEE your truth?

April 18

(Scene from the movie, *"Prince of Tides"*)

Savannah: *You sold yourself short—you could have been more than a teacher and a coach!*

Tom: *Listen to me, Savannah . . . there's no word in the language I revere more than "TEACHER"—none! My heart sings when a kid refers to me as his teacher—and it always has. I've honored myself and the entire family of man by being one . . . .*

Helen Keller called Anne Sullivan "Teacher" throughout the numerous yours they worked together. This is a term of great respect and integrity that some, like Helen Keller, may have found irreplaceable. I side with Tom, above...*teacher* has become one of my favorite words, going back to 1984 when I first became a volunteer teacher in urban Milwaukee. This experience has led to many forms of teaching—speeches, books, classroom instruction, leading on-the-job training, individual tutoring... once teaching is *in your blood*, it never lets you go!

We may have been teachers without knowing it. At times when we goof up, our subsequent behavior has most likely taught something important not only to us but to all those around you. At these times, did you get upset, bow your head in shame, blame another? Or admit the mistake, resolve to learn from it, and to do better in the future?

Actually, we are constantly each EXAMPLES for those around us— we are *constantly* teaching others. How do you want to teach others? With courage or *conceit*? Honesty or *orneriness*? Hopefulness or *helplessness*? It's your choice. How and who will YOU choose to teach?

April 19

It ain't enough to get the breaks—you gotta know how to use 'em.

Huey P. Long

A man hiking alone in the Colorado Rockies lost his footing and tumbled toward a cliff. Miraculously, he grabbed the root of a nearby bush, which left him dangling, stuck, looking down 5,000 feet.

Fearful and choking for breath, he called out for help, but, understandably, no one answered. He tenuously hung there for an hour and finally, in desperation although he was not a religious man—called to the sky:

"Is there *anyone* up there?!" Seconds seemed like days...

then, suddenly, to his surprise, a loud voice answered,

"Yes! What do you want?"

Shocked, but relieved, he sputtered, "Can't you see I'm in danger? What should I do?!"

The voice answered, "Just **let go** and I'll catch you."

"Let go?!!" The hiker thought it over, sighed deeply, then yelled again, "Is there anyone <u>else</u> up there?!"

In order to "get the breaks" in moments of hardship or desperation, sometimes it calls for **faith** . . . either faith in a higher power or simply faith in the goodness that rests within. If we are to hold an optimistic view of life, sure we have to "roll with the punches," but also it's best to pack the punch of faith in our hip pocket to help us through the tough times and rise to a place of safety, competence, . . . and even blessing.

When will you choose to *let go*?

April 20

Career is goal-oriented, but vocation focuses on the purpose for your life.

David McNally

The word EVOKE means *to draw out of,* and "vocation," according to author David McNally, implies bringing our life purpose out and into clear focus, which extends far beyond mere goal setting. To consult the inner-self is a component of a *spiritual way of life* which often leads to authentic decision-making, based <u>not</u> only on what we do, but on *who we are.*

In the public television portrayal of a fictional meeting between Martin Luther King, Jr. and Malcolm X, the King character stated, "If our purpose is clear, we will be able to endure much more." (Sounds, to me, like something King would have said). It is persistence and concentrated focus that lead us on the journey to find that which is the *purpose* of our lives— not to mention the importance of the opposite stance—relaxing and letting life develop around us. This paradox, this clash, seems irrational, but I believe both are essential!

With purpose comes clarity; with clarity, direction; with direction, promise. My hard-won purpose statement is very simple:

"Rich grows with <u>whatever</u> he's been given, and joyfully gives it back!"

This purpose statement came to me over many hours of searching and contemplation. Its simplicity makes it pointed and powerful for me, and is easy to remember and recite—good aspects of an effective purpose statement. It all started with just a few ideas—words, actually:

*Growth...give...joy...*and the notion of flexibility ("whatever"). Then, like stacking Lincoln Logs, it gradually came together. It's been a heart-phrase for me for over 15 years now.

Can you see yourself constructing a purpose statement? It doesn't need to be elaborate or over-symbolic—actually, the simpler the better. How could *you* define your purpose? What key words accurately describe you?

I challenge you to pick up a pen and begin jotting. You may be surprised (and eventually delighted) with what the paper before you reveals. It's well worth the effort. You may just find a powerful purpose longing to breathe the fresh air of your greatness!

April 21

I have come, more and more, to realize that being unwanted is the worst disease that any human being can ever experience!

Mother Teresa of Calcutta

Mother Teresa encountered this "unwantedness" in the daily suffering of the people she served...the dying, the desperate, the indigent, the weak in the slums of Calcutta. Many people would think, "What possible contribution could these destitute people make to society?" I believe this is the wrong question. The right question is, "How can we stop letting people get down so low that they end up like this?" I don't know the answer. But it has been said by psychologists that the greatest human need is *to be appreciated.* Social mores extend this concept as common courtesy, which calls us out to say "thank you" when receiving a goods or services from another.

I created the acronym "**NBA**" as a help...*NBA* = we Need to Be Appreciated. This can assist us in focusing on what we CAN DO, which is, show appreciation for gifts and presence of loved ones, and express thanks to those around us who serve and supply us. We need to recognize others' NBA and act accordingly to make them feel wanted and worthy. This is similar to the guideline *"treat others how **you** want to be treated."* Observing *The Golden Rule* goes far beyond ANY religious precept yet is a *spiritual* imperative!

There are countless *"NBA"* stories . . . here is one from my own life. When I first hit the ice on hockey skates at age 11 or so, I decided to join the local hockey team. But the year before I did so, I was so new to skating that I had <u>no idea</u> how to skate backwards. I had seen myriad others gliding in reverse and it looked fun. Skating in a public arena one winter afternoon, I blurted this skill-deficit to my older brother, and some other kids skating listening nearby began to tease me. I was burned—yet became motivated, in my anger, to learn how to take the risks to learn the challenging techniques.

Ironically, when I joined the Bantam team (age 13), my new coach made me a defenseman—the guy who spends much of his time *skating backwards!* I was forced to learn a crucial lesson: "Necessity is the mother of invention," and it didn't take long before I spun around and began mastering the skill. That first year, although I was a pretty weak skater and had absolutely no "stick handling" savvy, I became known as the toughest defenseman on the team! My specialty was knocking approaching opponents flat on the ice (known as "checking")—and my coach gave me the nick name "THE HAMMER"! It was the first nick name I had ever been blessed with, and it made me feel special—and essential! A previously unknown *NBA* was recognized and satisfied by this crucial recognition. From there, I went on to become captain of the high school hockey team, my senior year! *NBA*, when actualized, often builds confidence and purpose! How can *you* make someone you encounter feel appreciated? How can *you* lessen the "unwantedness" (of which Mother Teresa spoke) in someone nearby?

April 22

Some depressions can be caused by a chemical imbalance in the human brain, but often, pressures and stress can create "situational depression" which can cause just as much suffering and disillusionment   Below is a poem I wrote after coming out of a dark and dreary depression.

best cure for depression
I've ever found?
keep looking for life
around you
noticing every detail
every vein on new-sprung leaf
or sunset divine

from this
life will spring
  if you can express
    what you have seen, felt,
      smelled, tasted, touched

        freedom comes in the
          experiencing & expressing
          of such life
          and allowing the
          wonder
            to become
          life's road map
            once more

            seek life

          Corsair

April 23

It's better to keep your mouth shut and thought a fool,
than to open it and remove all doubt.

unknown

An unfortunate symptom of bipolar mania—a condition I've experienced many times—is definitely over-talkativeness. When mania is ruling the psyche, the person has so much to say and seemingly so little time to say it. The mega-creativity of mania supplies the person with seemingly endless ideas and a compulsive need to express them. A phenomenon known as "racing thoughts" provides ample fodder for ceaseless talkativeness.

The opposite is pretty much true when one is in depression. One has slowed thought and movement with very little to say. Bipolar is an illness of opposites—mood-wise and behavior-wise. From soaring glory and ecstasy when in mania, to depths of despair and hopelessness when in depression, bipolar is "cunning & baffling" (a phrase used in Alcoholics Anonymous to describe alcoholism).

The trick is to get the right medication and therapy that help one achieve balance—body, mind & spirit. It may be illusive at times but it IS possible! If you see these symptoms in your thoughts, emotions and behaviors, you may just want to get checked out for bipolar disorder. Getting the proper treatment can relieve much suffering and confusion! There may not be a cure, but there can be relief, a sense of control and ever-present HOPE!

Your health—your life—is worth it, and there's no shame in having a chemical imbalance in your brain—whether bipolar, major depression, or whatever! You CAN get help. I challenge you to have the courage to seek it!

April 24

"I said . . . a change—a change—will do you good!"

Sheryl Crow

Sometimes we just need a little change of scenery to refresh us. This is one major purpose for vacations. I remember our July 1970 family vacation like it was yesterday. Seven out of nine kids, and Mom & Dad, traveled to "the dunes" of south-eastern Lake Michigan for a week near the lake that seemed like an ocean.

We met many of our cousins there and had the time of our lives! The beach, the sand, the sun and...the rocks! Scattered on the shore were thousands of beautiful rocks—rocks that SPOKE to me and quickly became my "friends." I was found stashing them in pockets and filling cupped hands. Oh, the fantasy world of a curious 8-year-old boy!

Experiencing a comfortable solitude, I enjoyed my silent hand-held stone partners' "conversations" in this new-found language of texture, form and beauty. Also, I connected deeply with The Carpenters' #1 hit song, "Close To You," that seemed to play constantly on our old transistor radio during that sunny summer trip. The song spoke of someone realizing their preciousness and value—something of which I previously had had no concept. The song gave me a sense of self-esteem, although I had never heard of *self-esteem* before and had no words to describe those warm thoughts and feelings at the time. It was my first experience of self-love, an elusive—yet essential—entity which has floated in and out of my life ever since.

When it came time to go home to Minnesota, my older sister wouldn't let me bring my bucket of rocks home, so I secretly stuffed handful after handful in any space of the trailer I could find. Despite sisterly disapproval, my "friends"—the wonderful rocks I had collected—<u>did</u> make it home with me, as we crossed Lake Michigan on the ferry and sped from Milwaukee back to Minneapolis in the early morning haze.

As I recall my favorite childhood memories, the magical trip to *the dunes* at age eight is one of the most vibrant and retrievable. I thank God for vacations that bring life to Life, and provide wonderful new experiences and great memories!

April 25

Optimism means seeing the opportunity in every difficulty, while pessimism means seeing the difficulty in every opportunity.

Dr. Alan Zimmerman

This is one of the most challenging *and instructive* quotes I have ever encountered. I took a class from Dr. Zimmerman in 1983—my senior year of college—that changed my life forever!

The class was a 5-day, 8-hour per day seminar simply called *Interpersonal Communications*. The 35 participants were introduced to exercises in dealing with one another one-on-one, and although it seemed like real basic—almost obvious—material, we all gained great skills of interacting with one another that either hadn't existed in us before, or that had been dormant for years...unrecognized, undervalued.

This powerful seminar brought me a new optimism and belief in myself that I had never encountered before! I suddenly realized that, yes, I could start a conversation with *anyone,* or find the good qualities in a former enemy. Abe Lincoln said...'the best way to defeat an enemy is to make him your friend.' This applies to the self also. Eventually, I acknowledged that I had often been "my own worst enemy," but, because of the seminar content and exercises, had gratefully become *my own best friend!*

How can a seminar like this "change your life"? Well, I firmly believe that *Interpersonal Communications* made it possible for me to join the Jesuit Volunteer Corps (similar to the Peace Corps, but serving urban US communities) after graduation, seven months later, and venture into a life-changing experience as a teacher's aide in urban Milwaukee, starting in September 1984. Without these new people skills, and the confidence that accompanied them, I don't think I would have ever been able greet & meet the many challenges of culture-shock and classroom confusion that blasted me upon entering the old intimidating grade school building. Instantly, the experience became intriguing and joy-filled...clearly one of the most significant and fulfilling years of my life!

This class was a milestone event for me...it changed me—for the good—forever! What was a *milestone event* in YOUR life? How did it change you? When will you take the risk of attending a seminar that could potentially bring lasting positive change—and even adventure—to your life?

April 26

*I may not be perfect, but parts of me are excellent . . .
my mind is restored to a place others call brilliance.*

Each Day A New Beginning

I truly believe that <u>everyone</u> has a gift to bring to the table. While working as a special education teacher's aide a few years ago, I had an incredible experience while working with a *non-responsive* autistic 12-year-old boy named Jerry. He had never spoken and didn't respond to instruction of any type.

Well, Jerry and I were sitting in a small room and, to soothe him, I was slowly rubbing the index and middle fingers of my right hand on his right wrist. He seemed to become quite serene as I did this. After a few moments, I suddenly had a "special and spiritual broadening sense" that the love I was giving Jerry *at that moment* was reaching beyond time and space. *The world opened up* in front of me and it was as if this touch, this love, was flowing *through* him to others in the future and the past.

Being that Jerry was Jewish, it was as if I were touching and soothing an Auschwitz prisoner, suffering the perils of Nazi imprisonment. And also, it was as if I were calming and soothing a person who had yet to be born, in some future trauma he or she would experience.

This incredible spiritual experience has never left me. Although I will never be able to fully explain what happened between us that day, the event still encourages me to give my love to others as completely and as often as I can.

This transformative experience would not have happened without Jerry—a "severely handicapped" boy (and a *vision* catalyst)—a testament to the fact that "parts of him are excellent!"

April 27

We've
All
Got
Something

We've all got . . . *something* — such as an illness, a disability, a stutter, a scar, a dysfunctional past...*everyone* has something. And this can be good, in that it levels the playing field. You see, if *everyone* has some defect, we can find unity in our "brokenness."

What was it like for me, a person with bipolar disorder (manic-depression), to find out that Winston Churchill, Vincent Van Gogh and Vivian Leigh also had it? Freeing! No longer was I the lonely kid on the block with "a problem." I had company—even *famous* company.

It took many years of struggle, many "ups and downs" to come to this realization. Bipolar is a cave-ridden fiend, sometimes hiding in the dark for years, then pouncing with the fierceness of a hungry tiger. It's easy to blame yourself when you have a mood disorder because you may think you brought an episode on by your behavior or thought choices. Yet, these chemical imbalances can cycle, catching even the most health-seeking person by surprise.

When I came up with WAGS, I finally realized that everyone has some type of burden and that I was not alone in my suffering. The cage of shame had been rattled and lock broken—allowing the beast within to escape and set me free. Now, when I see someone upset or fearful, it just takes a realization of WAGS for empathy to arise, and compassion to flow.

Hey! We've All Got Somethin'! What have YOU got? And, though you may not pronounce it from the rooftops, does empathy find its way into your heart on account of this awareness?

April 28

> *...but somewhere along the line, Tim had been*
> *convinced, probably by someone whose love he*
> *needed very much, that he was worthless. I was only*
> *now beginning to see how feelings of unworthiness and*
> *mistrust keep innocent kids like Tim from accepting the help*
> *they need and deserve.*
>
> <u>*Children of Eve*</u>, *by Covenant House, NYC*

As we have seen, Mother Teresa was known to say that the worst "disease" is that of being *unwanted*. The above quote speaks of Tim feeling worth less, or worst—*worthless*.

I often wonder about the 5th graders I used to tutor as a teacher's aide. They seemed to have this grand need for attention from their peers and an overwhelming tendency to disrupt class, blaming others for their poor behavior. Could this be part of a lack of feeling significant?

Or could it also be part of what Dr. Ron Markman, (an expert on how violence affects people), points to as the cause of much violent behavior—*humiliation*? Humiliation creates rage. And rage—outbursts! I remember being humiliated many times as a youth, and having it come out in team sports—hockey & football. I wonder what I would have done if I hadn't had positive outlets.

As a teacher's aide at an urban Milwaukee grade/middle school, anger seemed to come out of the students from every direction, and mostly through classroom and hallway disruptions. But did these kids have any positive outlets for their anger? Grades 5-8 no longer even had time in the playground to work off some of their burgeoning energies.

My hope and prayer is that kids can find the structure, attention and love they need—along with common sense life-skills instruction—to assist in channeling their energies into positive outcomes.

What do YOU do when you feel "worth less"?

April 29

You don't get much in this world without an element of self-sacrifice.

Dr. Michael Ariss

One of the most compelling stories of self-sacrifice I've ever come across is that of a little black girl born two months early, who contracted double pneumonia and scarlet fever. Then she got polio which left one of her leg in a brace.

This little girl somehow got a notion that she was going to become the *fastest woman runner* in the world. They all laughed at her. But she would take her brace off and prance around the house when her mother wasn't home.

In junior high she decided she would join a race. Again they all laughed. She came in last. Next race, last. On & on. Until, one day, she came in second to last, then second. Then came the day in which she **won** a race—from then on, she won every race after that!

In the 1960 Olympics, in Rome, Wilma Rudolph won three gold medals the girl, the woman, who just wouldn't give up and who learned to use her self-sacrificing ways to achieve monumental goals. She had an indomitable spirit and enormous will power that carried her from being a thin, crippled girl to a world champion. I pray that I have even a tiny piece of the determination and giftedness she presented to a doubting world.

April 30

How does one become a butterfly?
You must want to fly so much that you're
willing to give up being a caterpillar.

Hope For the Flowers

Seems to me that *transformation* is the ultimate goal of any great teacher. We want to see those we teach change in positive ways—to be *transformed* from caterpillar into butterfly.

But the learner has to be open to this transformation, or at least to be somewhat flexible. Education is a 2-way street. In order for it to work, the student must "want to fly" while the teacher attempts to supply "the wind beneath their wings," as the popular song goes. All the teacher can do, really, is put it out there. Students must free themselves from the cocoon of inexperience as they consistently work to improve their skills and abilities.

Fr. Anthony de Mello, commented, "Say your thing and get out of there! If they profit from it—fine. If they don't—too bad!" Teaching is an art, but without open-minded students, the teacher cannot succeed. The student must grow to see that life in the cocoon is stifling and that being able to fly free IS the ultimate goal.

~ May ~

May 1

Sometimes it is necessary to teach a thing its loveliness.

Ko-Thi Dancers, Milwaukee, Wisconsin

This could be the most important lesson of all! So often we are unable (or unwilling) to see our greatness. Marianne Williamson wrote that we often most fear our brilliance, rather than our incompetence.

I remember showing the 5th graders with whom I worked—as a teacher's aide in urban Milwaukee—that they had great talents and power to do good. This was a process of working with groups of three or less, helping them see that they were EXAMPLES for their fellow students to follow. And as leaders, *they* had the power to *build or destroy* a classroom environment. I attempted to show them how to create the good, not bring on the bad.

These kids were so great, so special but only seemed to show it when they were "themselves," in the small groups I held in the hallway. They seemed to come alive in my small groups—becoming <u>kids</u> again--not showing this often-mutated adult façade, full of anger and destructiveness. I *saw* their **beauty** and prayed they would come to do the same.

My main goal was to help them see (and KNOW) these positive qualities, in themselves and one another, and live them out! EXAMPLE! Did I succeed? I'll never know. This is the nature of teaching—you may never see the outcome until 20 years later.

Yet, I hope they learned that..."*sometimes it <u>is</u> necessary to teach a thing its loveliness*" and found their greatness inside!

May 2

One good quote, properly placed in the mind and heart,
can change a life—and a _life_ properly placed
can change a world!

Corsair

I remember that in 6th grade, I memorized my first quote. Oh yes, I had tried to memorize quotes in religion class and even in history class, but it took until my piano teacher gave me a quote glued to a palm-held, oval rock—given as a gift—for me to really *grasp* the power of a quote. It read: "Be patient—God isn't finished with me yet!" I was 12-years-old when I received it—over 30 years ago! It still rings true today.

Collecting quotes began to grasp me in college, in the early 1980s, probably as I started writing my journal. But by the mid 1990s, I was in full swing, writing down quotes from TV shows, books I was reading and even scratching out notes in crowded, near-dark movie theatres.

Here's one I probably scribbled down in a theatre: *Integrity is what you do when no one else is looking.* *(unknown author)*

This makes me think.

Somewhere I picked up the power of the quotation, and it has led me to many great places, one of them being this book. Quotes—brief words of wisdom—can transform lives. They can bring out the best in us, and steer us away from the worst in us. I encourage anyone and everyone to pay attention to the type of quote that stirs and inspires them—and hold on to them with all their might. One quote—one simple phrase—may mean the difference between a moment of ultimate success or dismal failure.

Here's another favorite: *I have decided to banish, far away, all fear and all memory of past faults…no trace of dead sins left behind,… for in one second, Love can burn them to ashes.* *St. Therese*

This gives me hope.

One that has led me out of many-a-day of low moods and un-productivity came from my father's late business partner, Wayne. He said to me one day in 1978 that, *"There's always something to do!"* This simple advice was meant to motivate and instruct me on the jobsite at the family construction business, but it has proved helpful in EVERY area of my life! I've used it at other jobs, when struggling to fill "free time," and even in doing house duties. It has been a blessing—one Wayne never knew affected me so deeply.

It's no joke...a wise, instructive or comforting word, placed properly in time and atmosphere, can work wonders. Corral a quote & see.

May 3

If a man does not keep pace with his companions, perhaps it is because he hears the beat of a different drummer...let him step to the music which he hears, however measured or far away.

Henry David Thoreau

There is one thing we all have in common—that is, we're all **unique**. We ALL hear a different drummer—we have unique perspectives, interests, passions, aspirations, struggles. Contrary to common cultural belief, there is no average or "normal" person.

Kids (and even adults) tend to tease, even ridicule, those who seem to be "different," those who look or act *differently*—who "stick out in the crowd." Wouldn't it be great if we could all just *value the differences?* THIS is my definition of diversity—*"to value the differences, enjoy commonalities, and bring out the best in every person."*

I once heard of a kid who had no legs and tried out for the Minnesota Twins professional baseball team. He was out there "running" the 40-yard dash nearly as fast as the others (on his hands) and chasing down fly balls like the rest of them. When one reporter asked why he tried out for the team, he simply responded, "Well, I had nothing to do until 3 o'clock!"

What an awesome attitude! Just think of the image he had of himself going on inside his head. *He could* 'cause he thought he could!

Can't we just *step to the music we hear*, no matter how odd it may seem to others—*however measured or far away?* <u>This</u> is true diversity—valuing *oursleves* as unique individuals!

May 4

"...and then comes the confidence from truly not having a clue..."

Susan, National Public Radio

Every new parent probably has this confidence but quite possibly not much awareness of how much work it will be to rear their child.

I've never had kids of my own, but I have had a similar experience. Coming straight out a college in rural Minnesota in 1984 and entering volunteer teacher's aide position at an all-black grade school in urban Milwaukee, I had <u>no</u> <u>clue</u> of what I was getting into.

Everything was different: the skin colors, the hair styles, the black–English, the energy...it was a new world and my naiveté was my only *protection.* It kept me from experiencing massive culture shock! But I loved it! The kids were a bit rambunctious and over-active AND yet were very loving, most of the time. We learned from one another—but I ended up learning the most! You know how that goes.

I remember the day when one of my 5th grade math students, Rene, looked at me and said, "Mr. Melcher—you **act** black!" I had no idea what she was talking about, but I took at is a heart-felt compliment and went on teaching. Talk about not having a clue....

The *confidence from not having a clue* led to a confidence of getting to know them and what to do with and for them. It was one of the most moving and important years of my life.

What do you do when you find that you don't have a clue?

May 5

We can do no great things;
only small things with great love

Mother Teresa

It came to me while lifting weights in new program I'm embarking upon. The thirteen exercises, done on machines, challenge me with a combination of strength training and muscle toning. It occurred to me while lifting that I have often had a hard time following through on projects, such as this very type of weight training program I have started in the past and not persisted in continuing.

Then it came to me...the weights have a small ½-weight that slides down to give a more incremental strategy of lifting. And as I pondered my step-daughter's recent statement about "going to the next level," it occurred to me that I have most often seen moving up and forging ahead as being a process of taking giant leaps—huge strides—that of which have seemed too big to accomplish—even intimidating!

So I thought, "what if I were to '*Insist on Incremental Improvement* (I³)' and take baby steps toward my goals? Many baby steps equal a huge step, by the way! I thought about my struggles with reading. For 25 years or so I have seen myself as a poor reader. I have owned that label in my own heart and mind, and therefore carried it out with precision...therefore avoided reading more times than not.

What if I were to invest 10-15 minutes of time a day in reading—either aloud or silently—so that I can be putting effort into reading rather than complain about how I read so poorly? Wouldn't this be a better plan?

I have had an acronym in my back pocket for ten years (along with 31 other acronyms) that reads:

PUMP

Practice
Ultimately
Makes
Progress

Isn't now the time to live out this maxim? If I *"Insist on Incremental Improvement* (I³)" in this and other areas of my life, I believe that success in these areas will eventually be mine.

How can you get I³ working in your life?

May 6

God doesn't steer parked cars

John Ackerman.

Kevin had what one may call a *melancholy personality*. Junior high probably brings this out in many folks, but Kevin had a bad case. He would go to the beach in summer, see a girl he liked chumming with some other guy, and come home moping and full of angst. He would languish in the La-Z boy chair at home and think of his many troubles (of which he really had few). But he wouldn't act.

Kevin's non-assertiveness won him few friends and more fears—about girls, school, about Life. He stayed home a lot, watching TV shows that often made him feel more lonely because THEY had a life, and he didn't. Sometimes he chose exercise as an outlet, but you can only ride a bike so far, or swim laps for so long.

It took until senior high for Kevin to realize that his moping around was unproductive and so he decided to become more proactive - meeting friends after a game, making healthy choices, sharing himself more fully in conversations. This proved to be an excellent posture compared to his previous stance. God began to grace him with good friends and more productive attitudes. Kevin went from viewing to *doing*!

Remember, God doesn't steer parked cars.

May 7

Less

When you get in an argument ~
    Less is more.

When the plane is late ~
    Less is more.

When you need to write a theme paper ~
    Less is more.

When you're out in the hot sun ~
    Less is more.

When you've overslept on the morning
        of an important interview ~
    Less is more.

When the restaurant adds too much
        mayonnaise to your sandwich ~
    Less is more.

When your temper flairs at a loved one ~
    Less is more.

When you have to critique a co-worker ~
    Less is more.

When someone is showing disrespect to you ~
    Less is more.

All greed aside, sometimes LESS is a good thing!

                    Corsair

May 8

Know thyself.

Socrates

Another famous man wrote "The unaware life is not worth living"— maybe it was Socrates himself…sounds like this "knowing yourself" business was pretty important years ago. And it still is.

What are the ways you find helpful in getting to know yourself? Do you discover yourself in conversations with friends—hearing yourself speak your truth? Or do you get to know yourself through writing? I do. I started writing my journal on March 31, 1982 (yes, I remember the date!). Many born-again Christians can name the date of their conversion—I guess this was my "born-again" date. It was when my self-awareness started, and when my inner spiritual life really began to take root.

From these writings have sprung poetry and a wide variety of prose, including three books and numerous speeches. I have changed a lot over the years, and my writings have been a main reason for the positive change.

Glinda, the Good Witch of the South in the movie *The Wiz*, said, "When we know ourselves, we're *always* home—anywhere!" Awareness brings us to the doorstep of ourselves, and many wonderful gifts can come from the encounter.

May 9

True nobility is not about being better than others— it's about being better than you used to be.

Dr. Wayne Dyer

Wow, did this shake me up? Comparison is one of the biggest issues when it comes to self-esteem, and I have struggled with this monster all my life. As the youngest of nine, I had eight brothers and sisters to look up to, and I often got lost in the shuffle.

Our American society is filled with the *gotta beat him outs* and the *gotta look better than hers* that keep us separated from one another. It's so easy to compare ourselves with others and strive for moving toward the top, or end up spinning toward the bottom if expectations are not met. How many times have you been found comparing yourself to others? Did that make you feel stronger or weaker?

Isn't it true that it makes us stronger in the *weaker* parts of us—the insecure, burdened parts that have to WIN to feel free? Free of the bondage of incapability, and tied to the need for power—over others and over keeping that lead weight of inferiority balanced inside so it doesn't clumsily drop to the ground?

But when we focus on improving ourselves instead of rabid comparing, we can find peace—and the strength that comes from healthy progression. Dr. Dyer had it right: "It's about being better than you used to be!" Move to improve.

May 10

As the young move...horizons are breached,
the landscape is transformed; experiences are clarified.

Maxine Greene

Kids. We either were one, or we are one. Youth means change—movement. Looking back, I remember the struggles I had with over-activity, lack of accomplishment and lowered self-esteem. I didn't know why I was so restless, and I didn't know what "self-esteem" was, so how could I suffer from its absence? Well, we certainly can suffer from a disease that is unidentified, can't we?

But there is no standing still. We are either progressing or regressing. I believe it was Will Rogers who said, "Even if you're on the right track, the train will run over you if you're not moving!"

Surely, as in the quote at the top, "horizons are breached," and "landscapes are transformed," but—are experiences clarified? This seems to have happened very little for me in those early years. Only now, as I'm working with kids, do I come across with wisdom about MY adolescence... the attention-getting, the apathy, the struggle to read. Adolescence was a confusing and often painful time, with its hateful discouragers and multi-teasers.

It was a mix—there were many fun, even enchanting moments. It seems like such a blur now and passed quite quickly then. Sometimes clarity only comes in time, and youth surely flees with the wind.

May 11

Diversity is NOT a threat or distraction, but a great gift and—potentially—a powerful life- and hope-enhancing promise...bringing colorful beauty where chilling indifference and blind misunderstanding once stood.

Corsair

Why are we so afraid to be different? Possibly because we would stand out and therefore be in a position for ridicule or teasing. Even if this unique characteristic is a good one, it could cause jealousy, and so often, then, we hide our uniqueness.

I recently published a book, *Discerning Bipolar Grace*, which is a memoir about my chaotic and destructive year of 2008, due to an episode of bipolar mania. It is a big risk to put myself "out there" about a taboo topic such as mental illness, but I feel that if the wall of stigma is ever to be broken down, one must take radical steps to begin chipping away at the bricks of insensitivity and ignorance. So, I write on.

Stephen R. Covey, author of *The Seven Habits of Highly Effective People*, reflects that true diversity calls for *valuing the differences*—and this is where a group gains strength. When we all share our various talents and strengths—even our peculiarities—it creates a deeper and more powerful force. The cooperative spirit makes uniqueness valued *and* valuable.

"So don't be afraid to let them show—your true colors..." sings Phil Collins in a song about just *being ourselves*. ("True Colors"...his was actually the first song my wife and I danced to at our wedding in 2007). If we take the risks of sharing our uniqueness, the gift we have to bring to the table may just be the missing component for individual <u>and</u> group success!

May 12

Everyone wants a chance to be someone...

"Touched by an Angel," TV show

Rev. Jesse Jackson, while running for president of the United States in 1988, led crowds in a chant, "You ARE somebody! You are somebody!" Don't we all seek a life of significance? To BE SOMEBODY to someone... maybe we don't have dreams of being a national or international figure, but to be *somebody* in our community, our church, our family...this is true success.

I've heard that this is the same statement (if not sentiment) that Dr. Martin Luther King, Jr.'s grandmother used to tell him..."Martin, don't you ever forget that you are somebody!" This came in the heat of ugly segregation in Georgia, an evil that Dr. King went on to tackle and bring to the ground during his time as leader of the Civil Rights Movement in the United States.

This attitude is NOT arrogance, envy or unhealthy pride. It is a wholesome desire to make a difference and to demand dignity, in an often-racist and sexist society. What will be your stance as YOU decide to make a difference in your life? And WHEN will you get TO it?

May 13

It ain't where you come from—it's where you're goin'.

Madea, (Tyler Perry)

This idea has given me great hope lately. Sometimes I fall back into a hole, thinking that my past is actually more important and more influential than the present. This is a lie. If it were true, we would all be stuck with our past mistakes as reality, when it isn't. Some have even said that the past is an illusion.

An example? Well, as a teacher's aide for 5 years in Minnesota, I had been quite non-assertive, even apathetic, at times. When I was teacher's assistant in urban Milwaukee, I *had the tendency* to do the same—but finally decided NOT to act that way.

I remember one day when I had the *privilege* of working with a 5th grade girl who had been kicked out of her class for being insolent and violent. She was an angry young girl. I didn't know what to do with her at first, but then she noticed this leaflet that I always carried with me. It is comprised of creative art pieces, quotes and symbolic drawings, which helped me reach kids.

It sure reached her! She saw this diagram with six animals in a spiral figure, and I described how I had taken three "positive" animals (sea turtle, hawk, rabbit) and three "negative" animals (snake, scorpion, shark), and put descriptive words to each—to describe my emotions.

She quickly picked up a pencil and began drawing a spiral with the names of HER six animals, and named the emotions. Her mood went from distraught and upset to interested and even elated! The change was amazing—to both of us! I believe she surprised herself more than me. It was a wonderful transformation—the most radical and exciting I've ever seen.

Madea was right..."it's where you're going" that matters…an excellent attitude to keep us on track, isn't it?

May 14

I offer the gift of knowledge & wealth of mind
presented to me by many of the
masters of "thinkology."

(Scarecrow from The Wizard of Oz)

This, being my birthday, I find myself writing in gratitude for the many many gifts received from loved ones and from God. One gift is the ability to write, and also the "knowledge & wealth of mind" that come from writing from the heart.

One friend described the best communication—the most effective and enriching way of getting your point across—as speaking and writing "from heart to heart." Using this style, I have been blessed with a topic of importance that I am sharing in my new book *Discerning Bipolar Grace: a bipolar memoir.*

Bipolar Disorder used to be called manic-depression,
but I'm just going to refer to it as BIPOLAR. So, what exactly IS Bipolar?

Bipolar is a hereditary chemical imbalance in the human
brain that can cause dramatic mood fluctuations, thought
difficulties and behavioral disturbances.

Although I am not famous (so how could *I* write a memoir?), I believe this story about my experiences with bipolar can be very useful because it crosses several paths that many people find themselves on...depression, anxiety, spirituality, self-esteem—issues for a person with bipolar or issues for a loved one of one who has bipolar...really, for *anyone.*

So, why write this on my birthday? Well, because it is a giant leap to be coming out publically with a story on mental illness, AND because having bipolar is one of the things that makes me truly unique...offering me creativity, sensitivity and a sense of personal worth. Although nearly 2% of the population encounter this illness, I don't remember seeing many personal accounts about it—especially not from an *average Joe* such as myself.

My specialty is to speak "from heart to heart," and *Discerning Bipolar Grace* is probably my best "heart to heart" work because of its descriptions of personal events. The act of writing and the discipline of praying have given me at least a modicum of "*knowledge & wealth of mind*"...and I'm delighted <u>and</u> blessed to be able to share it with you! *Discerning Bipolar Grace* is available on *amazon.com*.

May 15

Fish discover water last.

(Stephen R. Covey)

This is exactly what happens to a person experiencing mania. Bipolar disorder, which is *a hereditary chemical imbalance in the human brain*, sometimes tilts toward mania. Mania is the energetic and overly-enthusiastic side of the illness—opposite of depression.

When in mania, the person usually has no idea he/she is in it, and is often the last to find it out. The manic side hides itself. A common attitude is "I don't have a problem—YOU have the problem!" I guess it makes sense that, when I was depressed for 5 months, then morphed into a manic state of optimism and energy, I exclaimed, "I'd take mania over depression anytime!" Mania feels much better than depression, although it has its own drawbacks.

This metamorphosis has occurred to me more than once. The mania feels so good and the confidence seems so real. But often it is a bloated self-esteem and a false confidence which come in to rule the roost. Because of the over-spending, over-creativity and over-talkativeness, mania can be TOO MUCH—especially for those around the one in mania.

Coming down from a high doesn't happen immediately. Actually, it has usually taken a medication change to help bring me down. And, as usual, the one in mania realizes it after everyone else—"fish discover water last!

May 16

*Persistence is not a long race…it is
many short races—one after another.*

Walter Elliot

This quote reminds me of my favorite NFL running back of old—the late Walter Payton. He was a man of integrity who had a spirited way of bouncing up after being tackled and beating everyone else back to the huddle. Payton understood that "persistence is not a long race" because he was not a marathoner, but a sprinter. He knew it was "many short races—one after another."

I remember the game where Payton's team, Chicago Bears, set a record—actually, HE did—running for nearly 300 yards against our Minnesota Vikings—in one game! He pranced and danced past linebackers and defensive backs, making them look like they were standing still.

Sometimes we need to sprint in life to get that job we want, to keep motivated to achieve our goals, and to avoid someone swerving into our path. It's a healthy stance, I believe, to look at life as many separate challenges, rather than being bogged down by seeing life as a huge burden. Breaking it down can be helpful.

My vote for the one who truly knew the definition of persistence goes to the late, great running back Walter Payton, who was always bouncing back to stride for the end zone.

May 17

*No one else has your answers! Only YOU have your answers—
the only truth that does you any good is YOUR truth.*

Earnie Larsen

Have you ever encountered *your* truth? Not merely something someone else gave you or told you, but an idea or posture that came directly from your experience? I've been blessed with this. . .

My truth comes in the form of acronyms. I know, you may be sick and tired of acronyms…CIA, FBI, **IRS**….Well, I'm going to give you a few *meaningful* and *purposeful* acronyms that have come out of my life:

My first is C.O.L.A. = **C**hoosing **O**ptimistic **L**oving
Attitudes…the key word is
"choosing" in that we have
a choice as to how we will
meet our day, and the people
and circumstances in it . . .

Then there's C.A.I.S. = **C**onnectedness with the **A**uthentic
Inner **S**elf…a spiritual idea for
anyone/everyone, not intimidating
by mentioning "God," but encouraging
us to build a bond with our *true self*, that
part of us that God inhabits our inner world—the soul . . .

Also, there's F.O.G. = **F**ocus **O**n the **G**ood…optimism is a key to
success, bringing strength and joy to most any
circumstance. This acronym can lift the spirits
and move a day into the win column in a hurry.

These are three of *my* truths that have come through having the courage to write down my creative ideas and use them. Could you create an acronym to speak *your* truth? What would it say?

May 18

Spirituality means . . . not being at the
mercy of any person, thing or event.

Fr. Anthony de Mello

De Mello had a way of getting to the heart of an
issue with just a few words. This is one of my favorites.
Why? Because I see it working in my life. When I
    make the decision not to be bothered by a person
or a situation, it is a *spiritual* event.

I remember many months ago when I
    was "asked" to take over the 5ᵗʰ grade class
        in my teacher's aide position—for the
        whole day! They left very few
            lesson plans and gave me
                no schedule to go by.

    But I met it
    with courage and
    enthusiasm
    even though
    I was scared to
death! Imagine—25 rambunctious
kids and no teaching experience!
But, this willingness to try
in this difficult circumstance
    brought me in touch with my gifts and
    abilities in a way I hadn't previously recognized.
I was NOT at the mercy of the children, but rather in
charge of them. It was a spiritual—an inner—event for me,
and I am a better person for it. Thank God for the courage to
stand tall and believe in myself and my abilities.

How do YOU stand tall?

May 19

> *We cannot reject ourselves and hope*
> *to have high self-esteem or happiness.*

> *Marsha Sinetar*

We've all probably had moments of self-rejection...we may have put ourselves down as a result of poor performance or negative emotional reactions. For me, such events as failing in sports, struggling with bipolar disorder or experiencing conflicts with people have held me back.

Just like many of us, I can't say I'm totally beyond it, but at least now I recognize the monster, and have choices as to how I will respond to downer situations. Most often I now try to *live in the present* and not let my past dictate what I will do. This frees me up to make healthy decisions and not "beat myself up" about a situation over which I have little or no control. What about you? Does living in the present help free you up to be your best self?

I have learned, though, that a quite fruitful posture is to *insulate* ourselves from negatives, and cultivate the positives. As Chuck Swindoll says, "*life is 10% what happens to me and 90% how I react to it... and so it is with you...we are in charge of our attitudes.*" So, if we have choices as to how we are going to respond to life's challenges, is it not best reach toward optimism?

This "reach toward optimism" is a multi-dimensional shift—body, mind and spirit—and it's all about learning to make this transition fluidly. It all starts with NOT rejecting ourselves and seeking positive solutions to problems, not wallowing in a negative soup. My belief is that we must move on and *find* ways to succeed—and not get stuck in the past. Hope comes from risking to step out confidently and discover our best selves.

May 20

*The kind of person we each become is just as important
as what we accomplish in the world around us.*

Each Day A New Beginning

We set goals of accomplishment—of getting things done—but do we ever think of who we are becoming as we strive to reach these goals?

If Abe Lincoln had focused on his accomplishments—or lack thereof— he would have been a great disappointment. He "failed" numerous times in his political career—so much so that any one of us in his situation may have been discouraged enough to throw in the towel. Yet it seems Lincoln was aware of WHO he was becoming with each failure—that he was learning from his mistakes, and achieving character in the process. It was this character-building process that made Lincoln one our most outstanding presidents. He was able to make failures work for him.

One of my favorite quotes comes from Fr. John Powell: "*The only REAL mistake is the one from which we learn nothing.*" This makes ANY moment we choose a lesson-learning moment, a character-building moment. Can you see how these are blessed times—where *becoming* is the main idea, the main goal? This is *my* stance.

May 21

Character is not made in a crisis—it is only exhibited.

Robert Freeman

A fireman rushing into a burning house must have courage acknowledged BEFORE going in—he doesn't gain it on the way in.

A baseball pitcher must have a sense of confidence in his competency before throwing his first pitch, or the "outside pitch" will become his companion.

An executive must have the confidence to wave the pen in a way that makes the organization thrive, if she is to be a good leader.

We build character after stretching-experiences, after a challenging moment—not necessarily during the moment of action. It's the process of *reflective pondering* that often creates character, so that it can be exhibited to a greater extent in the future.

I have an acronym that helps me in this area: "ETC" = *Excellent Test of Character.* When I get thrown into a challenging situation, I realize it's an ETC-moment, which helps me keep my focus on how I am growing, not on failing. It's these ETCs that make me into a better person so I can show my character when difficult situations appear. Do you have ETC-moments? What do you choose to do with them?

May 22

We need to build on our strengths!

Sandra Melcher

Sure we need to build on our strengths, but first we need to know what our strengths are. This is where friends, like Sandra, come in. A good friend is observant, aware of who the other is and can point out what powerful presence the friend is able to give.

Sandra has been this for me. While I was searching for my new teacher's aide job a few years ago, she was instrumental in emphasizing how I needed to become aware of my gifts, and strengths. She encouraged me to write out a list of 8-10 strengths, and I became fully acquainted with them.

Although the job interview was very brief—almost nonexistent—I was prepared and revved up. I see now that our gifts are extremely important because only when we are aware of them can we be proactive.

I thank Sandra for her assistance in my landing that job...a good friend is a precious gem!

(A year later, Sandra became my wife!)

May 23

Be awake to the songs of singing birds, the warmth
of the sun, and the small joys that have no words.

unknown

So often we may forget the little things, in this age of DVDs, woofers & tweeters, high definition TV, and mini laptops. It's so easy to pave over the simple beauties of everyday life.

I remember in fall 1983, a "natural" phenomenon occurred when a noisy wave of dried leaves suddenly—in my imaginative perception—transformed into a medieval horseback charge, as the leaves blew across an intersection in downtown Mankato, Minnesota.

The sound the crackling leaves became battle cries and the leafy wave's front line shifted as it traveled, much like a shifting "V" of Canada geese flying in an October sky. This medieval band of marauders (leaves) scorched across the fallow field towards a waiting enemy—raucous, unabashed. I stood in amazement, as I witnessed the "valiant charge," as if each leaf were a warrior on horseback in courageous stance, heading into heated battle!

But as the leaves crossed the street and the breeze died down, suddenly the warriors on horseback became leaves again, and hit the curb on the other side of the street—scene over.

I felt graced to witness this imaginary reenactment. It taught me to be open to the splendor of nature and the gifts we can receive when we let nature transport us to wherever *she* wants us to go.

May 24

The true self is always in motion, like music, a river
of life...changing, moving, failing, suffering, learning, shining.

Brenda Ueland

Who is this *true self?* How do you see yourself? Some people never ask these questions. Some see them as frivolous and a waste of time. But I believe we *need* to look at ourselves squarely in the face and see who we are and who we are becoming.

How do we do this? Millions of dollars have gone into the hands of psychologists to answer these very questions...but one less expensive way is through journaling...writing down thoughts, feelings and impressions about your day, your relationships, yourself. A journal can help you "talk to yourself" in ways that don't make you look, well...*crazy* (you know, like how talking to yourself out loud might make you look and sound "disturbed").

Journaling often leads to poetry, story-telling and other creative writing opportunities that may never have occurred if pen had never met paper.

Some people can tell you the exact date when they turned their life over to Jesus, or quit drinking...my date to remember is March 31, 1982 (it's mentioned a number of times in this book)—the day I began writing a journal. It was a day of freedom—a day of joy. From that day, I saw my life as significant.

From this journal emerges thousands of pages of inner-sharing AND all of my poetry—some of my most important writings. My life changed the moment I began taking myself seriously by writing a journal. Have you ever tried it? It may just be the break-through you've been looking for.

May 25

Every man dies...not every man lives!

movie, Braveheart

In the motion picture Braveheart, actor Mel Gibson plays Scottish rebel William Wallace who is a pillar of courage and stamina. As his band of rebels swept down from the Scottish highlands with great ferocity and tact, they put fear in the eyes of all they faced.

Wallace speaks a great truth with his words, *"Every man dies...but not every man lives!"* He was referring to his fearsome warriors who came together on a long-shot, hoping to win even a single battle. They won many! They were risk-takers, in a powerful sense of the term.

Are you a risk-taker? Not ridiculous risks, now, like jumping from an airborne airplane with no parachute, but healthy risks like attempting to switch professions, or trying a new sport like sailing or rollerblading. It is in our risk-taking that we build courage and character.

I remember when I was 16, I tenuously stepped out of the front boot of my water ski and began **barefoot waterskiing**. This exciting activity had became a comrade for the first time. It seemed a tremendous risk at that youthful moment, yet one that led to a brand new level of confidence that I still tout today.

"Barefooting" is a rare skill, and when I am asked (in a "getting to know you" exercise at a seminar or retreat) "What's something unique about you?"—I often share my unusual talent with the group. After all, I only know of a few people BESIDES JESUS who can "walk on water"! It was a risk well-taken, and I didn't just do it once, but numerous *enjoyable* times!

What positive risk can you take this week that may potentially lead to higher self-confidence and a better life?

May 26

*Between stimulus and response there is
A space to choose how we will think and act.*

Stephen R. Covey

Gotta go grocery shopping. Gotta fill up the car with gas. Gotta buy flowers for my wife because it's Valentine's Day...ever catch yourself thinking this way? It's when we have to that we don't want to. And often this "don't want to" gets built up in our heads as we repeat "gotta gotta gotta do it" consistently.

It's said that there are two things you gotta do—die and pay taxes. Fact is, you don't gotta do anything...but die. Many people get away without paying their taxes. Seriously, you didn't have to get out of bed this morning. Sure it may not have looked good on your job record that you blew off work, but you didn't <u>have</u> <u>to</u> get out of bed.

An alternative attitude is that you **get to** ("get-ta") do the things you do. If you choose to espouse this perspective, it can mean the difference between night and day. Here's an example.

For 35 years I've struggled with my reading skills. I tend to plod along, often needing to reread and refocus, as I stumble through a book or article. I often **have to** take breaks for:

- Feeling inadequate
- Wallowing in self-pity
- Delving into self-doubt
- Focusing on *that which I have not done*

But this morning I woke to a new view on this issue of *being a poor reader*. I no longer needed to carry the cloak of being a "poor reader"—this was a demeaning and disempowering stance in itself! I now choose to see that, in my reading, I GET-TA:

- Project confidence
- Acknowledge my progress
- Feel competent
- Recognize my worth

With this Get-ta Attitude I start the day with a new view of myself, and as I adopted a plan last night to start reading for an hour a day, my skills and confidence steadily improved. I get-ta see the progress!

You see, get-ta comes out of *gratitude*, and gotta comes out of grudgingly. When you gotta go grocery shopping or fill up the car, you focus on the negative. You overlook the facts that 1) you have the resources to do so, 2) you can usually get up the energy to do so and 3) you can enjoy doing so. The outcomes of doing these activities are positive.

Joy is one of the greatest outcomes of the Get-ta Attitude. When you are released from the obligations and brought into the *opportunities* of life, it all becomes much easier and much more enjoyable. And you can make that shift in the wink of an eye—IF you see the value in the switch.

Try it for a half an hour today. Consciously switch form a gotta attitude to a Get-ta Attitude, and see what it does for you. You're in for a pleasant surprise.

May 27

Victory belongs to those who believe in it the most—
and believe in it the longest.

(General Dolittle, movie, Pearl Harbor)

Persistence doesn't mean we are always moving in leaps and bounds, but we are moving in the right direction. If we are heading in the *wrong* direction, no matter how fast we are traveling, it's <u>anti</u>-progress.

How does one believe in victory? First we must describe what victory is for ourselves. I got a vision of this from my friend and former professor, Dr. Alan Zimmerman, who speaks of "little victories"—which I now call "mini-victories." These are small successes we have every day. In acknowledging them and thanking God for them, each day can be full of victory, as we travel down that road of success more quickly and enjoyably.

Like yesterday, when I finished my final edit on a book I'd been writing for seven months. I joyfully sent it off to be reviewed for publication. It was a memorable moment—a mini-victory I will always remember!

What are some of the *mini-victories* you have had today that have made your day worthwhile? Can you start observing them and showing gratitude for them? In my vision, THIS will lead to many more mini-victories, and ultimate victory for you!

May 28

> *How I see another at THIS moment <u>can</u> change*
> *the present interaction and may change—even if in*
> *a small way—the destiny of our world.*

> Corsair

You never really know how or if you are going to affect another. Have you ever realized that your actions today, in some small way, will affect another positively or negatively?

Therefore, I believe we need to strive to make *every* interaction—as much as possible— affirming and positive. What if someone was teetering on the edge of a personal disaster at the time you interacted with them. Would your actions and words be supportive and understanding? Or would you add to the discouragement, frustration and loss of hope for them?

"Example" - *consistently being at our personal best* - is one of the greatest gifts we can give to those we encounter. Will you brighten days, or throw a shadow on others? If you lead with optimism and follow with compassion, you will have done your part in the simplest and possibly most profound way. What type of example will *you* be today?

May 29

> *You eventually become what you think.*

> Dr. Phillip Fisher

Ever since 1984, when I was first a teacher's aide in urban Milwaukee, I have wanted to be a teacher. Actually, I have gone to grad school pursing a masters in education twice in Minnesota, and both times, decided against continuing.

But having been a teacher's aide here in Milwaukee in 2006-07, the state of affairs in a central city public school could possibly have discouraged me from even staying in education,…but it hasn't. I see how my unique contributions can be effective and fruitful for students. Yet something was missing.

Pondering on advancing in the field, I see that being a full-fledged teacher is NOT for me…too many responsibilities, too much stress. This TEACHER idea had been rollin' around in my head for 25 years, and I'm glad I finally came to the conclusion that it's not for me. At least I know where I stand.

By giving up the dream of becoming a full-fledged teacher, I felt a void in my life. So I have begun to fill it with the dream of being a *writer*—not only by writing this book, but working toward fulfilling several ideas for books for youth and adults. *Switching dreams* was effective for me…I've been visualizing myself as a writer for over 25 years now…and it's time to bring this dream into reality! So I'm now a teacher in a different, more appropriate (for me) way.

What dreams could you move toward making a reality?

May 30

*Obstacles are what you see
when you take your eye off the goal.*

unknown

Having a clear focus on what we want is paramount in achieving success in any field. Distractions can cloud our vision and pull us away from our purpose.

When bicyclist Lance Armstrong was in his winning ways at the Tour de France—wearing the victorious *gold shirt* 7 times—he and his team had <u>everything</u> worked out: From the type of material of his clothing, to cutting down on wind drag by using slightly tweaked body positions, to a finely tune racing machine. They had every move, every piece of equipment, every last water bottle or nutrition bar usage figured out for peak performance. Lance is a great example of an athlete, a person, who steered his eyes toward the prize and achieved the ultimate rewards.

"Begin with the end in mind"...wise words from author Stephen R. Covey. This is the second habit of Covey's book *The Seven Habits of Highly Effective People*, and it's all about priorities. Only if we have our priorities straight can we excel. Maybe this is what Jesus was talking about when he spoke of following His *narrow way*—knowing what is right and good, and seeking it at all times.

Recently, I took on a peculiar challenge of a friend. He said, "If you had 6 months to live, what would you do?" I thought deeply about it and came to the realization that—hey, what would it be like to live as if it were my last 6 months on Earth? So, after a few days of contemplation, I decided to dive in and make the commitment. On May 1st, I sat down and mapped out 20 goals I'd like to accomplish in the next 6 months, then chose 10 as my priorities. I've created a calendar to mark my deadlines and accomplishments, with the days counting down on a small erasable white-board.

Focus? Like NEVER before! I'm already near completion of one of the three books I planned on writing (including this one); I have already traveled to the Our Lady of Guadalupe shrine in La Crosse, Wisconsin (a birthday wish); I plan on getting ALL of my worldly belongings organized so I can either use them or get rid of them, and I am making plans to go horseback riding with my step-grandchildren this summer.

It's amazing what happens to you when you get serious about your goals, get your priorities straight and take action. I'm planning on living far beyond 6 months, but the "stimulus package" offered by this venture is truly motivating! I dare you to try it!

May 31

> *Treat people as assets to develop*
> *rather than costs to cut.*
>
> *Robert Reich*

A good friend of mine works in administration for a major public library system. Sadly, it seems that much of her time is spent in cutting the budget each year...less books, less staff, less hours of service.

Making these cuts is a tough job, and a painful one. I find it a shame that the public libraries are being cut at the same time we are spending billions of tax payer dollars on wars where the main goal is destruction and killing. I believe the *"costs to cut"* need to be that of the defense budget, not the public library budget.

"Assets to develop" would occur more fully if the library budgets were stabilized or even increased. It seems ironic that billions can go towards war while a library system is nickel & diming its way toward trying to keep libraries open. Buying books and keeping staff levels up seem to be better investments in the welfare of our communities than buying bullets.

What institution could be more service-oriented?

~ June ~

One good quote, properly placed in the mind
& heart, can change a life—and a life
properly placed can change the world.

Corsair

Why quotations? What's the use? I believe quotations are our link to the wisdom of the ages. Everyone has wisdom, and a quote allows that wisdom, that pithy thought, to live and breathe.

One of my favorite quotes comes from Dr. Alan Zimmerman: (I've doctored it up a bit)...

Optimism means seeking the opportunity in every difficulty;
while pessimism means spotting the difficulty in every opportunity.

This has been one of the most helpful quotes I have ever memorized... and what's the use of a good quote if you don't put it to memory? I have 4 or 5 favorites.

Another keeper is Fr. John Powell's *"The only REAL mistake is the one from which you learn nothing."* This quote has helped me persist and proceed even when I felt defeated. It has assisted me in re-evaluating a past failure and learn my lessons from a botched event or an embarrassing gaff.

Quotes are priceless! If you can put them to use in your life, they can lift you toward a brighter NOW.

June 2

> *There is a purpose for our lives far grander*
> *and more significant than perhaps*
> *we might ever have considered.*

> *David McNally*

What a God-given gift to know—really KNOW—that our lives have meaning. In the African American post-Christmas 7-day celebration called *Kwanzaa*, one day is symbolized by the word "**Nia**"—which means *Purpose.*

Purpose, NIA, is what gets me out of bed in the morning! Why Purpose? Because it means proactivity, direction and hope.

My **purpose** statement is...*Rich learns from and grows with whatever he is given, and joyfully gives it back.* This statement is a focal point of how I see myself interacting in the world around me. I'm a learner, and a teacher. (We all are, really). I also have an action statement...

My **action** statement is:

Think & Thank
Listen & Learn
Teach & Touch
Observe & Love
Gone & Go On . . .

Can you relate to this? What purpose statement and action statement could you write for YOUR life?

June 3

My thoughts create my experience.

unknown

We are "creators," whether we believe in an ultimate Creator or not. We create our world by the perspective we were given and molded into, and what we choose to see & believe & observe around us.

So, if "my thoughts create my experience," at any moment, I could choose new thoughts and have a different experience than ever before.

"Fake it 'til you make it" is one tenet that encourages us to try on new attitudes and activities, styles of communication and ways of being—even if we may not be comfortable with them. When we "fake it," we put faith in the belief that we <u>can</u> <u>be</u> anyone we want to be, or <u>do</u> anything we want to do—if we can believe it.

So take the chance…be the creator of your own masterpiece—your own best life, knowing that if it doesn't turn out, you can simply think & plan & create a new experience once again.

June 4

As long as you live, you'll never find
a better way of getting in touch with others
than to make them feel important.

Will Rogers

This is one of the most important proclamations one could ever hear, and it's so simple! Isn't it true that we value those who see us clearly, affirm us, and make us feel important?

It's so easy to do, to look at someone's efforts & accomplishments and let them know how you see them, <u>and</u> how you feel about them. Well, you may not tell EVERYONE how you feel about them, but you can affirm another's positive behavior...from a cheerful waitress, to a hard-working custodian, to a thoughtful loved one.

What if you had a mission to make others feel important? My guess is you would be the most admired person around, as you show genuine and consistent appreciation for others' efforts. Try it and see!

June 5

I am who I am
what I am
where I am
partly because of my struggles
suffering
but I don't go back and greet
those who shut me out
and labeled me unacceptable

I don't go back and chum with
the ones who smashed
my free-flowing
friendship on the
rocks of jealousy

I can only forgive them and
thank God for giving me
the wisdom and
TOLERANCE
to keep travlin' on

Corsair

June 6

When you shoot an arrow of truth,
dip its point in honey.

Arabic proverb

A few years ago, while serving as a teacher's aide in Minnesota, my principal called me into her office and reprimanded me for 40 minutes about six errors I was consistently making. I listened to point after negative point, struggling to take in all she was saying. I finally got out a notebook and wrote them down.

Yet, even with all my training as a member of Toastmasters International (which is a public speaking club), I had only once been treated in such a manner! In Toastmasters, I had been evaluated on speech performance dozens of times, and we tried to apply *the Oreo technique*: Give one compliment, even if very small...then offer the person the "meat" of the criticism, ending with a positive observation.

I was insulted by the principal but ultimately edified. Her criticisms hit home, and I made some huge positive changes in my life because of them! Ironically, the critique was one of the most crucial and helpful I've ever had.

The two changes that have been most helpful are:

1) I wasn't "in it;" I wasn't focused, observant or mindful, and
2) I wasn't asking enough questions; when I was in doubt I was stuffing it.

But I had been aware of *the Oreo Technique* and knew how to look beyond the criticism and into the value of the message...which could have been lost in the negativity of the comments.

It sure helps *"when you shoot an arrow of truth, to dip its point in honey"*—<u>and</u> to realize that when you look at a criticism non-defensively, you may just discover the gold hidden beneath!

June 7

If nothing changes—nothing changes.

Earnie Larsen

To pursue effective change, we need to make some *changes*. Change usually doesn't come through osmosis but through a conscious decision to try for something better.

Raphael had a tendency to sit back and watch life pass by—that was until his brother was killed in a motorcycle accident. This woke him up and, at age 37, he went back to school to do something he'd dreamed of all his life—become an architect.

He hit the books hard and, in three years, going to school ¾-time, he earned his degree. He got an excellent job in a suburban architectural firm and excelled. The tragedy had sparked his will to succeed, and he actually benefited from the unfortunate happening of losing his brother.

What spark needs to ignite inside you for you to discover (or uncover) *your* dream?

June 8

No one can take away your self-respect
if you do not give it to them.

Gandhi

Oh, how many times I have failed this test and thrown my self-respect into the dust at others' feet! The *second* day at my *first* job, age 16, I found myself in a humiliating situation when I was ordered to operate a forklift that I didn't know how use. Instead of admitting my ignorance and asking my new boss for assistance, I tried to "act as if." I only knew how to use the clutch and struggled to operate it on sheer observation—trial & error (mostly error).

My boss yelled at me for not knowing how to start the forklift, for not knowing how to raise the forks and for not knowing how to turn off the brake—demeaning me with nasty names in the process.

I have often thought about how mean this boss was and how I had been mistreated. Then, a few months ago, I realized, "Hey—I HAD options!" I could have dramatically changed the scene if I had only humbled myself and asked for help. Then the onus would have been on him to teach me! But my pride and "determination" created a scene where I was one down and my boss was one (or 10) up!

I had thrown my self-respect onto his dirty boots, and he had gladly trampled upon it. For 31 years I had thought *he* was the bad guy. Now, I truly believe that much of my angst in my 47 years has come from "disempowering myself" and empowering self-pity, apathy and envy..."*oh poor me, I'm not worth it; I wish I had the gifts others had*"... a pity-party partly stemming from this first work experience.

But now, today, I choose to empower my self-respect, to live a life of proactivity <u>and</u> humility—asking questions and uplifting & valuing my self-respect as the foundation of my personal life philosophy. When you think about it, without self-respect, what have you got?

It's never too late to learn a valuable lesson!

June 9

*If you compare yourself with others, you may
become vain & bitter, for always there will be greater
and lesser persons than yourself.*

Desiderata

The decision to compare can be extremely destructive. Not the comparison that occurs in healthy competition, but comparison based on envy—which can get a person nowhere but down & defeated.

My friend Jenny had this negative comparison hanging over her head. She was third oldest of six, having five brothers to contend with. She didn't hold jobs for very long…waitress, secretary, paralegal—even construction worker…she couldn't seem to find the right fit. All her brothers were successful in holding long-term jobs. In her mind, they were "successes."

She felt inferior to her brothers who—in fact—never made actual comparisons with her. They never spoke up to make her feel that she was less-than because of the jobs she held. This she was doing to herself.

Jenny finally came to a peaceful place when she stopped comparing herself to her brothers. In time, she found a job as grade school teacher's aide—and loved it! No more comparison & hello success—success the way she defined it.

June 10

The greatest gift we can give one another is rapt attention.

Each Day A New Beginning

When we are listened to—really *heard*—we are affirmed and come alive. Dr. Alan Zimmerman says, "When you really, really understand where someone's coming from, your natural response is *respect, empathy, caring*—not judgment."

Listening is one great way to build respect. I'm sure we can all recall times when someone took the time to *really* listen to us. These respectful encounters may have been with a friend, a parent, a pastor or counselor, and may often be remembered for a lifetime. This can be a breath of fresh air in a hurried, non-observant world.

But we must also be aware of *assuming*, when listening to others. A handily misplaced assumption can ruin the listening process. We need to be careful not to assume when we speak, or when we listen.

My wife and I just came through an emotional storm created when we made some broad assumptions, causing a deep misunderstanding. It took us a week to work through the mess created by the assumptions. Yet, we "heard each other out" and, through intense and honest sharing, our relationship has been strengthened and reaffirmed! We sure could have used Dr. Zimmerman's caveat…"When in doubt—check it out!" This could have saved us from this difficult and uncomfortable situation caused by assuming.

They say listening is one of the hardest things we can do. I agree. To communicate with full and accurate understanding IS one of our greatest challenges and yet most crucial skills. It takes time. It takes effort. But to truly build healthy relationships, listening with body, heart, mind and soul is invaluable.

How do you rate YOUR listening skills? Are you building respect and rapport, or listening with only ½-attention and ½-respect? If so, how could you improve your skills?

June 11

Maybe you can't change the direction of the wind,
but you CAN adjust the sails.

Adult Children of Alcoholics

Being stuck often involves believing we have no positive options. Yet we *always* have good options, if we have chosen a productive direction to sail our ship.

Tom thought he was lost when his job was eliminated at the auto parts manufacturer with which he worked for 20 years. He had no idea what to do with himself, as his job search dragged on and on. Then one day a friend asked him to help re-do some molding in a kitchen, and after doing an excellent job, the friend asked him if he wanted to be a part of his home refurbishing company.

With a little wind in his sails from doing the molding, Tom decided to take him up on the offer. Tom worked hard, asked lots of questions and quickly excelled to become a fine craftsman, re-doing dozens of homes and making a good living at it. The surprising turn of events helped Tom see that, by looking at his skills and taking some little risks, he could better his life and himself greatly.

Have you ever heard of the ol' *"Motivation: 2 X 10"* = *"if it is to be, it is up to me"*? We need to realize that we have the responsibility to make our lives successful. John Wooden was undoubtedly the most successful college basketball coach of all time. Wooden's father used to tell him "Make your life a masterpiece!" Leading with this attitude, Wooden led UCLA to 10 championships in 12 years! *Make your life a masterpiece!* Great advice for the aware person—that the power is in OUR hands, not the outer circumstances—to make each day a memorable one, a fantastic one!

WE can *adjust the sails,* and you are *not* powerless but power-full! Life is out there waiting for us to encounter it and make the best of it. *"We can't change the direction of the wind"*...we can't change the inevitable—the weather, the past or future, others' reactions—but we CAN steer them toward successful shores and a life of significance.

Sail On!

June 12

Never look down on anybody unless you're helping them up.

Jesse Jackson

I remember a time in my senior year of high school when I really blew it. There was this kid in math class, a junior, who had a sunken chest— probably a type of birth defect—and I decided to pick on him because of it. I pointed it out to some of my cronies, laughing as I ridiculed him behind his back. He tried to explain why he had the abnormality but gave up, probably thinking, "What's the use?"

What cruelty! What a judgmental way and an insensitivity to another's weakness. I think of him often when I am struggling with my own down feelings or challenging moments. He didn't ask for it. He didn't deserve it. I hadn't considered this bullying at the time, but now it is very clear that it was a form of abuse.

It was a low moment in my underdeveloped social and spiritual life. I have gone back in my mind and heart to ask him for forgiveness using a process I call *"spiritual amends,"* knowing I will probably never see him again, but praying that he will forgive my insolence and cruel behavior through a spiritual connectedness. I have found *spiritual amends* to be very effective and comforting.

This teasing was just plain wrong! "Sticks and stones may break my bones," but these harsh words can kill. It took lots of reflection, but I learned my lesson to never tease again. Ironically (and maybe not so) I've become a non-crisis mental health phone counselor. I volunteer time listening to other's troubles, longings and lonely moments. Upon reflection, the teasing event may have been a catalyst, unconsciously, for this type of service. Sometimes humiliating situations cause us much growth.

Where do you need growth when it comes to respecting others?

June 13

*Great works are performed not by
strength but by persistence.*

Samuel Johnson

ants

*look down sometime
in fact, get on your knees and stoop
to witness the most "faithful"
creatures on earth*

*ants
believe it
they are much more
than just hard workers
just think about it
people prancin' on down*

the sidewalk all day long
          never asking themselves
          "Hey! Am I going to ruin some ant
          colony's day by stepping on its house?"

          no
          and crunch—there goes 3-½ days
          of hard work...first rain floods
          then some careless pedestrian step
          but instantaneously, ants are back at it again
          rock by rock, carefully placing each boulder
          to make a symmetrical mound
          talk about FAITH—and "living in the now"
          just watch ants
          don't bother that half the neighborhood
          is looking at you on your hands and knees
          showing wonder and talking to yourself
they'll get over it—cuz these ants
are the most exciting group of go-getters
since Amway!

          Corsair

June 14

You'll never change your life if you wait until you feel like it.

Dr. Alan Zimmerman

"Action speaks louder than words" is a good depiction of what Dr. Zimmerman is speaking about. We need to act, not just talk about it.

In one of his most influential speeches, Dr. Zimmerman speaks of his father who had a mission of taking in alcoholics and giving them a place to sober up, re-organize, find a job and re-enter society again. Dr. Zimmerman talks about one man his father took in—Arthur—who spoke eloquently about what he WOULD DO when the right opportunity came along—when the perfect job opportunity arose or when Ed McMahon called him offering millions. Arthur had big dreams but no action. He ended up drunk, in the gutter, frozen to death in a mid-winter cold snap. Arthur's view of life was very limited.

Having goals in life—focusing on something we want to achieve—can be the pivotal component in reaching personal success. Yet many never put pen to paper and create worthy goals. Maybe they just didn't know how. I've got a cure for that.

You may have heard a version or two of "SMART Goals"...well, I've modified other versions a bit. See if you connect:

> *Specific:* What do you really want?
> (in detail)

> *Motivational:* What makes it exciting?
> How does it motivate you?

> *Achievable:* Can you see yourself accomplishing it?
> Is it realistic?

> *Respectful:* Are all parties involved being respected?
> Is it for a good cause?

> *Time-focused:* When will it be accomplished?

We must get beyond making plans and into following through on them. A plan with no propulsion is a boat dead in the water. The follow-through is the toughest *and* most rewarding part of any plan. *SMART Goals* can help you get there!

Do YOU have big plans? Have you written down the goals it will take to fulfill these plans? When will you put your motor in the water and create a wake? Give SMART Goals a try and reach for your success!

June 15

What you reinforce and pay attention to tends to reoccur.

(Minnesota State University, Mankato, Counseling Center)

One day, years ago, I realized that the more I chose to think about a particular thing, the deeper the "groove" it created inside my brain—which would more easily bring that thought back. (It seemed so simple—why hadn't I gotten it before?) And I realized this could work for me or against me...think good—positive groove, think negative—bad groove.

One evening in 1994, while mopping a boys' bathroom floor as a part of my duty as school janitor, I was playing with the thought of creating an *acronym* to describe the thoughts that were tumbling around inside my head:

"Choosing Good Thoughts: *CGT* . . . no.
Deciding to Think Positively: *DTP* . . . no!
Optimism and Being Positive Works: *OBPW* . . .no!!"
None of these "worked"...

Then, it came out of my mouth:
"Choosing Optimistic Loving Attitudes . . . COLA!!"

Now THAT was an acronym to be remembered and used. Coca-Cola was my favorite drink! Easy to remember, with words that had great meaning!

I have given talks on COLA, thought about it hundreds and hundreds of times, even adding "COLAAA" ("and actions") to it for a greater and more holistic affect. It has been a positive force in focusing my attention on the good in others and situations.

Meaningful acronyms can be a great way to reinforce positive ideas, and to build a healthy "groove" in your mind. Have you ever created your own personal acronym for self improvement?

Try it. You'll like it!

June 16

> *The greatest gift we can bring to any relationship*
> *wherever we go is being who we are.*

The Language of Love,
Gary Smalley

and if I told you I was a teacher, would you believe it?

TEACHER? WHAT VALUE IS THERE IN THAT?
CORRECTING PAPERS AND TELLING KIDS TO
SIT DOWN.

wait a minute...when you were 10 or 11, who did you spend more time with? Your mother or your teachers?

DON'T SIDETRACK ME! HOW MUCH MONEY DO
YOU MAKE?

not much but what are you going to leave for this world when you are gone? what are you going to pass on?

HEY, I'LL HAVE LOTS OF MONEY TO PASS ON
TO MY KIDS. AND YOU? YOU'VE GOT BRAINS,
YOU COULD BE MAKING <u>REAL</u> MONEY!

it always seems to come back to money...one question...what did Jesus leave when he died?

JESUS? WHAT DOES HE HAVE TO DO WITH IT?
HE WAS JUST A
Teacher . . .
and as teacher, he left Himself; He left stories
of His life; He gave knowledge, & inspiration, & Presence...
and He left lives changed forever—He had little money...

GO AHEAD. TAKE THE GARBAGE FROM THE
KIDS. TAKE THE LOW PAY. TAKE THE LONG
HOURS. IF THAT'S WHAT YOU SEE AS BEING
HAPPY—YOU CAN HAVE IT!

and if you told me I was a teacher, I would believe it.

Corsair

June 17

As long as you live, you'll never find a better way of getting in touch with others than to make them feel important.

Will Rogers

Sometimes nicknames can be very endearing. As a young hockey player in Minnesota in the mid-1970s, my coaches gave me the nickname "The Hammer," due to my ability to check and stand-up-straight any opposing attackers—many times knocking them flat on the ice.

As I grew older, the nickname became "Melch," one I prized highly. I once had a student call me "Mr. Melch," not knowing if he had just forgotten my full name (Melcher) or if it was a term of endearment. Knowing my status at the time, it was probably the former. A friend in high school, Troy, sure seemed to like being called "Troyzie," and another friend's nickname jokingly became "Ting."

I saw the opposite in the urban school at which I was once a teacher's aide. Cruel teasing was the most prevalent and destructive force at the school. It led to arguments, scuffles and even fights. I finally realized its real name—**bullying**—where terms of endearment turned into terms of "*undermine-ment*" and scorching ugliness!

Sticks & stones may break my bones, but words…can kill! If there is one lesson I needed to teach my 5th graders, it was how "to make one another feel important" by eliminating all the unnecessary and often vicious teasing. I pray I was effective in this venture.

June 18

Wherever you look, there's something to be seen.

the Talmud

If there's always *something to be seen*, then observation is one of our most important activities. There is another word for this—*awareness.* Becoming aware of our surroundings and our inner landscape makes life come alive. As a novelist describes the inner-workings of the main character, or a documentary producer finds details never seen before, so we see that *observation is the key to discovery.*

If "wherever you look there's something to be seen," this opens up all the possibilities. Suddenly, the mundane becomes magnificent, and the dull and nondescript come alive! Nature is full of amazing features!

I'm amazed at how a field full of sun flowers can follow the sun across the sky. I've also been told that the sunflowers follow the sun across the sky on a cloudy day—peering through the clouds to follow their sun god! It's amazing that when we look at the stars, we're looking at light that took light-years to reach us. Scientists say that even the sun's rays take eight minutes to reach Earth! That means, when we look up in the sky, we're seeing the past, not the present! Actually, some of those stars may no longer be there!

Wonder is a great quality...the wonders of nature, the wonders of the mind, the wonders of the heart. Awareness and observation bring life to Life. How alive are *your* senses? Can you name one wonder-full thing that happened to you today?

June 19

A mind stretched to a new idea
never goes back to its original dimensions.

Oliver Wendell Holmes, Jr.

God Planned This One! When I served as a 5th grade teacher's aide in an urban Milwaukee K-8 school a few years ago, I was often given the duty of "covering" other classes while the regular teacher was in a parent's meeting or off to an appointment. I had covered 8th grade, 6th grade, both of my 5th grade classes and a 2nd grade class.

Then one day came the call for me to cover a 10-student *kindergarten* class. Memories of Arnold Schwarzenegger's "Kindergarten Cop" popped into mind—where he played a cop posing as a kindergarten teacher (and he was *taken to the cleaners!*). I mentally prepared for this duty. I had my doubts, but mostly *excitement*...I <u>love</u> little kids!

Our first activity of the afternoon turned out to be the most rewarding. Before the teacher left, the she had showed me these big picture books in the front of the classroom that promised possibilities for lots of reading exercises for the kids and a way to get them immediately interested. As I read the colorful pages, each student took a turn reading the page after me. I asked them all kinds of questions about what they saw and read. They were eager and excited, gleefully raising their hands and bubbling over like hastily poured champagne glasses. *It was magical!* The rest of the day was filled with videos, reading in small groups with their 7th grade "reading buddies" and...suddenly, it was time to go home!

This experience changed how I saw "covering" other teachers' classes. Encountering these kindergarten students was such a blessing—a serendipitous event I will always remember with joy. It built my confidence and encouraged me to take on more opportunities to cover classes with gusto and enthusiasm! You just never know when God is going to throw a pearl in your direction!

The next day, I surprised them with a box full of used books. You should have seen the looks on their faces as they picked out their very own like-new, colorful books. I will cherish that moment forever. Children are the sparkle in the diamonds of life!

June 20

Once we know that suffering has a purpose,
or at least, once we can believe that there is a
meaning to it, we can endure much more.

Van Breeman

What could this *"meaning"* be? How could suffering have a purpose?

I, for one, believe it can, and it does. But it only has this meaning if we decide that it does. We all have suffering. We all reach those moments in life when we are challenged by the circumstances of struggle and even tragedy. When the tough times come—and they come to us all—we must choose how we will respond. Emotional loss caused by death or injury to a loved one can cause much pain and upheaval. We can lose our positive vision of life for a while, but we need to always come back to a clearer vision that will bring us through.

Personally, having bipolar illness, I have had pain and disillusionment the size of towering mountains, at times. My faith in God and encouragement from my family and friends (along with proper medications) have been the factors that have brought me back to a balanced state. They have restored my clear vision of living, propelling me into a successful future.

The pain has *meaning* in the sense that, when I think I'm having a rough go of it, I can always think back about the *rougher* times and see how God pulled me through those difficulties. Yes, as the gospel song proclaims, "Jesus **is** a rock in the weary land!" This view lifts me above the treetops to view, with gratitude, all the blessings I have received.

I thank God for my struggles, knowing they have taught me how to be a loving man, an observant man, a grateful man. Believe it or not, it could be that *gratitude* is the greatest gift we can gain from painful moments. This has been my path.

June 21

I am not perfect, but parts of me are excellent!

Each Day A New Beginning

This is one of the tenets I carry into any new job. Surprisingly, some previous employers only found ways for me to "improve"—actually, they were not that kind. They were critical and pointed me towards how I could *do better*, yes, showing me only deficiencies but rarely pointed out a single proficiency. In my opinion, this does not build one's competence or confidence.

Yet, I know what aspects of my efforts had been successful. I ultimately don't need an employer to tell me I work well with customers or with children. I don't need 'em to tell me how successfully I carry out my duties…I don't need 'em to tell me how well I work as a team member. (It would be nice, though). These I can see in me.

But I guess I'm a bit sad that management sees reprimand and fault-exposing to be their primary way of interacting with staff, as if pointing out the negative *alone* was going to bring the results they expect. Having a thick skin is paramount in the job market these days because management is most often not going to compliment on a job well done but criticize unmet expectations.

As the quote above hints, you need to see your good side because you may be the only cheerleader you will have.

June 22

Faith trumps fear!

Mark T.

I heard these words in the context of a Bible study tonight and it struck me hard. I had just finished professing how fear has played such a pivotal and often-destructive role in my life, dragging me down and creating doubt and confusion.

But Mark's comment cut through this fog so sharply that I could feel the blade on my skin. He spoke truth—a truth that I so often have needed and will forever use now that it has been revealed. My gift of faith HAS pulled me through some very tough times. Is this true for you also?

I think of a statement by St. Therese..."(I have decided) to banish all fear and all memory of past faults—no trace of dead sins left behind—for in one second, LOVE can burn them to ashes." Oh how this phrase has shaped my life. Often I (as possibly you) have struggled with past mistakes—goofs and gaffes that were embarrassing or self-defeating or even harmful to others. And the fear of repeating these mistakes, or inventing others, has often gripped me.

But there is no need to fear when we have faith. Not only does love conquer all—*faith conquers all*...the faith in a loving God who will never abandon us nor leave us faltering in a dreary past.

It's true—faith trumps fear—as long as you believe...for faith is belief in action.

June 23

You can run but you can't hide what's inside you.

Steely Dan

Melancholy seems to follow me at times, tugging on worn emotional strings. I don't know if it's a part of my bipolar illness or not, but *the blues* seem to ride along my side often, these days.

It could be that I've experienced dissatisfaction in finding the right type of employment; or it could be this struggle to find an appropriate exercise routine and commit to and follow through on; or it could just be the *winter blues*. Whatever it is, it can grate on the soul.

But I do know that ever since I can remember, I've had a BLUE streak in me—possibly the part of me that makes poetry stream from my heart, mind and soul at times. Since I can't just ditch these moderately depressive tendencies, my option is to watch them, while I seek a more optimistic stance—actively moving towards a future of promise.

Recently, I was procrastinating on creating a speech I will be giving in the near future. My lethargy was holding me back from putting in a full effort. Then I realized the responsibility I had of giving the youth I was to present to a valuable and interesting message. This helped me break out of the blue mood and create some unique features to the speech that will most likely prove successful in reaching the students. I chose to get busy and make something special, rather than rush at the last minute and make something mediocre.

Sure the blues can be present, even on a sunny day. But it's how we deal with them that counts—not just lyin' back & takin' it—but standing tall and asserting our positive options. The blues may make for good sad songs but not for a good daily companions.

Do the blues ever get you down? What do YOU do about it?

June 24

You gotta get busy livin' or get busy dyin'!

movie, "Shawshank Redemption

In this movie, Andy Duphresne, played by Timothy Robbins, has found out he has lost the only witness who could have freed him from prison. He had been in prison over 20 years for a murder he did not commit and suddenly realized that his time for a 10-year-planned jail break had come…he wanted to *get busy livin'!*

A few years ago, I reached this same conclusion. I had been in a less-than-adequate—or so I had thought—job situation as an elementary school teacher's assistant that was heavily taxing my patience and leading to substantial anxiety. I had blamed the school & the kids' disrespectful ways for my discomfort.

Then I realized the real culprit—**my attitudes.** I had been putting "new wine into old wineskins"—as The Bible puts it—and acting out helplessness and hopelessness of previous job situations. Also, although I had been "building the ultimate classroom environment" that I call *"ICY: the Inward Curriculum for Youth"*…I was not living the prescription I had tried so hard to formulate.

I soon discovered, it wasn't the school or the kids that needed to change, but ME! I finally decided to take full OWNERSHIP of my job and to start being more calm, curious and courteous as I walked on the school grounds and in the crowded hallways. A new person began living *ICY*…stressing proactivity, awareness and gratitude as I chose to become a positive example by living what I had previously prescribed for others.

I decided to "get busy LIVIN'!"

Rich Melcher

June 25

> *If you can just observe what you are*
> *and move with it, then you will find that it is*
> *possible to go infinitely far.*
>
> *Krishnumurti*

    will I run
   or will I fly
    take root, seek shelter to hide
   or water to swim
    see sun set or rise
   or disappear into lofty cloud?

  it takes a keen eye and open ear
  to know when the journey calls for change
 do I choose safety in numbers
or risk being the lonely rider on desert trails?

          only God knows which way is best to turn
          to sprout…to reach…to duck…or run
          God sees the way within me
if only I quiet myself enough to hear
  the soothing voice of silence inside

     Corsair

June 26

I've always believed that failures
are the second greatest teachers in life;
mentors are the first!

Steven Scott

In his book, <u>Simple Steps To Impossible Dreams</u>, Steven Scott has a section on partnering with good mentors. Scott states, "Every person I've ever met, known or read about who achieved his or her dreams in any area of life had at least one mentor in that particular area."

Henry Ford had Thomas Edison; George Lucas, (creator of Star Wars), had Francis Ford Coppola; Steven Spielberg had Sid Shineberg. Mentors are crucial if we are to discover our true potential and lasting success.

Helen Keller would have remained in obscure darkness if it hadn't been for Anne Sullivan, and Anne Sullivan would have remained in obscurity if it hadn't been for a soon-to-retire nurse who wanted to make a difference with *someone* before she retired, coaxing and encouraging Anne out of a pitiful existence.

The amazing and sobering thing is that, we may be a "mentor," in a way, to others simply by living a value-driven, integrity-filled life. Fact is, we may never know the positive affects we have on others who witness our *example* and emulate our actions. This is how God works in & through us!

Who are *your* mentors? And how is your *example* affecting those around you?

June 27

You perform exactly as you see yourself.

Dr. Alan Zimmerman

Visualization is a powerful force in reaching toward success. Bruce Jenner is a living example of how this process works. Before he entered the 1976 Olympic Decathlon, he visualized every move, every step, every throw and every finish line in full color inside his mind.

Jenner practiced visualization in every area of the competition so completely that when he actually entered the arena, it was simply a matter of following through and putting his imagination into real-life actions.

Sure, he got his body in shape and practiced on a track. But off the track he used his imagination to create a winning pattern in his mind, like creating a groove on vinyl for the record stylus to follow...creating beautiful music.

Jenner experienced success in his mind first, then brought it into reality by "following the groove." He won the 1976 Olympic Decathlon because he *saw it* over and over in his mind, then simply turned imagination into reality. "We become what we think about most!" a wise person once stated. Jenner lived it!

June 28

You can never talk yourself out of problems
you behaved yourself into.

Stephen R. Covey

It amazes me how many of the 5th graders with whom I once worked, as teacher's aide, point fingers at others even when they got caught red-handed bothering another student or talking out of turn. They blamed others immediately, without taking any responsibility for their actions.

"Responsibility," says Stephen R. Covey, "is *the ability to respond*." What rises from this definition is that we have *choices*—something my 5th graders didn't seem to understand—or weren't willing to look at. It's as if they were on an auto pilot for disaster, in which much of the teaching time was wasted on attempts of teacher and me to create an orderly learning atmosphere.

But seeing the bad behavior go on, day after day—talking, laughing, teasing, threatening—they didn't seem to get it that no teacher or teacher's aide could *create* this essential orderliness without their cooperation.

I had hoped that, before these students stood on the threshold of 6th grade, they would have come to understand that no one could make them learn—they must do it themselves. I think some of them learned it. And if they chose not to allow the learning to take place by creating constant disruptions, they would not be able to *TALK their way into the next level*. Some may have found that it was too late to **behave** their way into it! But I do hope they all have learned their lessons and are progressing to higher levels of awareness.

June 29

Little things don't mean a lot—they mean EVERYTHING!

Harvey McKay

Just a little thing that may grow to mean a lot…an acronym I wanted to present in a past educational job. The acronym is "R.R.O.C.K.S."----it started at a previous grade school position in a Minneapolis suburb, that had a poster in the hallway stating 4 important words: **Respect, Responsibility, Cooperation and Safety.** This concept struck me as relevant and helpful. So I added 3 more words, *Knowledge, Observation* and *Service* to create R.R.O.C.K.S.S.…

Respect
Responsibility

Observation
Cooperation
Knowledge
Safety
Service

Being *observant* and *safe*? Good reminder; always seeking *knowledge* leads to life-time learners—good stuff. *Respectful, responsible* and *cooperative*? Couldn't our government use that instead of getting into ridiculous wars? *Service*...be it customer service or giving service to those in need, we could all be a little better at this.

In the classroom, I wanted to create a RROCKSS environment for youth to have simple guidelines for attitude and behavior. Simple to remember, challenging to implement. Well, although I have left the field of classroom education, my wife and I have started a business to go into schools and social agencies to teach (among other things) *RROCKSS Creative Writing Program*, using the above acronym as a base for getting young students to write. And it's a great success!

Funny how one simple idea can lead to much bigger things! God is good! All the time!

June 30

The way to make a man rich is to decrease his wants.

Ozzie Davis

It's our wants, our desires, our cravings that can get us into trouble. When we want something so badly that we can taste it, but it's nowhere to be found or to be seen, it can cause suffering.

In my view, inner suffering often can be felt deeper than physical pain because it involves our spirituality. Suffering can wear us down in spirit, as well as body & mind. Having uncontrollable desires can create this suffering—longing. Yet if we can let go of desire and give it up for *reality*—for what *is*, we may even find a peace indescribable.

In the movie <u>Sister Act</u>, Whoopi Goldberg's character, Sr. Mary Clarence, created a new reality by giving up her old night club ways and found that she could be a catalyst for dramatic, positive change with the other nuns and the entire neighborhood. Her "giving up" led her to become the choir director, and she instilled in the other nuns the confidence and inspiration to sing way beyond their previous abilities—and go out in the community to serve others. All of Sr. Mary Clarence's influence came from *giving up* a negative lifestyle and adopting HOPE and proactivity.

She had a rebirth as the choir quickly became well known because it brought popular music *with a* *spiritual twist* to a hungry, thirsty public that had previously shunned the church. <u>Sister Act</u> is a great example of how one person can make a gigantic difference simply by "letting go" and deciding to *risk the moment.*

~ July ~

July 1

> *It's not what you get that's important, but what you give.*
>
> *unknown*

This seems to be a pillar of any spiritual way of life—that one gives to others with a generous heart. Is it just me or is it everyone who thinks of their mother in these terms?

Like many mothers of her generation, my mom never had "a job" outside of the home. She served on the school board and as a religion teacher, and even worked with women in the local jail, helping them with their spiritual journeys—but she has never had a "paying" job.

It was a true gift when she shared the story of *Jonah and the Whale* with the women in the jail. She appealed to their creative gifts as she likened their jail stay to being in the belly of the whale, and, like Jonah, they now had time to think about their lives. I believe she even called it a "retreat" experience for them. This was a twist for these incarcerated women who often seemed to have little hope for the future.

For a woman who "never had a job," my mom has been involved in some very praise-worthy activities—such as rearing 9 kids and making bedrolls for the homeless in Minneapolis! And if she were to have been paid monetarily, she would be a very wealthy woman. Yet, she IS wealthy, in heart, in mind, in spirit...for all the good she has done for others— outside the home, as well as inside.

What's YOUR "mother story"?

July 2

Be the change you want to see in the world.

Gandhi

Shepherd Walk

Lord, You see me in my broken ways
under pressure
inner blindness occurs
& the ordinary routines
get blocked by an anxious mist–
lead me in Your ways
guide me all my days

Lord, You know me in ever-special ways
that no one else sees or feels
You have given me a joy
beyond all social extravagancies
and worldly pleasures
You lead me in Your ways
and guide me all my days

Thank You, Lord
for bringing me on this shepherd walk today

Corsair

July 3

We can do no great things;
only small things with great love

Mother Teresa

It came to me while lifting weights in a new program I'm embarking upon. The thirteen exercises, done on machines, challenge me with a combination of strength training and muscle toning. It occurred to me while lifting that I have a hard time following through on projects, such as this very type of weight training program I have started in the past and not persisted in continuing.

Then it came to me...the weights have a small ½-weight that slides down to give a more incremental strategy of lifting. And as I pondered my step-daughter's recent statement about "going to the next level," it occurred to me that I have most often seen moving up and forging on as being a process of taking giant leaps—huge strides—that of which have seemed too big to accomplish—even intimidating!

So I thought, "what if I were to '*Insist on Incremental Improvement* (I³)?' and take baby steps toward my goals. Many baby steps equal a huge step, by the way! I thought about my struggles with reading. For 25 years or so I have seen myself as a poor reader. I have owned that label in my own heart and mind, and therefore carried it out with precision...therefore avoided reading more times than not.

What if I were to invest 10-15 minutes of time, to begin with, in reading—either aloud or silently—so that I can be putting effort into reading rather than complain about how I read so poorly? Wouldn't this be a better plan?

I have had an acronym in my back pocket for ten years (along with 31 others) that reads:

PUMP

Practice
Ultimately
Makes
Progress

Is it now not time to live out this maxim? If I *"Insist on Incremental Improvement* (I³)" in this and other areas of my life, I believe that success in these areas will eventually be mine.

How can you get I³ working in your life?

People need responsibility—they resist assuming it,
but they cannot get along without it.

John Steinbeck

"Response-ability" helps us see anew a heavy word that many don't want to accept. The "ability to respond" brings the word *responsibility* down to the level even a kindergartener can understand. Understanding *responsibility* opens the door to new learning, based on the attitude we take. Even little ones can be brought to be "responsible" in the choices they make each day...putting the building blocks away, or cleaning up some spilled Kool Aid. Taking responsibility is a learned habit.

Freddie, a fourth grader who was struggling to keep up in math, had a defensive attitude of "I know it already—so I don't have to do it." This side-ways view of his studies was channeled into successful behavior once he came to see that *practice makes progress,* and that his previous attitude reflected a fearful stance. At this early age, he decided he didn't want to be run by fear.

From there, Freddie decided to get involved in his math assignments with a new fervor, and he eventually became the best math student in the class! He had begun to see the *fun* in response-ability and this success led to many other successes.

July 4

The best criticism of the bad is the practice of the better.

Fr. Pat Griffin

It's so easy to ride on the high horse of superiority when we see the actions of others as either making no sense or as being destructive. A better way than just criticizing would be to look inside and see if we have some similar ways WE need to improve. This can lead to real progress and a better attitude towards those we see as deficient. Maybe *they* aren't deficient, but our perspective is.

To see others with compassion and wisdom means never giving up the possibility that *we* may actually be in the same boat, in a similar but invisible way.

Oh, how I remember the humbling—even humiliating—affect my first depression had on me. My self-esteem was so low that I suddenly began seeing those I had previously ruled out as worth-less as being superior to me. It made me wonder why I ever saw ANYONE as less-than, and me more-than. This depression changed me forever. I finally saw that we are all alike, with only differing gifts and struggles. I saw, for the first time (and not the last) that we are one.

I believe that our challenge is to seek to do our best and let go of comparing ourselves to others. We need to work toward accepting—even nurturing—diversity, as we strive to find the good in others, while we reach toward our own best selves.

July 5

No one can make you feel inferior without your consent.

Eleanor Roosevelt

What power and even joy can come through the revelations of this quote. Mrs. Roosevelt makes clear an amazing truth—that we have control over how we will be affected (or not) by others. <u>We</u> have the power!

Do we give the power away by "getting mad" at others, or do we pull in the reins by understanding where the other may be coming from—choosing empathy over negativity?

I was once given some great advice by a supervisor whose statement I've made into an acronym: D-TIP...

Don't Take It Personally!!

This idea has helped me so many times when I've been tempted to blame or shame myself, or to take someone's criticism too seriously. Even when it's "given personally," I don't have to TAKE it personally!

In 2004, while working as a special education teacher's aide in a suburban Minneapolis school, my principal pulled me aside and reprimanded me for 45 minutes about six major areas where I was not fulfilling my duties. After 2 or 3 pointed comments, I asked to take out my mini-notebook so I could record what she was saying.

It was a tough 45 minutes, but I still remember (and have often used) two of her criticisms:

1) Rich, you are not "in it"...you are not focused or fully aware of what is going on around you...

2) You are not asking enough questions. You are left in the blind because you are unwilling to get clarification.

These crucial critiques have helped me in every job—and most any situation—since. Who would I be if I had <u>NOT</u> taken it personally, listened and acted? I really don't know. So next time you're receiving a neck-tingling criticism, try *D-TIP* and let go. It may bring a surprising breakthrough!

July 6

> *When you have nothing, you have nothing to worry about.*
>
> *The Buddha*

The quote above seems to be referring to the power of the Spirit that Jesus was talking about in the Sermon on the Mount. Jesus established a fresh and awakening way of looking at spirituality..."blessed are the poor in spirit." What does this mean—"poor in spirit"?

Because of a former relationship where my partner had somewhat of a "Gimme Gimme" attitude—grasping for more and more material possessions—I adopted an acronym to counteract the selfish behavior.."CLAM."

Choose
Less
As
More

Now, I am not always the best at following my own advice, but CLAM has been a help when I get off into possessing things that are really beyond my established budget, or when I stop using the things I have in order to possess more stuff—buying for buying's sake.

The late John Lennon, in his song *Imagine*, speaks of imagining a world with no possessions—"I wonder if you can"—sings Lennon. This helps put me in the place to realize that all I really own is <u>my self</u>—my body, my mind...and the blessing of housing my spirit.

Have you ever seen the sarcastic bumper sticker that reads, "The one with the most toys wins!"? Have you ever met people who have so many possessions that they don't have enough time to use them? It's a sad scene. This flies in the face of Jesus' "poverty of spirit," doesn't it?

But I guess we can make decisions that de-personalize and "devalue" our possessions—promoting the notion that people are more important than things. I think this is what Jesus was talking about.

July 7

*When I was playing, I had a coach who used to tell me
to keep my priorities straight..."You figure out what's important
and you push everything else aside!"*

Coach Jones, movie RADIO

In the movie City Slickers, Mitch (Billy Crystal) is challenged by the rough & tough cowboy, Curly (Jack Palance) to find his "ONE THING"—the thing that brought meaning and fulfillment to his life. Mitch sat stunned in his saddle, as Curly held up his index finger..."You know your ONE THING and all the other don't matter crap!"

Have YOU found your *one thing* yet—that activity that brings *life* to your life? I've been blessed to find my *one thing*—mine is actually two-fold...teaching & writing! In every job I've had since my first teacher's aide job in 1984, I have loved showing people how to do things. Some of these have been educational jobs—such as a teacher's assistant—and some have not. Teaching is near and dear to my heart—and I've found myself to be pretty good at it, specifically as a communications consultant on self-esteem, goal-setting and bipolar disorder.

Along with teaching goes writing—a very important skill I have been working on for 25 years since graduating with a degree in mass communications in the early 1980s. I've found that writing is a form of teaching, since my books and poetry often focus on learning lessons in life—*education.*

Finding valuable employment has always come down to the fact that I love writing and teaching. I ask my Lord for the graces to fulfill my *one thing,* through actual hands-on teaching, and writing books, poetry and articles that educate.

Have you discovered your <u>one</u> <u>thing</u> yet?
If so, what are you doing about it?
If not, what ARE you going to do about it?

July 8

*We are prisoners of the
prisoners we have taken.*

Johnny Klegg & Suvuka

often I take myself prisoner
it is true
that the things I thought
I had control over
may have control over me

    such as
    fear
I go for a long time with
    NO FEAR
      then suddenly I find myself
      10, 15 years back
      in seemingly the same position
     failing as a far past person
    how can this happen?
    haven't I outgrown this?
  and security is temporarily shaken
but I go on and realize
it was just a glitch

yet even with this I can learn
(isn't that the point?)
so I choose to learn
and plan
and let go of the controls
into the hands of God
for "surrender" is
often my only recourse
in a world of uncontrollable
controllability

in the end, I see God as *in control*

Corsair

July 9

*It is a spiritual truth that our love for and praise
of others will improve our own self-image.*

Each Day A New Beginning

What a great incentive to share our praise, knowing that it will not only lift the other but bolster <u>our</u> own self-esteem!

It's a great give & take...to give another *"uppers"* and receive uppers in return. I know this feeling of giving another honest and appropriate praise and, in the expression, feeling good about myself too. Recently I composed a note of appreciation and praise to my wife and, although she will see it in the morning on the dining room table, I already feel uplifted by the simple act of love.

I'm no hero for doing this—only giving a lift to the one I love. But this is exactly the opposite scene as "crabs in a barrel,"...people pulling one another down the moment they make any progress. I saw too much of this in my job as teacher's assistant...kids dragging one another down with ceaseless criticism and ugly teasing.

I thank God for the gift of "reciprocal uplifting" that comes with praising others. When have you felt this praise/lift feeling about another's thoughtful actions?

Do you act on it?

July 10

"Remember—no man is a failure who has friends..."

It's a Wonderful Life (movie)

This movie is one of the most life-affirming shows I have ever seen—and one of my favorites. Let me briefly tell you the story.

George Bailey (played by the ever-enjoyable Jimmy Stewart) gets a unique opportunity/challenge to see what life would be like in his little town if he had never been born.

George's uncle had misplaced $8,000 and after a frantic search, George came to believe that, since he was liable for the loss, a $15,000 life insurance policy was more important than his life. He decided to throw himself off a bridge into a raging river. But before he could, an old man jumped into the water and began thrashing around. Being the good-hearted soul that he was, George saved the man—who happened to be his guardian angel—Clarence.

When George insisted that his guardian angel, Clarence, was a phony and that he thought his troubles were so deep that he wished he'd never been born, Clarence granted him the wish.

Suddenly, none of his friends knew him, nor did his mother, and most strikingly, neither did his wife Mary. Why? *Because he had never been born.* The town's name had changed also...from Bedford Falls to Pottersville, the name of George's nemesis, Mr. Potter—the richest man in the county who owned almost everything.

George's brother had died at age ten because George was not there to save him from drowning. And the druggist, Mr. Gauer, went to prison for accidentally poisoning a kid. Yet George distinctly remembered saving his brother and catching the druggist's mistake. He scrambled around town in disbelief.

Upon realizing his guardian angel wasn't kidding about how the world had changed because he hadn't been born, he ran to the bridge where he had earlier readied himself to jump and commit suicide, and, in desperation, begged Clarence to give him his life back. Through divine intervention, George received a second chance. His "old life" reappeared.

When he joyfully ran home, he greeted his kids, then his wife. "Mary! Are you real?" he cried out! It was a miracle! Then suddenly another miracle occurred...people came flooding into their home with money, having heard he needed it. His friends appeared from *everywhere* to help pay the $8,000 and keep him from losing everything!

It's true—*no man is a failure who has friends*. Awakened by his "nearly-unborn" experience, George was overcome with the awareness that *he surely did have a wonderful life!*

July 11

*The greatest contribution we can make
to the lives of others is to be affirming.*

Each Day A New Beginning

The opposite is so recognizable—those who aren't affirming tend to drive us away, most likely without knowing it. To be affirming means to SEE the real person—the triumphs & struggles, the long-held beliefs and the dusky doubts—and to love the whole person, blemishes and all.

Teachers get the biggest chance to be affirmers. They work so closely with students and see aptitudes and altitudes better than most others. Therefore it is most important that teachers be affirming, even in their correcting.

One teacher in high school was extremely influential. Mrs. Nolan, my English Literature teacher, made the topic come alive! I'll never forget when she read from Beowulf, pronouncing the intriguing Old English with fluency and poise. It was many years later that I realized how my decision to become a mass communications major was influenced by this excellent teacher.

It is true that the greatest contribution we can make is to be an affirming teacher—and because we're all **examples** to one another—WE'RE ALL TEACHERS!

July 12

Your ultimate goal is to become your best self.

Marsha Sinetar

A wise psychologist once challenged me to "CBS"— **C**onnect with my **B**est **S**elf. He pointed out that when I disconnected myself from my greatness, I experienced unhappiness.

Do you *CBS (Connect with your best self?)*? Many people don't even know what I'm talking about. Your Best Self is that YOU in its resilient state—when you are living from the inside out. Some call it "performing at peak"...I call it "living a spiritual life." Why "spiritual"? I see spirituality as being in contact with our essence, our inner selves, our Authentic Greatness...being in touch with our Higher Power resting within. When we live authentically, we live with integrity and dignity.

My friend Tom is a great example. He is a now-retired Catholic priest who, over the 25 years I have known him, has stayed in touch consistently. Although I lived in a different city for 18 of those 25 years, he never dropped the relationship—although his has been an extremely busy life and he knows many hundreds of people! More than any other friend, Tom has been there for me—bringing me to the hospital twice (15 years apart) when I was having difficulty with my bipolar disorder. Loyalty is no stranger to Tom!

Sometimes it takes many years to learn a lesson. This lesson of how to *CBS* took 16 years for me to learn. But, as my mother recently pointed out to me, the seed had been planted in fertile soil and has just now sprouted. She observed that I never gave up hope or simply dismissed *CBS* as a frivolous acronym that was of no use to anyone—not even myself.

God let the roots grow, unseen, these past 16 years and only now, in writing this meditation book, did it surface and become real! I have learned how to *CBS*, and have been able to acknowledge my strengths and weaknesses, focusing on changing the latter and accentuating the former.

If our ultimate goal is to become our Best Selves, we need to revisit those un-germinated lessons that wait in dusty closets, and coax them to come out & sprout. What better way is there to praise God—to give God the Glory?

July 13

It is only with the heart that one can see rightly—
what is essential is invisible to the eye.

The Little Prince, Antoine de Saint Exupery

This is one of our greatest challenges in life—learning to give *unconditional love*. I'm not always very good at it—are you? Oh yes, I have unconditional love for my wife, who is my lover, my confidant and my best friend. And I have unconditional love for my mother, who has been there for me through everything! But to always "see rightly"? This is a struggle for me.

I recently had a business dealing turn sour, and the negative feelings generated were quite over-powering. It's been difficult to get the other party out of my mind. But, then I realized that *"what is essential is invisible to the eye,"* and I remembered how my wife and I had seen such a lack of character and professionalism in the other party! It had been somewhat hidden from us at first, but became totally apparent at our final business meeting—after which we decided this was not in our best interests.

After much thought, I decided that an earnest prayer for him and a dismissal from the mind was appropriate. No need to go further. I see this as an extension of unconditional love—to not judge or continually criticize, but to let go.

When I said above that "I'm not always very good at it" (giving unconditional love), it probably resonates with many people. Often, many people—like me—are self-centered, not necessarily "selfish," but simply focusing on themselves first. This is a natural human trait. After all, we are trained to feed ourselves, dress ourselves, groom ourselves...self-sufficiency takes a great amount of focusing on ourselves! But having unconditional love means putting others first—at least to some extent.

A college buddy of mine caught me being critical about him behind his back. I was pretty harsh, and he had every reason to be angry—and even had enough "evidence" to break off the relationship. Nearly immediately, after we had both cooled down from the moment of his discovering my disloyalty, he wanted to hear my side. He expressed how much he was hurt by my comments, and when I apologized sincerely, he forgave me. He has never brought up the incident since!

This was a clear picture of unconditional love applied in the moment. My buddy got beyond his anger and forgave me in my most negligible moment. He saw my essential goodness and overlooked the rest.

How are you doing with your unconditional love lately?

July 14

*Visualization is...the conscious creation
of desired outcomes in your life.*

unknown

Can you visualize your ultimate success? Close your eyes and look in your mind's eye at yourself completing a huge task...climbing to the summit of a great accomplishment, or flying high in the success of achieving a dream. Can you feel the sensations?...taste the flavors?...feel the vibrations?...smell the fragrances?...see the sights?...hear the sounds of your successful venture?

My wife Sandra saw herself, many years ago, as a successful library administrator. She visualized herself leading people successfully, fulfilling administrative duties with poise and accuracy, AND pulling in a paycheck commiserate to her skills and efforts. She succeeded with flying colors—all because she saw it in her mind's eye and followed the vision!

See it. Hear it. Feel it...if you repeat your visualizations often enough they can lead to incredible outcomes. Scientists have discovered that *the mind can't tell between a real event and one vividly imagined.* This makes visualization not only practical but essential for future success.

What is important enough to you for you
to visualize yourself into success?

July 15

We are unique in our gifts and united in our struggles.

Corsair

The only thing we all have in common is...*we're all different!* This uniqueness can be a cause for joy and excitement when we see our gifts as valuable and when we observe that we all have different gifts to bring to the table.

Yet often, we try to hide our uniqueness behind the guise of conformity and sameness, matching others' moods, clothes, hair styles and actions in order to fit in. In this "fitting in" we can lose our greatest gifts, in fear that we will be "found out," and seen as "different." After all, who wants to be *"terminally unique?"*

But as we share our struggles with trusted friends, we find that we are actually quite similar to others, not stranded on the desert isle of a lost self. Here, our uniqueness can rest and even *play* because we know the other has experienced similar pain and disillusionment and come through it—with the help of others.

I remember that, before I "came out" about having bipolar disorder, I felt very isolated and *negatively unique*. But when I became open about the illness and no longer hid it, I discovered how common it was and how willing people were to talk about it—and not judge me. It has been an incredible ride since bipolar is no longer hidden in some long-forgotten coal mine of my psyche! I have even given many speeches on the topic.

We are NOT dependent upon others when we share our "tough stuff," our struggles and downfalls. By sharing our true selves, we become *interdependent* and KNOWN for who we truly are. This is one of the greatest gifts of friendship—that vulnerability in sharing that turns into understanding and strength.

I don't know where I would be in life had I not had good friends and loving family members to talk to—in times of joy <u>and</u> struggle! I'm sure that we can all relate to the experience of being seen for who we are (unique) and for feeling united with others while achieving a common cause or the great feelings of getting together with others in social situations.

In essence, we are one..."UNI"...**uni**que <u>and</u> **uni**ted, through taking the risks of intimacy and giving it a chance to change our lives.

July 16

Don't push the river - let it flow by itself.

Adult Children of Alcoholics

Spirituality. Not religion, but…*Spirituality*. Fr. Anthony de Mello once said that "Spirituality means no longer being at the mercy of any person, thing or event." In this quote, de Mello expresses a simple but profound truth…that spirituality does not necessarily mean religion. Religion is often filled with rules and dogma, structures and hierarchies. Spirituality is something more basic, alive and free. One can experience spirituality while walking through a field and resting among the rustling weeds and wild flowers.

To me, spirituality is making a connection between myself, my life, my surroundings and my God. At times, it arises in the most unlikely places. Recently I experienced a change of heart and renewal of identity while writing, from memory, some words of the movie The Wiz (the African-American version of The Wizard of Oz) into my journal. I experienced anew important words like, "I believe there's a reason to be!" and "I choose to believe in myself—right from the start!" These highly motivating, memorized quotes brought me a new sense of connection with my life, my future and my God.

Another spiritual awakening occurred on a snowy February walk in 2009. It was a *"Wiz thing"* again. I had recalled the words of Dorothy, "Is there a way for me to find home?"...and asked God the same question. I had been feeling pretty disillusioned, having been unemployed for months and coming out from under a year of huge mental health difficulties.

As I trudged through the new-fallen snow, my acronyms (of which I have created 35-40) began to come to mind. I questioned what this had to do with HOME. Then it hit me. I reached into my wallet and pulled out a business card-size laminated copy of 32 of my personally-created acronyms. I had been *"sitting on my wisdom,"* rarely having pulled them out to look at <u>my</u> truth, <u>my</u> way of looking at the world! The answer was inside my pocket all the time!

On that afternoon, self-validation became my charge—not waiting for others to affirm me, but seeing MY good and valuing MY truth. This became a new perspective of how I value myself. The acronym occurrence was a "GOD THING" that I will never forget!

The moving words from The Wiz had rested in my mind and heart for years, and when it was time for them to shine once again, they bubbled up in an instant, giving me new energy and direction. *This* is spirituality, to me...a great blessing of personal significance from my Highest Power.

July 17

Wisdom is <u>not</u> experience—wisdom comes from not being influenced by experience . . . wisdom is not applying yesterday's solution to today's problem . . . wisdom is to be sensitive to <u>this</u> situation, to <u>this</u> person—uninfluenced by any carry-over from the past—no residue from the experience of the past... quite unlike what most people are accustomed to thinking.

Fr. Anthony de Mello

After listening to this quote probably 15-20 times in the past 10 years or so, tonight it finally hit home! What was different? I was ready to hear it. You know how that works, don't you? How many times have you heard Jesus' parable about "taking the plank out of your eye before you take the speck out of your brother's eye"...I heard this on the tape just before the above quote. And I GOT IT!

In my endeavors with a loved one, I had been extremely critical and judgmental about a set of behaviors, attitudes and attributes that were "driving me crazy"! I didn't feel comfortable around this person because I felt used, and that ingratitude was rampant. WISDOM, de Mello-style, came to the rescue.

When I heard of "the plank" tonight, I realized that I often demonstrate many of the same characteristics—or, at least, had done so—dramatically—in the past. Instantly my heart was softened and forgiveness was nurtured. I no longer dislike being near this person, and actually (and surprisingly) now find it enjoyable. I can even deal with the previously-distancing attitudes. I'm not bothered by previously perceived annoying attributes. And with my change, positive change has surrounded the relationship. God is good!

This, I believe, is what Fr. de Mello was talking about. To let go of past sufferings and prejudices and just deal with the moment—in the moment! It has now begun to seep into my body, mind and soul...and I know God is doing a great work within me.

Do you see how this *wisdom* can play an important—even crucial—role in your development? Wow, what a difference it has begun to make in my life!

July 18

Optimism is a little thing that makes a BIG difference.

unknown

Dr. Alan Zimmerman offers a definition of optimism (which I modified): "Optimism means seeking the opportunity in every difficulty, while pessimism means spotting the difficulty in every opportunity." This has been one of the most life-enhancing quotes for me—in my top ten! It is a powerful quote, isn't it?

Why powerful? Because no other quote I know can spin me in a "180" with so few words. Many times I have caught myself in a pessimistic way and have simply repeated the words "optimism means seeking the opportunity in every difficulty" and steered myself away from negative ways of thinking and acting.

Optimism is really NOT a little thing, but actually one of the biggest things—it can make the difference between finding our true path and getting lost in the negative thoughts and decisions that can, in time, make life miserable.

My most recent hero of optimism is President Barack Obama who rose to influence through his integrity, honesty and poise. "Yes we can," a primary theme of his 2008 campaign, smacks of hope and optimism—like no other politician I have ever seen! I believe he will be one of America's most successful presidents, partly because of the optimistic stance he projects in all he does.

Optimism clears the way for a lifetime of healthy living. "Looking at the bright side" may be an over-used phrase, but a bit of optimism can make all the difference as we *seek opportunities instead of always spotting the difficulties.*

July 19

*"...It's never a mistake to care about someone—
that's <u>always</u> a good thing."*

Coach Jones' wife, movie "Radio"

In the movie "Radio," Cuba Gooding, Jr., plays a mentally handicapped young man who is befriended by the local football coach (Ed Harris). The young man goes by the name *Radio*, a name the coaches gave him when he showed interest in their radio.

The head coach, Coach Jones, takes a liking to Radio...why? He can't explain fully, but he does explain to Radio's mother that "it seemed like the right thing to do." The coach gave Radio duties on the football squad that made him feel valuable. Coach Jones surely understood the words of will Rogers—displayed through his kind actions...*"As long as you live, you'll never find a better way of getting in touch with others than to make them feel important."* Coach Jones had this down!

Radio ends up being sort of a mascot for the team, with his enthusiasm and friendly, gentle ways. The once-silent Radio becomes quite talkative, making friends on and off the football field and even began doing the announcements in the morning at the high school!

When Coach Jones starts getting heat about having Radio involved in the school activities, the coach begins to question whether he should have ever reached out to him at all. His wife immediately remarked, "It's never a mistake to care about someone—that's <u>always</u> a good thing." With this encouragement, Coach Jones fights to keep Radio in the school environment—and wins!

This true story continues today as Radio is still involved with Hanna High...a beloved and welcomed fixture, *all because someone believed in him.*

Do you have an opportunity to reach out and believe in someone today?
What's stopping you?

July 20

"One small step for man—one giant leap for mankind."

NASA astronaut Neil Armstrong

When Neil Armstrong stepped onto the lunar surface on July 20, 1969, the world entered a new era. After seeing the Earth from the surface of the moon, never again were we to see our world as compartmentalized, with totally distant neighbors—no more impermeable political borders.

But even with our global view—and now global economy—we are still so separated. War, famine, crime and hatred pervade our societies, even though we have massive technological resources that could solve most—if not all—of our problems. But how does one solve the problems of the human heart?

You've probably heard this spiel before, but I want to repeat what Neil Armstrong said as he first tapped the moon's surface..."one *giant leap* for mankind"—was this a leap forward or a leap backward? It seems that—since even before the dawn of man's walk on Earth—technologies have harmed human life as much as helped. Just as an example, as soon as the Wright brothers invented the airplane, the new invention was probably being groomed for warfare—the new wonderful weapon of the air. And, these days, computer software and hardware is probably being used just as much (if not more) for warfare purposes as for purposes of education.

My hope and prayer is that man can find a way to create and utilize technologies *only* for peaceful means, not for means of destruction. The moment we move our major resources in this direction, I believe this is when we will have accomplished the true "Giant Leap."

July 21

> *To be wronged is* nothing *unless you insist on remembering it.*
>
> *Fr. Anthony de Mello*

Have you ever had someone "do you wrong" and you just can't get it out of your mind? Traumatic events can get etched in the lens with which we view our world. How could we ever get the etching off the glass?

Fr. Tom Weston said, "The only way to get rid of bad, old ideas is to replace them with new, good ones." Is this possible? Sure. Look at all of the Holocaust survivors who have gone on to live happy, productive lives. Or, look at the many American veterans of foreign wars who survived with honor, overcoming the horrors of battle to return to their lives here at home.

Most of us have had far less trauma in our lives—but we have had trauma, none the less—and we have found ways to overcome these deficits. It's human nature to try to forget such events, and this is probably a good thing. But I remember a movie in the late 1970s called *Ordinary People* where a high schooler was repressing the grief of losing his brother in a sailing accident. He only began to come around when, in desperation, he admitted to his psychologist that he was infuriated that his brother had let go of his hand and slid into the foamy waters.

It was this admittance, this cathartic moment, that broke him free of the anguish he had felt—the pain and guilt of being the one who survived the accident. Only then did he start to heal. Up until that point he had been trapped by the shame of having watched his brother slip into oblivion and being left the only one holding onto the boat.

Sure we need to *replace bad old ideas with new good ones.* But at times it helps to revisit a traumatic event, in a supportive atmosphere—not to dwell on it over and over, but to see it for what it was and take the sting out of it by letting the light of truth shine in and lighten the dark corners of our memory. This may just make it possible to let go of the memory's grip once and for all.

July 22

Let us look for the good in others and ourselves
and, in time, it is all that will catch our attention.

Each New Day A Beginning

This is what the best teachers do. In college, I had a professor whom I respected a great deal and is, today, a good friend of mine. She had a way of bringing the best out in me, as I studied mass communications law and creative writing under her tutelage at our southern Minnesota university, 27 years ago. This was one of my first poems, written in 1982 about a grade school teacher on an Indian reservation in South Dakota. It reminds me of the role my college professor played in my life:

Teacher Student

a teacher is a student
learning much from the pupils
the way to enjoy life—good time spent
opening the heart so happiness fills

yes the teacher is to be taught
an opposite role
in order to find what is sought
fulfillment—through making another whole

oh yes the teacher is example
yet the example is in front of you
the answer seems so simple
to become a learner again is true virtue

Corsair

I remember the wonderful conversations we shared in her office. She had a great sense of humor, so I would tape wacky cartoons to her door—of which she always showed her appreciation—and laughter.

After college, especially in the past 10 years, my teacher-friend has been there for me in some pretty tough times, always offering encouragement and support. She has a way of finding the good in me—and affirming it!

Have you ever had a teacher-turned-friend? Was he/she an "encourager"?

July 23

We shall never cease from striving—
and at the end of all our striving, we will arrive
where we began—and know the place for the first time.

T.S. Elliot

Sometimes when we feel like we're going in circles, we may just be in what *The Lion King* calls the Circle of Life. Life is a process with many stages. As we put effort in, we will gain strength and experience. Simple enough. It's almost as if a wheel were turning beneath us—not like a gerbil on a spinning wheel—but, hopefully, a wheel of progression and growth.

A few years ago, I experienced this in my own *symbolic/spiritual* life. A name came back to life in my journaling process—a name—*Corsair*—that arose as a preference at age 14. This is the name of my favorite World War II fighter plane that came flying back into my mind during my journaling process. It came to mean "FAITH;" so I chose the name as the pen name for my poetic writings. Corsair, a 33-year-old preference came back to me into my own personal Circle of Life.

Journal entry:

Fri. Dec. 29, 2006

(While writing in a coffee shop)...I had a "born-again experience"
*just now that brought back an old name (**CORSAIR**) and a new*
*attribute of **FAITH**, arising from the past symbolic spiritual*
*spiral encircled with the words **F**=Freedom, **A**=Authenticity,*
***I**=Integrity, **T**=Truth & **H**=Honesty...I discovered that these*

5 words express what is deep within me...this name, this plane,
this preference has brought me back to myself!

Sometimes we can be pleasantly surprised as *the circle* can bring great gifts that appear around the bend and present themselves at our feet. We need not make HUGE changes in our lives, but a little engine-tweaking can make a big difference.

This Circle of Life brought me back to 5 attributes I've acquired over the years. And I was so moved by the experience that, in 2008, I had my middle name legally changed to *Corsair.* It is my realization of the significant connection—*the Corsair Connection*—that called me to the name change. It feels right—and good. *Corsair* is now not just a pen name but a part of my REAL name...and I have come home to my self!

July 24

There's nothing stronger than the heart of a volunteer.

Gen. Dolittle, movie, Pearl Harbor

Serving others—isn't this what it's all about? My mother is the spiritual leader of a group of women in Buffalo, Minnesota (my home town, near Minneapolis) who create bedrolls for the homeless in the St. Paul/Minneapolis area. These women get together every Thursday to contribute their time, talent and effort in sewing these sturdy bedrolls. They also include a bag with a T-shirt and some toiletries for the homeless folk who receive the bedrolls.

This project began over ten years ago when my mother read a magazine heard from a close friend about someone making bedrolls for the poor. "That's for me!" my mom exclaimed, and proceeded to get the ball rolling in the basement of the local Catholic church.

These fine bedrolls get distributed to the homeless for no cost to the recipients—giving these fine women peace and joy in their hearts for a job well done. Dolittle was right—"There's nothing stronger than the heart of a volunteer."

July 25

*In a Charlie Brown comic strip, Linus says to Charlie Brown,
"Charlie Brown, the trouble with you is that
you don't want to know the trouble with you."*

Awareness. This is the main theme in many of Fr. Anthony de Mello's presentations. De Mello, a Jesuit priest from India, spoke with meaning and authority until his untimely death in 1987, at age 56.

His philosophy of SEEING—being **aware** of all that is going on in us and around us—led him to formulate the best definition for LOVE I have ever heard: *"Love is clarity of perception and accuracy of response."* This description of love has been a very important part of my life because it is so practical—so true. How can we love that which we do not know…and once we know, how can we keep from loving?

Linus' proclamation to Charlie Brown is a wake-up call to all of us who don't like looking within and becoming aware of our inner worlds. Even though I have been journal-writing for 28 years, I still find that, at times, I'm not willing to look at my true reflection in the mirror of my heart.

Recently, I caught myself in the hypocrisy of being judgmental of a loved one. I was so caught up in the emotion of feeling taken advantage of that I made a huge deal out of nothing, and the result was alienation. After a number of days, I realized my folly and apologized, which led to our relationship being mended. I had not had clarity of perception, and my response had not been accurate!

God, please help us have the courage to see who we truly are, as with look for the good in others and ourselves…seeking *"clarity of perception and accuracy of response."*

July 26

I'm very seriously kidding!

Corsair

My brother John once told me "nothing is so tragic if you can get a good story from it!" Stories are the most meaningful and interesting things in the world.

John was on the Pine Ridge Indian Reservation years ago, teaching at Red Cloud Indian School, when the kids decided to give him a Lakota nickname…"Zintkala Nasula," which they told him meant *proud eagle.*

He was so proud of his new name until he told the elders of this newnick name—*Zintkala Nasula.* They laughed to themselves, and when John inquired why, they told him Zintkala Nasula didn't mean "proud eagle, but "*bird brain*"!

Playwright August Wilson said, "If you're going to tell someone a story, and if you want to keep information alive, you have to make it memorable so that the person hearing it will go tell someone else." Humor is one of the best ways to get a message across.

…There's the story of Grandpa & Grandma Mardy, tired from their 60th anniversary celebration, resting on the porch. Grandpa felt moved, you see, and said, "Grandma, I'm proud of you." Grandma replied, "Speak louder—you know I can't hear you without my hearing aid!" "I'm PROUD of you," exclaimed Grandpa. Grandma retorted, "That's OK…I'm *tired* of you too."

My brother John was right…"Nothing is so tragic if you can get a good story from it"!

July 27

If we fill our hours with regrets over failures of yesterday,
and with the worries over the problems of tomorrow,
we have no today in which to be thankful.

Adult Children of Alcoholics

It is the moment—this moment—in which we live. "NIATI"...Now Is All There Is! There is no other moment than the present. *Here (snap fingers)*—& it's gone...*here (snap)*—& it's gone. So we need to use it wisely.

Regret and worry are two major *now-killers* that, along with fear, create a threesome of destruction like no other. Regret keeps us thinking about a negative past, while worry traps our thoughts and feelings in a negative, unknown future—both wasting time enormously.

Fear is the biggest now-killer of all. Fear creates an atmosphere of inner-mistrust and often an unwillingness to look at all the good that may be happening around the scene. I love the quote by St. Therese ..."*I have decided to banish, far away, all fear and all memory of past faults—no trace of dead sins left behind—for in one second, love can burn them to ashes.*" This puts fear into perspective.

I have found the practice of gratitude to be the best way to counter my regret, worry and fear. There are so many times just in this past year that I have been blessed with the gift of gratitude—which has brought me back to a place of peacefulness and love. I've experienced and expressed gratitude for others, for my place in life and for a God who loves me through all my moods and inconsistencies—loving me out of my brokenness.

Recently I started a new job at a group home for young men. Having been unemployed for over a year, it was a welcomed change to be back at work. Yet it was bound to be somewhat stressful because this was home for youth who have recognizable troubles with personal and social behaviors. I became quite worried that I may not be able to handle the job.

So I prayed. I prayed that it would work out for the best for everyone, and, so far, the blessings have been overflowing. My worries and fears have melted away as a sincere thankfulness now emanates from my heart and mind. Being brought through the waterfall of fear and to the other side is an exhilarating experience!

The expression of gratitude is uplifting to the giver as well as the receiver. The great thing is...there's ALWAYS something to be thankful for—if we only look for it! Nothing like having *just a little somethin'* to be grateful for.

July 28

Only a person of deep faith can afford the luxury of skepticism.

Nietzsche

The above sounds like an oxymoron...like "jumbo shrimp, lengthy brief, tall shortcake, or...<u>faith-filled skepticism</u>." But it makes sense in *my* spiritual life.

In the movie, the Sound of Music, Mother Superior tells the wavering Maria something to the effect of "I like to keep some faith in the midst of my doubts." I believe it's more difficult (and important) to struggle with issues, rather than just *believe and never question*. It's in the struggling that true, orange-hot issues are hammered into shape...faith being forged through heat and pressure.

Archie Bunker, a grouchy character in the 1970s show *All in the Family,* was a *cynic*—always finding the bad in most every situation—and constantly verbalizing his dissatisfaction. His step-son was a *skeptic*—always questioning the status quo, never satisfied with how things looked on the surface. Which would you rather be?

Skepticism means you do not know and want to find out, while *cynicism* means making a negative value judgment about a situation. Skepticism means being cautious and observant. If we are never the skeptic, are we the sponge, who just accepts at face value all that we hear and see? If so, we may be missing the most important activity of life—making up our own minds, choosing for ourselves what we will make a part of our lives.

Viktor Frankyl, Auschwitz survivor, stated, "They could take from me everything but the last of human freedoms—to make my own decisions in any set of circumstances—to choose my own way." Frankyl's hard-won truth shows how faith can bring a *holy skepticism*, which can be a bridge over many a troubled time.

I tend to have some pretty descriptive and empowering dreams—and I can often interpret them quite well. A few weeks ago, I had a disturbing dream about a business deal in which have I was involved. Although I *KNEW* I should have listened to the dream, I shrugged it off, ignoring my gift of holy skepticism. A day later, the business deal blew up in my face, as the other party was found to be untrustworthy. I immediately got out of the deal. Being more skeptical may have allowed me to pull out of the deal before it got nasty.

It's empowering to know that my dreams don't lead me astray, but guide me onto the right path. This event bolstered my belief in holy skepticism, and the need to follow my heart.

July 29

Every experience can move us forward in understanding ourselves.

Each Day A New Beginning

If we choose it, we can learn from EVERY experience, good or bad, positive or negative. Like with the stock market, you can make money when the prices are moving up, and, if you play the game right, you can win when the prices are moving down!

Every experience can be "positive" when we *learn our lessons*. As previously mentioned, John Powell, SJ, once wrote, "*The only REAL mistake is the one from which we learn nothing!*" This is one of my top five favorite quotes because it makes it possible for me to realize I can learn a lesson at any moment in which I reflect on the situation—no matter how far in the past or recent the event—and reach new plateaus of understanding and acceptance.

My struggles with bipolar disorder have <u>not</u> been in vain because I decided—long ago—to "learn my lessons" from some pretty harrowing experiences, and to apply these lessons to everyday life. One lesson was learning my "manic clues"—writing down my symptoms and precipitating events that arise when I begin to become *manic*—this over-symbolic, over-creative, spinning-mind state that cause an extremely unbalanced lifestyle and may lead to an eventual hospitalization.

It is because of these *manic clues* that I have learned how to recognize and avoid mania. This single effort of creating a list of my manic clues has been enormously helpful in keeping my balance as a person with bipolar disorder!

This *"learning life's lessons"* is, to me, a good
definition of successful living.

July 30

To live without hope is to cease to live.

Dostoyevsky

Being in full-fledged depression is, to me, the most hopeless and painful state in which to be. Spring, 1980 was the first (and the most severe) depression that I've ever struggled through. A huge factor was because I didn't know I HAD bipolar disorder—or even what it was. What is bipolar? Once called manic-depression, bipolar is a hereditary brain-chemistry disorder that can cause dramatic mood fluctuations, from depression to elation and anywhere in between.

The symptoms of mania include over-activity, irritability, over-creativity, sleep deprivation, rapid thought/speech patterns, grandiosity, impulsiveness, overspending, etc. Depressive symptoms are completely opposite...sluggishness, slowed speech and thought processes, pessimism, lack of creativity, lack of ambition, emotional anguish, self-shaming, etc.

As referred to above, in early 1980, my senior year of high school, I found myself drowning in a sea of regret and shame, having no idea I was in depression. It's such an all-encompassing state that even though I was living, I "ceased to live." There was rarely any relief from the torments of this depressive state. I didn't even want to get out of bed—the hardest part of the day. What was there to get out of bed *for*?

I thank God for proper medications AND an unconquerable mother who saw me through the very worst moments. She said three crucial things to me: 1) I can see you're suffering, 2) you're NOT alone and 3) this, too, shall pass. It may be that these statements seemed to have fallen on deaf ears, but I *was* listening...and eventually, I came through the storm.

Bipolar is extremely treatable with medications, so if you or someone you know has these symptoms or behaviors, get help. You can save yourself or someone else a lot of pain and anguish—or even save your/their life—with appropriate treatment. There is always hope!

July 31

"...doing everything for the love of God and for no other reason."

St. Vincent de Paul

What a stance in life, to do everything for God, out of the love we have for God. Personally, I am a Christian but I don't have God, or Christ, on my mind at all times. I guess I think it would be overkill, and the sentiment would be in danger of losing its meaning.

But I do follow Jesus' WAY of thanking God for all the gifts bestowed and graces rendered. It was Jesus' example to praise God, His father, for life's blessings—and life itself—that latches onto my spirituality, like a barnacle on a barge.

The St. Vincent de Paul Society, of which I am a member, has five tenets—of which I have added two:

Selflessness, Simplicity, Humility, Gentleness and Zeal...with my two offerings of Authenticity and *Gratitude*. It is this last one—GRATITUDE—that has extreme meaning in my life. Gratitude is my call to surrender, my call to uplifting God's Presence, and my call to worship. I see gratitude as a primary attribute—represented in the Last Supper, the Eucharist (which means "thanksgiving").

"Praise God always," and in all ways, is the Bible's proclamation... seems strange to praise God even when things aren't going so well. But who knows...maybe this "bad thing" will bring about one of our most treasured blessings.

God Is Good...All The Time!

All the time...God is good!

~ August ~

August 1

We must have purpose in our lives, for the flame
that warms the soul is an everlasting vision—
every man __must__ have his goal!

Art Holst

What is YOUR purpose? What is *your* life about?
Have you thought about it much?

Most goals come from small beginnings. For me, I took a life-altering volunteer job, just out of college, as a teacher's aide in a predominantly African American grade school in urban Milwaukee, fall 1984. I was so fascinated by the culture and encouraged by the children that, quickly, my goal became to achieve my grade school teacher's license.

It's been about 26 years since this inspirational time and, after 2 previous attempts to get my teacher's license, I've decided it's *not for me*. It would be too much pressure and impose too many responsibilities. Sometimes you have to let go of a dream to latch on to a new one.

So I've decided to modify this dream. My wife Sandra and I are venturing out as public speakers in the Milwaukee community to speak on all aspects of RESPECT—self-respect, respect of others, mental health respect, intercultural respect. We will most likely be reaching more people—youth and adults—than I could have ever reached as teacher. My actual influence and ideas will most likely reach a far greater audience because I'm following my heart and following through on my talents to meet the needs of others effectively.

Isn't it interesting that if we keep the fire of passion burning in whatever way we can, the flame will embroil our goals in time, and we can move forward with our plans—even though they may be very different than first imagined. This is what has happened to me, and I feel this recent movement toward my dreams is much more realistic and plausible. If we follow our heart, I believe God will have a way with us. Believe it!

August 2

Enough days committed to the completion of enough small objectives will bring the attainment of any goal—large or small.

Each Day A New Beginning

In high school football, we had this occasional call-out by the coach to "break down!" When we heard *"Break Down!"*, we were to immediately lower our center of gravity, straighten our backs, lean forward, and drop our arms by our sides. Not bad advice to "mentally *break down"* when we meet challenges—breaking them down into smaller, do-able tasks.

This is common sense. You don't eat a whole loaf of bread at one time—or even a whole slice of bread. We break it down into manageable bites.

In his book to Simple Steps to Impossible Dreams, author Steven Scott calls this *the process of dream conversion.* Applying it, he shows how to dream big, then break the dreams down into goals, then divide goals into steps, and finally the break the steps into tasks (bites). It's a challenging process that takes some real time and attention to construct, but, as Scott acknowledges, it really works. Scott went from corporate underdog to millionaire in just a few years using this process.

I finished writing my third book a month ago—Discerning Bipolar Grace—concluding a process that lasted ten months. It is a memoir about my struggles with bipolar disorder. I accomplished it by breaking down the dream of producing the book into bite-size pieces. It was a "what am I going to write about today?"-process, with no real plot or specific direction—to begin with.

207

But as I wrote chapter after chapter, it took the form of sharing *teachable moments* about my struggles and triumphs with the illness. When the first version was completed, after considerable effort, my wife and edited it; then we got feedback from my parents and we edited it again; then I edited it fully two more times—just me, hearing the words in my solitary presence. Finally, it was done!

It was this layered, step-by-step approach that made the process of creating <u>Discerning Bipolar Grace</u> so special. It was truly a blessed series of writing and editing events.

Do YOU have dreams? Why not give the *dream conversion process* a shot!

August 3

> *You cannot NOT communicate.*
>
> *Dr. Alan Zimmerman*

s i l e   n   c   e

no sighs or violence
stillness absolute
not a breeze whispering through complaisant pine
nor gently folding lap on rocky shore
lonely hawk's absent plea cheats the cool night air
and cricket chirping choir rests voiceless
ear grasping the nothingness
   (loudest sound never heard)

to be motionless
noiseless
loud as running sap
or ant scurrying
eardrums crying for lack of a drummer

once *silence* is heard
the beat
the melody
the rhythm
the tone

it leaves its impression forever

(the trees will know you then)

Corsair

August 4

*Humor is a way of standing back and putting
yourself and your recovery in perspective.*

Patrick Lair

Humor can break the tension—or the boredom—that often surrounds us in everyday life. Fr. Anthony de Mello has a few good ones I'd like to share:

A man escaped from prison by digging a tunnel and came out in the middle of a children's playground. He couldn't help himself and called out "I'm free! I'm free! I'm free!"

A little girl, watching nearby, looked at him scornfully and retorted, "That's nothing—I'm four!!"

****

(Then there's the one)...Two friends were talking about the up-coming election. John said, "David, are you planning on voting Republican?"

David said, "No. I'm planning on voting Democrat."

"Why?" called out John.

"*Well, you know, my father was a Democrat, my grandfather was a Democrat, and his father was a Democrat—so I'm voting Democrat.*"

John retorted, "That's crazy logic, David! Let me put it this way…if your father was a horse thief, and your grandfather was a horse thief, and HIS father was a horse thief, what would that make you?"

"*Oh,*" *replied David,* "*Then I'd be a Republican!*"

August 5

Things may get easier with time,
but it doesn't mean they become easy.

Corsair

Mistaking "easier" for "easy" can mean folly. We always need to be challenged in some way, or we lose "the green edge," the growing potential. With "easy" can come complacency and even laziness.

Jenny moved from a 9-to-5 job to a second shift job, 2-10 p.m. She thought this would be *easy*, not having to get up early in the morning—sleeping in. But it backfired when she began sleeping until 10 or 11 a.m. With "nothing to get up for," this *easy* life had become her enemy.

She got fed up with this and decided to find events and activities that would get her out of bed by 7 a.m. and motivate her to keep busy during those long morning hours. She began attending Catholic Mass, got involved in writing and craft projects, and even went for long walks. Soon, her *easy* life shifted into "functional"—and even *productive*. Her life was once again more balanced and on track.

Sometimes simple semantics play a huge part in success.

August 6

Between stimulus and response, there is a space
(a "freedom space") to choose how we will think and act.

Stephen R. Covey

It was 64 years ago today that the United States dropped the atom bomb on Hiroshima, Japan. Could it be that America lost its "freedom space"—its tolerance—and felt compelled to use *the bomb* once it was invented? We all need a measure of restraint in our dealings with others. To fly off the handle in the face of opposition or conflict usually leaves a situation in much worse shape. If only restraint had been applied in some extreme cases, our world would be very different.

Hopefully the two atom bombs dropped on Japan in 1945 will be the only nuclear weapons used on this earth. My hope is that we can expand our "freedom spaces" to tolerate those who are different. The 10 words below were spoken by a Japanese poet:

ahh
Hiroshima
let us make clean
our hands by our-
selves
///
///
//
///

powerful
words on a day of
anti-celebration when we
realize only a bit of what we've done
—this falling out of the sky bringing
a world of death into a new world
that can never to go back to ancient
"primitive" ways of solving
our vast problems----just

a new way of deciding
and "compromising"
/////
////
///
//
///

now only beyond brute strength
will solve arguments
and differences of policy and opinion
this new way of cruel quick solutions shows
worldly mega force of how ugly human beings can be

now we need a **real peace**
we need to find *a solution to the solution*
in time for the times ahead
seems we are approaching hell with our
military madness
can't you see it?

God, help us with an answer!

*Corsair journal, August 6, 2009   (64 years after the atom bomb
destroyed Hiroshima)*

August 7

*The change of one simple behavior can affect
other behaviors and thus change many things.*

Jean Baer

In 12th grade science, our teacher filled a 30-inch-high beaker with
water on a Friday afternoon during class and dropped one single drop of
dark ink into the standing water. We didn't think much about it.

But when we came into class on Monday, the entire beaker had transformed into purple-colored water. Our teacher called it "diffusion." I called it "amazing!" How could that one drop of colored ink affect the whole beaker—with NO stirring? Diffusion!

This is exactly what the above quote is talking about. One change of attitude or behavior can have enormous affects on us and our environments. Like the ink, a "concentrated" effort is all it takes.

When Matthew returned to expressing himself through painting, his whole life changed. He had neglected his painting efforts for years and had been itching to get back into it. It took an encounter with unemployment for him to have the time to express his creativity through abstract art again. He came alive—giving him the energy and ambition to re-do the entire interior of his home...woodwork, plumbing, painting—the works!

He began to have more energy for his relationship for his wife, and even for walking the dogs more consistently. His artwork thrived and he even shifted into painting on larger canvases, using more elaborate color schemes. His painting passion affected every area of his life.

What small aspect of *your* life can you change for the better? It may just change everything!

August 8

There is no such thing as sacrifice—only opportunity to serve.

(attributed to Dr. Martin Luther King, Jr.)

What an inspiration to realize that we are not merely called to "sacrifice" but to "serve"! This takes life to a whole 'nother level—the level of *mission*.

To have a mission in life, not just a goal or even a dream, brings in the spiritual side of a life-calling. With a "calling," someone or something has to *do the calling*. For me, this is the God of my understanding, my Highest Power.

My mission is—you guessed it—*to teach.* I have decided that to become a certified teacher was too stressful for me. But I have served as a teacher's aide, which has allowed me opportunities to teach and shape young lives, without all the pressure of being the main teacher.

Goals may fall by the wayside, but I believe missions live on. This mission to teach has been defined and expressed in different ways for me over the years—from writing prose, to teaching, to public speaking, to writing poetry…yes, I have been blessed with a mission!

What skills do *you* bring to the table? What is YOUR *opportunity to serve*—your mission?

August 9

*With each new day I put away the past and discover
the new beginnings I have been given.*

Each Day A New Beginning

Journal entry, 2007:

Today is a day of new beginnings for me. I have been the object of abusive behavior and and have witnessed so much disrespect as a teacher's assistant at the school in which I work! Yet I have not known how to create order. The first word in my scholastic acronym— "*R*.R.O.C.K.S.S."—is "*Respect*," and it's occurred to me that without this power-word, my students will have no ability to continue successfully in their education.

Stephen R. Covey, in his tape series "Living the Seven Habits," states, "*RESPECT of person and property is the foundation of all society.*" This simple truth goes unnoticed and un-heeded in many of the encounters with the 5th graders as the regular teacher, and I experience these students' every-day interactions.

"*Respect for person and property*" is often smothered in incessant student-to-student teasing, jabbering and even taunting, during the school day. My decision today is to COMMAND respect with these unruly students so that if they learn one thing this year, it will be how to respect the teaching staff, themselves…and one another.

Big job, I know. But, for me as teacher's assistant, it looks like my premier aim and most important activity. I care about these kids and to send them on to 6th grade with no respect for authority, property or one another would be a travesty. God, please help us in this aim!

August 10

The pain of change is a reality. But so is
the pain of no change when change is called for.

Each Day A New Beginning

Life, to me, is about learning our lessons. Sometimes we can learn them at the moment of interaction, sometimes not. At times, the pain is too great—the fog of confusion too thick to learn our lessons at the exact moment. Maybe we need some distance—linear, temporal and/or spiritual—to figure things out.

Many people stuff stressful or painful learning-pregnant moments so deep that they don't come up for air for years, if ever. This is sad because the potential seed-in-fertile-soil is lost to abandonment or inattention.

One experience for me stands out, as far as a learning-moment that was nearly lost in the mundane. It was 1994, and after experiencing non-inspiring services at the only black Catholic parish in Minnesota, I stuffed and hid my "Milwaukee Self," a man who had spent 3 years in the vibrant African American community in Milwaukee, Wisconsin.

In Milwaukee, 1984-1987, my life had been forever changed—for the better—because of my interaction with blacks, and a black Catholic parish there, where I had joined the gospel choir. But when I came back to Minnesota in 1987, no one could relate to my excitement over my experiences in Milwaukee—not my family, or friends, or acquaintances. So I unconsciously decided to bury this "Milwaukee Self"—my authentic self—deep in my psyche after 7 years of Minnesota exposure.

But in 2004, the repression broke open like a breaking dam, and I could hold my *Milwaukee Self* in no longer! Months later, I ended up moving back to Milwaukee—the city of my success, having been a teacher's aide AND teacher there in the mid-'80s. Once again my spirituality came alive as I joined a black Catholic church, its choir and the St. Vincent de Paul society, once again serving the disadvantaged black population in urban Milwaukee. Change had changed my life—never to go back!

It is a process of "dying to self" that comes the moment we choose to change or have it forced upon us by circumstances. My hope is that we can learn our lessons as close to the precipitating event as possible. This way, our lessons don't turn into the stone of indifference or the ice of avoidance, but are confronted with a vigor and insight of a challenge to be met. This lesson had finally been learned and my *Milwaukee Self* is now back in Milwaukee!

August 11

Nothing beats a failure but a try.

Henry Johnson

My good friend Henry spoke to me of giving up an unwanted bad habit by persisting, encouraging me that even after a failure I need to keep trying, again and again. And how many of us give up trying to quit smoking or over-eating or drinking once—then, after experiencing a costly side-effect, give up our efforts?

Yoda, in the motion picture *Return of the Jedi* (the third movie in the Star Wars trilogy) told Luke Skywalker, "There is no 'try'—only 'do'!" I had held onto that theory for many years, feeling guiltier and guiltier as time passed because I was rarely able to follow through on it. "Only DO"?

Sure, this type of regimentation came from a respected figure, Yoda (although he was only a muppet), and he was wise and pithy. I respected that. But I finally had to give in to the realization that ALL WE CAN DO IS TRY. There are no guarantees that we will succeed, and we need not put ourselves under such pressure and permanence with this "do or die" self-defeating stance. Another good friend speaks of living every day for itself, and only by itself—that we only have *the moment* in which to live.

In 1982, I was highly influenced by Dale Carnegie's How To Win Friends and Influence People, a great book about interpersonal communications that got me excited about the topic. In it he speaks of having "day-tight compartments" in which we live our lives with only today in mind. No yesterday, no tomorrow—only today. How does this relate to "trying"? It puts the emphasis on the moment, on the individual efforts, on the ability to *try* to make things work. We TRY, never having the audacity to predict absolute victory, but putting in our best effort, just the same.

Indeed, *nothing beats a failure but a try.* What have you been putting off for fear of failure, or because you live in a world where perfection is the only perspective—thereby keeping you from trying?

Remember the old maxim: If at first you don't succeed, try try again!

August 12

Meet life's challenges with a zest for adventure...

Dynamics of Personal Motivation

By now, you probably realize that I create acronyms to guide me on my quest. This past week I had been telling my wife that I wanted to create an acronym using the word "experience." So I started conjuring up ideas—the best one being "KEEP: Knowing that Every Experience = Progress."

But I wasn't satisfied...until I remembered the above quote about having a *zest for adventure*. But what acronym could I make from "ZA"? I thought of "Pizza"—no! Too corny. It baffled me for a few days. Then, during lunch break at work one day, as I worked on these ideas, my thoughts suddenly focused on the biggest pyramids in the world, at *GIZA*—in Cairo, Egypt. Hmmmm.

Soon, I had it!

    Gladly

      Investing a

        Zest for

          Adventure

This acronym is easy to remember and very motivating! It can help with enriching many attitudes and activities—not actually mentioning "experience," but assisting in creating life-enhancing experiences. This ZEST is a personal energy that can take a difficult or mundane experience and transform it into a positive, energy-filled experience just in the realization that we have to power within us to motivate and uplift—no matter what the circumstances.

Encouragement is the greatest gift of GIZA—the encouragement to make a way out of no way, bolstered by a belief that the *adventure-attitude* will create the zest and see us through. How can you apply GIZA today?

August 13

> *It's God's design that we live fully*
> *each moment as it comes. Therein lies*
> *the richness of our lives.*
>
> *Each Day A New Beginning*

Here is a poem in remembrance
of a peaceful moment that flew

onto paper:

> *I remember*
> *the joy*
> *of solid solitude*
> *to be alive and in air*

& water swimming
in a body free from chains
or molasses stick
in the mud

and bird without feather
oh yes I remember

        that feeling of being free!

    Corsair

August 14

> *You can choose your attitude even in a set*
> *of circumstances you can do nothing about.*
>
> *Stephen R. Covey*

The 1991 Halloween blizzard in Minneapolis/St. Paul, Minnesota, dumped 30 inches of glistening snow. People were seen trying to finish raking their leaves on the wind-blown evening, while trick-or-treaters reluctantly covered up their creative costumes with winter coats and hats, as they trudged door-to-door in the near white-out conditions.

These undaunted Halloween celebrators are good examples of what Covey was talking about. They could do nothing about the storm but chose to move ahead anyway.

But what is this about wearing costumes in a snow storm?

Some of us disguise ourselves from showing our true selves. It's natural to want to protect ourselves when a situation becomes uncomfortable. I was "in disguise" the last four months of my high school career in 1980 because I found myself suffering from depression. If I were to have shown on the outside what was going on on the inside, I would have been the most hideous goblin ever to walk the streets.

I chose the attitude of "don't ask—don't tell"—possibly a mistake, but I <u>did</u> make it through that tough time without cracking. It was the most difficult time of my life—especially since I didn't have a clue I had bipolar disorder, or that it even existed! But I made it. Depression was something I could do little about—it just <u>was</u>. Still, my choices (and the grace of God) led to the emergence from depression into a brighter, healthier world.

Sometimes we have to just ride out the storm, knowing that, "maybe we can't change the direction of the wind, but we CAN adjust the sails." And if we keep in mind that we have choices—that we don't have to get stuck in previous patterns or predicaments—we will more than likely discover that we are capable of making choices that will lead toward health and happiness.

Disguising our suffering selves can lead to uncovering our magnificent selves in time. Being true to ourselves is the key in knowing when it is time for either one. This takes courage and self-awareness which lead to those good choices that reach beyond circumstances.

What circumstances will you overcome with
the choices you make today?

August 15

*Recovery is renewal, change; it is
dying to the old and rising to the new.*

<u>*Letting God*</u>

Isn't this a good definition for forgiveness? By letting go of resentment or fear, we are refreshed by *the new*.

Some of the time—maybe *most* of the time—forgiveness is not instantaneous. In fact, often it never happens at all. We can get so caught up in our own self-righteousness and confusion that trying to forgive isn't even in the works. I bet this makes God feel sad, when people refuse to "let go and let God" and allow forgiveness to sprout from within.

Dan found himself encountering an acquaintance who was experiencing a manic episode due to his bipolar illness. Being a school psychologist, Dan recognized the behavior immediately—the rapid speech, the lack of judgment, the over-creativity. One day, the acquaintance lashed out at Dan for not being as forthright and friendly as the man imagined he should be.

Dan faced a dilemma in his Christian life—how to be compassionate and not offended at the same time. But Dan, knowing the illness, found himself able to forgive the man for his infraction because he knew the man was being controlled by the manic phase and couldn't help himself. Dan chose forgiveness through understanding, rather than resentment through being close-minded. He also saw to it that the man got the help he needed in dealing with the illness.

For many, the personal challenge is to forgive themselves for past failings and short-falls. This is often harder to do than to forgive a worst enemy because who IS often the worst enemy? One's self. Self-esteem is hardest to build in a self-sabotaging system of thinking.

Have you come to realize you have a hard time forgiving yourself? Maybe it's time for you—as it is for me—to Let Go and Let God! Now is always a good time to *die to the old and rise to the new.*

August 16

> *Pleasure disappoints—possibility never.*
> *And what wine is so foaming, what so fragrant,*
> *what so intoxicating as possibility?*
>
> *Soren Kierkegaard*

Any person who has been manic, due to bipolar disorder, probably understands this quote all too well. Mania—this excited, unrealistic jubilance—is BUILT ON *possibility.* The reality may be falling down all around, *but the possibilities are endless.*

I remember a time when I ran out of money for food but still I had the creativity to be planning speeches for an unknown audience, at an unknown venue, for an unknown event. In mania, creativity is at a premium and realism at a minimum.

Possibility rules over reality when mania grips tightly. Only cure is to come down out of the clouds to reality—through proper medication, sleep and counseling—often to see how *possibility* has left life in a mess. Time to start rebuilding, again.

August 17

We are what we pretend to be.

Kurt Vonnegut, Jr.

There was a 1970s episode of "Love: American Style" where impersonator Rich Little played—of all things—*an impersonator* who couldn't stop impersonating. He was <u>always</u> somebody else.

His girlfriend finally gave him an ultimatum: "Stop impersonating while we're together or the relationship is over!" He implored that she wouldn't like him, that he was boring just as himself. But she insisted.

So the next time they were together, he was *just himself,* and she was bored out of her gourd! He WAS boring and unlikable as his normal self...so she encouraged him to go back to his constant impressionistic self—sometimes Richard Nixon, then Walter Cronkite, or even Winston Churchill—acceptable and funny again.

I approach this episode now with sadness that Rich Little had to be something other than himself to be acceptable, unless his impressions WERE his true self...sometimes it gets confusing!

August 18

> *If everything is going right, any jerk can be positive...*
> *it's when things aren't going so well that you find out*
> *if you really do have a positive attitude.*

> *Dr. Alan Zimmerman*

I remember in 1990, watching my roommate, Paul, come in from a tough day at work on a snowy January afternoon. The snow, which had accumulated on his garage door, emptied out on his head and shoulders, spilling down his back. I remember the forlorn look on his face as he stepped inside. Then his grimace turned to a toothy smile, and humor filled the room as we laughed together about his misfortune!

Sometimes a bit of *good humor* means much more than an ice cream bar on a sizzling summer day...a saving grace in stressful situations.

Paul snickered as he pulled off his overcoat and told me of his perfectly looooonnggg day at work. Then he laughed and called out, "Wouldn't ya know! THIS is how my day's been going!" And as quickly as he kicked off his dress shoes, he forgot "the day" and started pealing through a Newsweek.

He had everything to complain about, but his massive positive attitude knew better! When things weren't going well, he did it up right!

August 19

> *Take note of everything but don't be amazed at anything.*

> *Epictetus, Greek Stoic philosopher*

What may keep us from experiencing, even accepting, certain important situations is our surprise—even denial of—such happenings. Are you one who sets aside the positive or ignores the negative? Epictetus seems to be saying that observation is more important than analysis. Observation is what great authors and playwrights do so well. They bring you into the scene through vibrant description. They notice everything and bring it to life—to *your* life—through artistic expression.

Observation is also what brings love to *Love*. Fr. Anthony de Mello, spoke often of Love as *"clarity of perception and accuracy of response."* This clarity of perception comes from being acutely observant and seeing fully who the loved-other is and is becoming.

I remember three moments in my life when my father has said something like "you are the best writer in the family!" These are cherished, uplifting words—written on my heart with indelible ink!

Isn't it great when someone sees the good in us and "responds accurately" by acknowledging these encouraging details? Affirmation helps us grow and branch out, especially coming from one who has truly observed our goodness accurately and shared their perceptions honestly and forthrightly.

August 20

I'm listening for the message, not the mistakes.

(a patient parishioner)

What do you pay attention to when you listen to others? Do you listen for others to make mistakes, just for the facts, or for the main idea?

Years ago, listeners were studied at the University of Minnesota to see what were their worst listening habits...among them were:

~ calling the topic uninteresting

~ criticizing the speaker's delivery

~ showing no energy output

~ becoming easily distracted

~ inexperience in hearing difficult material

~ letting the mind wander

Many of the listeners only got 25-50% of the material right when given a brief multiple choice test after short lectures—that's no better than guess-work!

An opposing list of *HOW TO* listen would include:

*seeing the topic as interesting
*acknowledging the speaker's strengths
*investing energy
    *avoiding distractions
    *challenging yourself with difficult material
*staying focused

You may be amazed by what a list of 6 short suggestions could do for your listening habits. Are these skills YOU need to improve? Come again? I didn't catch that.

August 21

No one else can do it for us. We must do it for ourselves.

Stephen R. Covey

The individual must take the responsibility to get things done. Sounds simple, but some people don't get it, or choose not to. I have faced this as a teacher's assistant many times. A student blames *me* for the classroom being too loud, when I have made it very clear to all the students that they need to lower their voices. Some students saw it as easier to blame me than to be a good example and restrain themselves—leading the way for fellow noise-making colleagues to act up also.

Fr. Anthony de Mello once said, "Not even the greatest guru can take one step for you—you must do it yourself!" I realized this one day while covering a class for an 8th grade teacher where the kids became somewhat unruly. No one was coming on a white horse to rescue me from this difficult situation. It was up to me to do my best with the resources I had. So I put my full attention into being creative and optimistic, and the morning went quite well.

We all must make up our minds who we want to be and get busy becoming that person. As Viktor Frankyl wrote in <u>Man's Search For Meaning</u>, one must "choose one's own way."

Persistence is the attribute that fits this philosophy the best, and Christopher Reeve—who played *Superman*—was a great example of a man with persistence. Reeve became a quadriplegic after a horseback riding accident and invested himself in finding a cure for spinal cord injury as a response to his dilemma. I saw Reeve at a motivational speaker's conference in Minneapolis, Minnesota in 2002, and although he spoke that morning with some great speakers such as Zig Ziglar and Brian Tracy, Reeve out-shone them all. His dignity and candidness was refreshing and enlightening!

It is folks like Christopher Reeve who amaze me with their ability to just be themselves. He learned how to bring people together to rally the cause of curing spinal cord injuries, and took on the responsibility of being their spokesperson—despite his disability. I pray I can be an example of resiliency and grace like this brave man was.

August 22

*If you follow your bliss, you put yourself on a
kind of a track that has been there the whole while,
waiting for you, and the life you ought to be living
is the one you are living.*

Joseph Campbell

Can you remember the day that was most pivotal in molding your life? I remember mine: March 31, 1982. That's the day I started to follow my bliss. It was on that sunny Thursday afternoon that I picked up a pen and an 80-page notebook and began writing a journal. From this journal has sprouted thousands of pages of journal entries, hundreds of poems, and numerous speeches. Also, two weeks later, I joined a public speaking organization called Toastmasters International. These two new passions melded into a vision of communicating effectively with others that I have developed ever since.

Over the past 28 years, writing has become my passion, and speaking remains an interest as well. Today, in 2010, I have found myself coming full-circle, as I have published my third book (not including this one) and as my wife and I have ventured into our community as a public speaking duo.

When you "follow your bliss," you *find* yourself!

August 23

*Every time we consciously choose something,
however insignificant it may seem, in line
with what we feel is highest and best in
ourselves, we support our true life goals.*

Marsha Sinetar

We have almost all been given enough advice in our lives to fill the Grand Canyon: What to wear, how to eat properly, how to drive & walk & talk! But there is one piece of advice that I will never forget, and always treasure. It wasn't easy to hear, nor did I understand it at first. But it rings clear to me again today.

This observation came from a housemate, Sarah, with whom I served as volunteer in urban Milwaukee back in 1984-85. She pulled me aside one day and very delicately yet poignantly said:

*"Rich, the difference between you and me is
that when you walk into a room, you're more concerned
about how others are going to affect you; and when I walk into a room,
I'm more concerned about how I'm going to affect others."*

I had no clue what she was talking about at the time. In fact, it wasn't until 2005 or so that I began to see how I had come into many-a-room thinking only of myself—only concerned about how others were going to affect me—what they were going to offer <u>me</u>.

It's all about self-awareness. It never occurred to me that I may be having an influence on my environment.

This is actually a very disempowering stance—to feel that you don't have an influence, that you don't really make a difference. It was in recognizing that I had the power to affect my environment that I could make decisions about how to make a positive difference. Laughing too loudly, invading others' space, playing the wall flower—these were three previous behaviors that I now recognize as significantly unwelcomed.

But since I have now identified them as not appropriate, I can avoid them. This awareness of self is so freeing. It doesn't always come naturally but it sure beats the alternative. It involves caring about how I come across to others, and being able to excuse myself when any boundaries are broken. I don't like to be seen as a bull in a China shop—which may have been a good descriptor in past days.

How do *you* "come into a room"? Are you aware of how you come across? Something to think about.

August 24

> *I have decided to banish—far away—all fear*
> *and all memory of past faults,…no trace*
> *of dead sins left behind, for in one second,*
> *LOVE can burn them to ashes.*
>
> *St. Therese*

Do you have fears? Do they inhibit your growth? Fear was explained by world-renowned speaker Zig Ziglar as being:

<u>F</u>alse <u>E</u>vidence <u>A</u>ppearing <u>R</u>eal…

This is
all fine & good

but what if the "evidence"
<u>IS</u> real? What if you're up against
some pretty horrific situations?

I believe we need to choose to "banish this fear—far away" and look at the realities that we face. Whether it's money problems, inferior feelings or body-image challenges, the fear only constricts our abilities to see clearly and act responsibly. When we *banish fear*, we give ourselves the chance to use our common sense and God-given gifts to solve our problems. We can also reach out to others and utilize their resources to help solve the challenges we face.

St. Therese's quote is one I encourage you to put into your memory. It has helped me enormously over the years!

August 25

*Asking a "stupid" question is better
than making a "stupid" mistake!*

unknown

You know how there are some dates you remember—not just your birthday, but other significant dates?

A date to remember for me....November 9, 2004 . . .

As a teacher's aide
at a grade school in
a suburb west of Minneapolis,
Minnesota, I was ushered into my
principal's office, and with my silent
supervisor looking on, the principal admonished—
nearly lambasted me—for 40 minutes about what a lousy
employee I was (or at least that's the impression I got of how she saw me).

After a few of her "suggestions," I asked if I could take out my mini-notebook and begin writing them down...some details so I could remember them. She told me 6 major things, two of which, I took totally to heart. One was "you're not engaged"—and I admitted to her that, yes, at times I would lose my focus (I didn't say a peep about how tedious and boring the job was). The second was that "I don't ask enough questions." This was also hard for me to do. My upbringing did not encourage question-asking—I was just supposed TO KNOW!

As mentioned above, I took these two criticisms to heart and I have made huge changes, for the good. I even coined a little phrase I now use when I sense someone is struggling whether to ask a question: "NQDQ".... *No Question's a Dumb Question.* This often puts the other at ease and they are able to ask questions more freely.

This discouraging yet instructive critique changed my life! Do you have any "big dates" that you easily remember because you were forever changed that day?

August 26

*It's your choice—either you go somewhere
deliberately or you go <u>no</u>where fast.*

Corsair

*I see it now
I know it now that
I am who I am
what I am
where I am
because of my struggles*

suffering

*but I don't go back and greet
those who shut me out...*

Corsair

Recently I wrote down my *visualization script*—how I see myself succeeding in the most important areas of my life. I have often suffered from a lack of positive visioning, so I decided it was time to clearly define my future success in the present time. It was quite empowering.

A visualization script is simply taking 4 or 5 of the most important areas of your life and writing out exactly how you see each being lived out successfully. This script includes all the details you envision—outcomes as well as processes—the fruits as well as the journey along the way. It is not only a great goal-setting technique but can set up a positive self-fulfilling prophecy system that moves you steadily towards these goals.

Can you define your future successes? Are you willing to take the time and effort to complete this exercise that may just change your life?

I truly believe that we become what we think about most, so it's time to shift my focus from what I can't do to what I want to do—and WILL do. Since "the 1,000 mile journey begins with a single step," I've taken that first step of deciding who I want to be and have begun to visualize my ultimate success.

Since so many changes are happening in my life—new job, expanded writing opportunities—I am going to (today) rewrite this visualization script to fit the current circumstances. It's exciting to be moving forward in positive ways, and this is one tool we can use in doing so.

Do YOU know what you really want? Can you visualize it? To do so is to take a giant leap in the direction of freedom and success!

August 27

*Even our failures may turn out to be
important learning experiences.*

unknown

One of my heroes, Fr. Anthony de Mello, once said, "Failure is the only way to learn." I agree that failure can help us mold good behavior...

like when I fell off my bike at age 7 or 8, learning—real quick—not to look back over my shoulder while riding—especially on asphalt! My face soon kissed that tar.

Another guiding phrase is "nothing fails like success"…like trying to raise child #2 just like child #1. There's nothing wrong with being consistent, but if we only rely on previous successes, we may not be open to the changes needed in a present situation—a flexibility that can lead to a *future* success.

But I don't agree with de Mello's assertion that we can ONLY learn from failure. We also grow from our successes. When we win a game or other competition, or score well on a test, we learn how to win, and this can give us the confidence to put in another best effort, which leads to another success. Winning can become a habit—it can be contagious, leap-frogging from success to success.

We need successes to keep up encouragement, to move forward. We can also learn a great deal from *others'* successes. When Forrest Gump (in the movie of the same name) won a world championship ping pong tournament <u>and</u> became a millionaire as a shrimpin' boat captain, it inspired me on to move toward my dreams. It was a great motivator! Even a movie can help us find the best in ourselves!

This may just be one of the best ways to learn. And others may be looking our way for a good example, learning from <u>our</u> successes or failures. We're always teaching one another, so we need take seriously the *example* we put before others.

August 28

"…the sweetest thing is actin' after makin' a decision…"

Indigo Girls

Viktor Frankyl, a Nazi death camp survivor, wrote about some surprising and enlightening conclusions he came upon after living through the horrors of Auschwitz. A psychiatrist, Frankyl wrote, in his book <u>Man's Search For Meaning</u>:

> "We who lived in concentration camps can remember
> the men who walked through the huts, comforting
> others, giving away their last piece of bread. They may have
> been few in number, but they offer sufficient proof that
> ***everything can be taken from a man but one thing: the last
> of human freedoms—to choose one's attitude in any given set
> of circumstances, <u>to choose one's own way</u>.***"

The choice is ours and no one else's. When Hamlet pronounced, "To be, or not to be," he spoke of the very decision every Nazi death camp prisoner had to make every day—to live or not. We are no different. We meet each day with an attitude of "I'm going to MAKE something of this day," or possibly, "oh no, not another crummy day"—or somewhere in between.

So what choices will YOU make today?...hopefully, yes, to live—but also to carry an attitude of excitement for life and a hope for the future that propels you through your day with a modicum of joy and a good measure of confidence. In the end, we must "choose our own way."

What way will YOU choose?

August 29

Maturity means no longer blaming others or yourself.

Fr. Anthony de Mello

When we blame, we shrug responsibility. And we avoid *learning our lessons* that can lead to maturity.

This type of maturity means learning past lessons that went ignored or were simply swept under the rug in past days. One of my favorite life-changing quotes (a popular theme in this book) comes from John Powell, SJ: *"The only REAL mistake is the one from which we learn nothing."*

Why is this so important? Because it allows us to look back at our lives, our experiences, and learn our lessons from these past happenings. By re-experiencing, modifying and reconstructing these past events in our minds, (learning our lessons, then letting go of outcomes) we gain the wisdom and hope that has been lying there, dormant, fallow, just waiting to be rediscovered.

This process allows us to see what has gone wrong so that we can avoid such folly in the present and future. Without this rediscovery, we may be left with repetition of past failures because lessons may go unlearned. "Learning our lessons"—taking our unique experiences and finding the golden nuggets of growth in them—can be one of the most exhilarating events of our lives. Why? Because we can suddenly possess a piece of God...to become the *creator* of our own successful growth opportunities... and what is more important than that?

We can all have a "*born again* experience" if we but take a look back and use the view to correct a NOW attitude or action. Don't let anyone tell you to "*leave the past behind you*"—it can become, in a sense, a great friend and teacher! We need not get stuck in the past but a little look here and there can work wonders.

August 30

To the extent to which we avoid and deny and disown
our own experiences, it's clear that we impoverish
and diminish our sense of self.

Dr. Nathaniel Brandon

A friend of mine never sends out a Christmas letter. Cards, maybe— letter, never...claiming he has a boring life. This boring life keeps him busy with playing in an orchestra, a jazz band, playing hockey once a week, playing on a pool team and singing in his church choir. There has *got* to be a little drama brewing there! But not to my friend.

The above quote seems to fit him well...the diminishment & concealment of self, as if he has *nothing* to talk about. It may be that he's humble and feels writing about his life would be a self-exultant act. Or it may be that he's too lazy, or that introspection is not his gig.

But a Christmas letter is neither a journal entry nor a novel—it doesn't have to be edited by a professional or meet a publisher's standards. Whatever the reason, I'd love to get his recap of the year, knowing that it would be anything but boring.

Do you deny or disown your experiences? A Christmas letter is one way to make sure that doesn't happen. Write On!

August 31

If you have no confidence in self,
you are twice defeated in the race of life.
With confidence, you have won even
before you have started.

Marcus Garvey

The word "confidence" comes from the Latin—*confide*—which means *to have faith in* and is probably one of the most important words in the successful person's vocabulary. How could you NOT see this word, this concept, as important? To believe in yourself is the basic building block of self-esteem, the belief in your own goodness and competence.

Marcus Garvey points to the fact that confidence creates a state of success in the mind. I believe it must be based on reality or, at least a "fake it 'til you make it" stance of affirmation and belief. When we believe we have success—over and over—we move toward it. This leads toward its realization. This is how the mind works . . . *association brings assimilation*!

Dr. Phil McGraw says, "You have to behave yourself into success," and this behavior comes from confidence in self. One wise woman once said, "The key IS that my thinking creates my experience." I have confidence she was right.

~September ~

September 1

The 3 great questions:

> *Who are you?*
> *Where did you come from?*
> *Where are you going?*

(Artie Shaw)

Let's first focus on question #1, *who are you?* This probably has an endless answer, since we are always in formation. This question takes personal awareness in order to answer. To be aware of *where you came from?*—question #2—advances at every moment also. So we need to be honest with our past and learn to take past events and gain from our mistakes.

My question #1 is *Who do you WANT to be?* Life is an endless decision-making process where we get to decide who we are going to be now, and in the future. This leads to question #3, *Where are you going?* If you don't live your NOWs with integrity and balance, you will find it difficult to live with integrity in the future, especially since the future quickly slides through the now and into the past.

"Who do you WANT to be?" shifts the focus onto a now-centered, future-facing attitude that makes it possible to see who you are AND improve yourself for the future. This allows you to be proactive about "where are you going?" and look back again on "where did you come from?"

This victorious cycle can lead you to success in any goal you choose. How would YOU answer these questions?

September 2

...me, myself—I've got nothing to prove...

musical artist Tracy Chapman

Trying to *prove*, rather than *improve*, causes all kinds of trouble. I remember my blurry junior high years when I was constantly on edge, trying to prove to others I was likeable and worthy—worthy of respect, worthy of love.

Be it on a hockey rink, in the classroom or at the ballpark—I spent most of my time trying to impress others. I thought others would like me if I made baskets in the gym where our homeroom met, while others engaged themselves in conversation. I didn't see interaction as the way to make friends, but that showing-off was where it was at. This made NO sense 'cause I was lousy at basketball! If I was really trying to impress anyone, shooting hoops was not my forte.

My current challenge is trying to work my way out a hole with my new employer. The other day I missed ½ of an important meeting, and today I missed my first day at my regular shift because I read my schedule wrong. I am struggling to keep my self-confidence—feeling I now have to prove myself to my employer that I am a worthy employee. My wife suggested I just start out tomorrow as a new day and pray for God's guidance—and just move forward. "They need you, and you need them," she said. And, you know, I think she's right.

The opposite of *proving* seems to be to have a strong sense of self, gradually moving toward success. I remember a guy I first met in junior high who, in 11th grade, became an Eagle Scout. His patient humility made me jealous—jealousy, which is a sister to *proving*.

One solution for me is to focus not on proving, but on <u>im</u>proving and reaching out (and reaching in) to be my best self. My former counselor gave this acronym to me...CBS...<u>C</u>onnect with your <u>B</u>est <u>S</u>elf! This disengages *proving* every time and has been an agent of empowerment, over the years. Now I need it more than ever! *So I move forward.*

September 3

*We can cultivate feelings of compassion
for those who annoy, anger and upset us
by remembering that we are ALL wounded.*

Touched By an Angel

"Cultivate"—to till the soil, to de-weed…these "feelings of compassion" don't always come naturally. The "soil" has to be de-weeded and must be turned over for these compassionate feelings to appear, to be discovered.

But how often do we give a break to those who annoy and anger us? It's so much less effort to build resentments and to act out of anger than to try to understand another. Yet when we realize the reality that "we are all wounded," we can learn to empathize with another and "walk a mile in their moccasins" in order to understand their point of view.

I came near tears recently when I realized that a person who really annoyed me was very much like me and has a similar background. Talk about walking in someone's moccasins! I was walking in my own! How humbling—and shocking! It has brought me down off my high horse of criticism and judgment-slinging to see how my brokenness is connected with her brokenness. My annoyance and disapproval have nearly dissipated because of my new awareness.

Yes, WE'VE ALL GOT SOMETHING—in our past, in our present life, or coming down the track in our near future—that upsets us. Wouldn't you like someone to be patient and understanding with you at your weaker moments?

September 4

Experiencing *BASS* . . .

Becoming
Aware through the
Senses and
Silence

Fr. Anthony de Mello speaks of a human phenomenon called "the *Observer.*" This is a part of the human psych that plays the role of *documenter.* It's the part of the brain that watches, listens—simply recording whatever is going on, in and around us. It does not judge—good or bad—just observes.

The Observer encompasses a unique part of the memory that can "play back" the sights and sounds—actually, all five senses—and even the emotional state of a moment in time so we can look at it objectively. So, what's important about the Observer's gift? With it, we can re-view a specific moment in time, looking beyond our perspective at the time, and see what we missed.

Example...when I recently had some bipolar complications, I said and did many things that I wouldn't normally say or do. With help from my Observer—which holds the "objective recorded tapes" in my memory bank—I have been able to see just how things went wrong. I could hear the tenseness and fear in the another's voice and see key facial expressions that had gone unnoticed at the moment of anger. And I could revisit the quivering sensation in my chest muscles that were there to warn me that my anger was reaching a peak. From this data, I was able to analyze what happened and how I got there, so that if this type of situation were to occur again, I would be alerted and can re-evaluate the situation—hopefully able to choose healthier options. The Observer at work!

It is through keen awareness of the senses that allows the Observer to work—in the now-moment. Sure I know now that there was a voice inflection, a facial expression and a body sensation that were overlooked, as seen in the previous example. But by paying attention to what I am seeing, hearing, feeling, smelling and tasting—in the moment—not only can I gain the greatness of what it is to be human, but I can also gather the data that will help me make clear and appropriate decisions. And so it is with you!

I see that I can now choose. The next time I become angry, I can consult this ever-watching Observer, cue into my senses, and make sure I don't make the mistakes I made the last time.

Yet this connection with the Observer takes a silence—a stillness—*inside,* so that the cues of the senses are not missed. Sometimes it takes actual silence...no radio blaring, or constant chatter. At other times it takes a silence of the mind. Either way, I believe this attention paid to the senses and the sense of inner-peacefulness can give us a great opportunity to put our Observers to work—assisting us in making the most accurate and thought-filled decisions possible.

Will you give *your Observer* a chance to help
you reach your greatest potential?

September 5

*If you need to be out of prison in order
to be free, you are a prisoner indeed!
Freedom is not in exterior circumstances—
freedom resides in the heart.*

Fr. Anthony de Mello

This statement recently turned my boat around. Have you ever had it happen to you that you recognize a dramatic change in a relationship?

When I heard this quote last night, I realized my folly instantly. I had felt for months that I was being held captive by a close relationship—that, with this person around, I didn't feel comfortable. This was my claim... the reality is that *I* was putting myself in that prison.

The other party had no hand cuffs, no prison bars, no huge rusty gates. All of these were in my mind, built up by my imagination, my resentment, my anger and my pride. Yes, I had had judgmental thoughts about this person—not wanting bad to fall upon them, but, then again, wanting no more negative circumstances to befall me. I had spoken to a friend of my anger and feelings of being used, and how I often felt uncomfortable.

Now, none of this matters! The gates of fear have been toppled and the shackles of mistrust broken off. God has made a way out of no way! I let myself out of the prison because I <u>never</u> <u>was</u> in prison!

Now, I see a bright future of laying down my fear and foreboding, and picking up the banner of freedom—a freedom that was within me all the time, but I never recognized it. I can see "freedom from" playing a greater part of my life...

Freedom From

Freedom From . . . now becomes

FREEDOM TO

Freedom To

Freedom To be my Best Self

in a world of my choosing

Freedom To

Freedom To

Freedom <u>To See</u> & <u>be free</u> to be my Authentic Self

and THIS ~ I promise to BE!

Corsair

September 6

Life is good when goodness meets goodness!

Corsair

My writings call me "*Corsair*"...most everyone else calls me "Rich," but four young ladies call me "Grandpa." This is what happens when you marry into a family—now I, the youngest of nine, am *the second* to have grandchildren! Step-Grandchildren.

I had been working on an idea for many weeks...the concept that we need to meet others with our goodness to bring out their goodness. The final (I had thought) quote had become:

> *"Display the courage and insight it takes to bring out the best in others by offering the best in yourself."*

Awful wordy, I know, but I couldn't seem to simplify the main idea. That was until yesterday...Labor Day evening, 2009...and a day with my step-daughter and the family.

I had not expected to see my oldest granddaughter, but there she was—nearly 16 and resilient as ever! Have you ever had one of those occasions where you get to have 3-4 significant conversations with someone you love? This was yesterday. It was like meeting someone I'd never met before, yet I knew her well. Nearing adulthood, speaking so eloquently about her prospects for future successes, smiling with a new confidence and twinkle in her eye.

She reconstructed within me the meaning of the stretched-out quote above about "displaying the courage and insight." It suddenly became:

> *Life is good when goodness meets goodness!*

My granddaughter had reaffirmed within me one of the greatest lessons of all—that *sharing the true self in an honest and open way can bring an unbreakable connectedness.* We shared meaningful conversation like we had never done before, and both grew in the process. Truth is, it makes me so proud to be called "Grandpa." Yesterday was a testament to the maxim, "Love (truly) conquers all!" And I love it!

September 7

*Success is to be measured not so much by the position
that one has reached in life as by the obstacles that one
has overcome while trying to succeed.*

Booker T. Washington

Obstacles. Mountains. Challenges. Struggles.

International public speaker, W Mitchell, once said that "It's not what happens to us that matters but what we do about it." Our stance, our perspective, can be the key to success <u>or</u> the anchor that keeps us stuck in unsuccessful waters.

Perspective, the way we SEE life, is the chosen hue of the lenses we put in our glasses. Some choose the fabled rose-colored glasses, only seeing the Polly Ann-ish, over-optimistic, unrealistic view of life and events. Others have very dark lenses that dampen the scene with pessimistic and depressive attitudes that rub off on anyone who doesn't avoid the charcoal roughness.

Still others have a clear lens of healthy optimism and firm realism. This perspective allows for the negative to be a part of the scene, yes, but chooses to focus on the good and hopeful aspects of virtually every situation.

This is the lens I attempt to wear in my *perspective-glasses.* The "position I have reached" (as Washington referred to) is <u>not</u> the most important aspect of my reality, but rather *the lessons I have learned* and focus on—as I move toward that which gives my life meaning. These are the stars that brighten my midnight sky. Where do you stand? What perspective do you take?

Last year—2008—was a year of dire struggle for me. Have you ever had a time in your life when you felt you were in a capsizing boat, and the waves just kept on crashing in? That was my 2008. Bipolar disorder can do some mean things to one's system, affecting EVERY area of life. It took until October for a balanced medication regimen and some consistent, healthy sleep to pull me around. But, with my wife and family's help, I weathered the storm and found myself on dry land.

Washington was right…the important part of life is "the obstacles that one has overcome while trying to succeed." And often our biggest obstacle is our attitude—the hardest AND the easiest thing to change.

September 8

Self-esteem means to appreciate yourself
as a unique human being with your own
special talents and abilities.

Reni Witt

Angelena, a fourth grade African American girl in an urban Midwestern city, found herself in an uncomfortable position. She was enrolled in a summer creative writing course that was testing her courage and belief in herself. How could SHE be a writer? Her home life was a mess, her best friend was acting distant, and she had never really done any creative writing before.

After the second day of class, while writing what her teacher thought was a good sentence, Angelena scribbled . . .

I CANT WRITE
BECAUSE I'M
STUPID

Upon discovering this in her notebook, the instructor was aghast! "How could this young, seemingly bright girl, see herself as dumb? How could her self-esteem stoop so low?"

The third class arrived, and with a short rebuttal and some encouraging words, Angelena took up her pen once more. She wrote on the topic of the day—which happened to be self-esteem . . .

A day when I was very happy was on my birthday.
Everybody cared for me and it was a day just for me...
and I will remember it fore ever and ever
and for as long as I live.

Angelina had discovered a new part of herself—through writing! And such a great job she did! It's amazing how a teacher can find a painful spot in a child and so quickly be a part of the healing—AND how quickly a child can respond! Angelena went on to write some incredible stories with her new-found friend—creative writing. A moment of greatness came alive!

September 9

The flower that follows the sun does so even on cloudy days.

unknown

Isn't this what *faith* is all about? And I bet we all struggle with this sometimes. One day recently, after three of my closest friends didn't return calls, I was feeling a quite frustrated and left out. Upon hearing of my frustration, my best friend—my wife—said to me, "Have you prayed about it?"

I was a bit startled, even miffed, by this question. Who made her guardian of my spiritual life? But you know, I hadn't. I hadn't offered my disappointment up to God. I hadn't placed it before Jesus and asked for healing. Also, I now see the judgmental attitude I had, expecting my friends to call right back when they might have some distractions or stressors in their lives that had preempted them from calling me back in a *timely* manner.

Then I looked at my own behavior. I recently didn't call my brother back promptly. I may have had my reasons—further evidence that my friends probably had good reason for not calling me back on MY time schedule.

This happened to be true. One friend was out of town, another had been stressed out by a college course she was taking, and the third—it just slipped his mind. I had no reason to be upset. And it showed how insecure I was acting when I didn't get my emotional and social needs met immediately. I had to grow up!

Just goes to show that WAGS = <u>W</u>e've <u>A</u>ll <u>G</u>ot <u>S</u>omething…some setback, some illness, some struggle, some bad habit. When we realize we are all broken in some way, it's so much easier to give someone a break, to allow them to be human.

Who do you need to *give a break* to today?

September 10

> *A stranger is just a friend we have not met yet.*
>
> *unknown*

I met my wife in 2006, we got married in 2007…and somewhere between that time, I met her neighbors Danny and Cynthia. I had said HI to Danny a number of times—for probably six months—until, one afternoon, we struck up a conversation in the condo driveway we shared.

It was very enlightening to converse with this intelligent, interesting guy who, before, I had no real opinion about other than he seemed friendly and had a great smile. We talked for 45 minutes that afternoon! That was the longest conversation—in person—that I had had since coming to Milwaukee a few years earlier—that is, except for conversations with my wife, Sandra.

My step-daughter reminded me today that "God puts people in our lives at the right time"…and I replied that "someone once said, '*a stranger is just a friend we have not yet met.*'" I continued with, "maybe friends are all around us—we just haven't discovered them yet."

Danny and I have become very close friends, sharing many interests, information and opinions. He was right there, next door, waiting to be discovered. It just goes to show that, if we just look around and reach out

246

a bit, we can find friends—even develop close relationships. Danny and I are proof positive!

September 11

You can achieve anything you can consistently think of as possible.

William James

Why do we not envision our *successes*? Not that it's hard to do, or that it takes a long time. It's probably that we either haven't been shown how, or we're out of practice. Did you know that the human mind can't tell the difference between a real event and *one that's vividly imagined*? When we keep this fact on the positive side, we can see that visualization can become a treasured friend.

All we have to do is imagine our successes in every detail and repeat this process over and over. It helps to be in a relaxed state and in a quiet atmosphere. Soon it will make an imprint in the mind that, when practiced, becomes a groove. And the groove a track—and the track a train—a train of positive thoughts that can bring productive outcomes in every area of our lives. This train of our imagined successes can lead the way to enjoying car loads of high achievement and happiness.

This flies in the face of worry. Worry and fear are now-killers. They usually consist of negative visualizations and can build up nonproductive habits that may become hard to break.

In the original "Rocky" movie, Sylvester Stallone plays a washed-up boxer who gets a second chance at making himself a winner in the ring. In a famous scene, he sprints down a riverside sidewalk, donning a sweaty gray sweat top and pants, charging up a ton of stairs to a concrete platform—holding his fists above his head in an imaginary victory moment. This imagery brought him to a future victory beyond his wildest expectations. There's nothing like the power of imagination!

James' quote, above, points to how we can condition our minds and shape our attitudes for success. I encourage you to try visualization and see if your imagined winning ways lead to successful outcomes.

September 12

. . . if you don't put faith in what you believe in,
it's getting' you nowhere . . .

Phil Collins

In the 1990s movie *With Honors,* Brendon Frazier (in one of his earliest roles) plays a Harvard senior who is doing all he can to make the grade and graduate *with honors.* One evening, his computer crashes, and his masters thesis goes down in flames as the computer memory is destroyed. But he has one copy of the nearly-completed masterpiece in hiding.

Frazzled, he runs off to a copy shop to secure an extra copy for his files. On the way there, he trips over a tree stump and falls in the snow, dropping his paper down a window ledge. He watches it slide into the basement of the library. Madly, he pursues his paper, winding his way through the corridors of the library basement. He finally discovers "some street person" using it for kindling in the furnace room.

Treating the bearded, scruffily dressed man like a thing, Frazier demands that he give him his paper back, as the man crumples up a sheet and tosses it into the furnace. Aghast and bewildered, Frazier agrees to a deal that with every favor granted, the street person, Alvin, would give him a page back. Deal.

Throughout the movie, Frazier is found granting graces far beyond the specified "deal," moving Alvin in from the van in the winter-scorned back yard of their house to take the attic as his own. This kindness leads to friendship, and respect.

Nearing the end of winter, revived by the new relationship, Frazier tosses out the idea of ever getting back his thesis and begins anew. He forges on with great success, yet his ambition is challenged when he discovers that Alvin is in the last stages of cancer. Frazier is ever so near his goal of graduating with honors, and only needs to turn in his thesis. But that day, Alvin's last wish is to take a 200 mile trek to visit the son he left behind at age 10.

Although he knows it will cost him his *Honors* recognition, Frazier decides to honor Alvin's wish—and his clamoring roommates all pile into the van for the trip. Alvin's son rejects him on the spot, saying he "never had a father," and it seems to be a wasted trip. But not to Alvin, who is satisfied that at least he did his best to reconnect.

In Alvin's last days, his friends—who formerly had seen him as "some street person," read Whitman to him as he lay gasping in the attic bedroom. They all missed their opportunity to graduate with honors at Harvard, but at Alvin's funeral, realized they had graduated with honors in learning how to respect another.

This is TRUE learning!

September 13

If I cannot do great things,
I will do small things in a great way!

unknown

We don't have to erect a sky scraper, invent a solar-powered car or climb Mount McKinley to do something great. Living an honest, virtuous life is great in itself.

In the movie *Crash*, a Latino locksmith gives us a great example of this. With an Arabic customer, his patience and endurance were tested to the extreme. The man wanted a lock put on a door—simple request. But the door itself was sprung and needed replacing.

Our locksmith friend told the bad news to the customer who began to yell and accuse him that he had a door salesman friend on the side and that he was being ripped off. After explaining over and over, the locksmith just gave in and gave him the lock & labor for free. He cut his losses and left.

That night the store was broken into—caused by that broken door—and the store owner blamed the locksmith. The customer went wacko and hunted down the poor locksmith with a loaded gun. Not realizing he had blanks in his gun, he "shot" the locksmith's daughter. They were all amazed at the *miracle* that she was unharmed and the locksmith and family re-entered their home safe and sound.

This locksmith had done a great thing by giving his goods and services to the customer in the heat of argument and was repaid by getting a possible killer who had blanks in his gun. Strange situation. Good outcome. He had done a small thing in a great way!

September 14

". . . and justa's for all . . ."

Had a dream last night...that I was justa janitor. I was trying to re-learn all the skills I had achieved when I WAS a janitor for 10 years—when, at the time, in real life, I had seen myself as "justa janitor." Some see low paying jobs as "justa" jobs. There's the guy who's justa cab driver. The young woman who's justa waitress. The older man who's justa doorman. Or the middle-aged woman who's justa drugstore clerk.

Wouldn't it be great if there were no justa jobs, no justa attitudes or justa people? If instead there were "giving-blessings jobs," "giving-blessings attitudes" and "giving-blessings people"!

Imagine it, if we all saw the myriad jobs people do as giving blessings. The butcher, the used car salesman, the secretary, the street sweeper—all doing jobs to bless themselves, others and the world around them!

Or if we all were to give blessings in thought—in attitude—to all those in the various cultures and locations of the Earth...how much more understanding, acceptance and love we would encounter, and how few wars we would be waging—avoiding the "justa" attitudes.

And if we were to give blessing to all others—not that they are justa 'nuther guy, or woman, or kid, but our own brothers and sisters to be treated fairly and lovingly. That doesn't mean that we play Good Samaritan to every stranded motorist on the freeway, but that we at least try to reach out to our fellow humans in any way we can.

A municipal administrator I know had a special connection with the janitorial staff. To her, *people were people*, no matter what the position or stature. She knew how to value people, living out the statement by Will Rogers: "As long as you live, you'll never find a better way of getting in touch with others than to make them feel important."

NOBODY was just a "justa" to her. I think we can all take to heart her example, and get rid of *justa's for all!*

September 15

>   pathways
>   from here to there
>   and I am thankful
>   for the guidance of a loving God
>   who sends me
>   and encourages me
>   and provides the light at the end of the tunnel
>   so I may continue to grow beyond my present limits
>   oh how wonderful it is to be on the path
>   way on down the road in search of self
>   seeking the authentic life
>   some call it searching (I think it is much more)
>   to be aware of self—watching, listening,
>   feeling, touching—
>   is to know the soul
>   and how important it is to observe and breathe in
>   the words, actions, feelings of others
>   and encourage them to be their best selves
>   a blessed mission—this I call...*creatively building souls*
>   the results of such depth of love are many and wondrous

for who can tell who we will influence positively
like the maple's helicopters spinning down
from a generous autumn branch to hungry earth below
as small seed may produce a majestic tree
(such as each of our relationships) many are
the mysteries of life we meet
upon our
pathways

Corsair

September 16

*Love the moment, and the energy of that
moment will spread beyond all boundaries.*

Corita Kent

Have you met people who exude this precept? Are you one? Many of us struggle, off & on, with motivation. It's not a given that we always feel up and ready to go.

There is one person who fits this quote quite well. Coreen is a woman who works as an office manager back in my home state of Minnesota. I've never met anyone who is more energetic and optimistic than she.

When I stop into her place of work while visiting in Minnesota, Coreen's right there with a smile and a hug, no matter how business has been—up or down, busy or slow—always the same enthusiasm and interest in how I'm doing.

This type of person may be rare but surely appreciated by me. She "loves the moment" and energy flows from her like the *mighty Mississip.* We can all gain an example of how to live from Coreen...she has been a positive force in my life for many years, living out Norman Vincent Peale's *Power of Positive Thinking* every day.

Do you have at least one "Coreen" in your life?

September 17

> *It's not what happens to you that makes*
> *the difference, it's how you react to it.*
>
> Dr. Alan Zimmerman

A reality of having bipolar disorder is that, sometimes, one may need to seek treatment in a formal setting. In 1989, after a particularly severe bout with mania, I was sent to a treatment center in the small west-central Minnesota town of Willmar.

On the ride there, I decided I would make the best of this stay, to try my very best to cooperate and participate. This was a great decision. At Willmar, I made the biggest gains <u>ever</u> in understanding and controlling my illness.

The greatest breakthrough occurred when I began writing a list of "manic and depressive *clues*"—the symptoms that occur when I'm heading for trouble. This list has not only been helpful to me but to many people with whom I have shared it, as I've spoken in schools and other venues over the past 18 years.

<u>Manic Clues</u> (symptoms)

1) Racing thoughts

2) Heightened energy

3) Pressured speech

4) Extreme creativity

5) *Lack of sleep*

6) *Lack of judgment*

7) *Destructive of relationships*

8) Quick to anger/irritability

9) Sense of urgency

10) Manipulative/aggressive

11) Med non-compliance

12) Delusions of grandeur & unrealistic self-esteem

13) Mood fluctuations

14) Personality shifts

15) Feel called to the extraordinary & sense of new-found power

16) Agitation/continual action

Depressive Clues

1) Feeling hopeless/helpless/worthless

2) Inability to focus/concentrate

3) Preoccupied with negative thoughts

4) Avoidance of physical exercise

5) Sleep/appetite disturbances

6) Avoidance of social situations

7) Destructive daydreaming/suicidal ideation

8) Indecisive

Life has dealt me a weak hand at times, but with God's help, I've ended up with a royal flush! The list has helped me identify the signs of relapse and therefore move to avoid such a happening. This stay at Willmar strengthened my confidence and coping abilities enormously. Sometimes, I guess, you just have to go with what you've been dealt and make the best of it.

When is a time *you* chose to respond positively to a difficult situation? Have you had a "Willmar" recently?

September 18

Nobody knows the trouble I've seen!

Negro Spiritual

African Americans have given the world the gifts of a wide variety of music, which originates from their vast native land of Africa. Their gifts in America started during the time of slavery with field songs and "negro spirituals," morphing into jazz, gospel and blues.

The irony disturbs my spirit in that these forms of musical expression may never have developed if not for the mistreatment of blacks in America. From slave songs came jazz, gospel, and the blues—connections that may never have been formed if it weren't for the ugly, violent demeaning conditions from whence this music sprung. They say "necessity is the mother of invention," and this is ever-apparent with the formation of African American music.

Don't get me wrong, I do not condone the hateful world of white supremacy. It sickens me to see ANY group of people showing hatred toward—and claiming they are better than— another.

But we are all blessed by the African American ways of expressing themselves through music! I sing in a mixed-race gospel choir that allows me, a white man, to participate in the joy and meaningful expression of my Christian faith through the exuberance and emotion of gospel music. I am honored to sing in this music that has its roots in African American struggles and triumphs.

I am grateful that God found ways for African American creativity to develop and flourish, even in the trying times of the past in a country that often misused them. And I pray that these dreadful conditions <u>never</u> be repeated—even if a new form of music were to be created in the process.

September 19

> *The only way to get rid of old, bad habits is*
> *to actively recruit new, good ones.*
>
> *Fr. Tom Weston*

The psychological concept called *displacement* works well with the statement above. Imagine taking a full bucket of water and, one-by-one, adding thumb-size rocks to the bucket. The rocks *displace* the water, until soon you have a bucket full of rocks with very little water.

This is the same with thoughts. If you continually fill your mind with good healthy, productive thoughts, they will displace many negative thoughts that have rested there and controlled your life-outcomes.

The displacement theory works because no two things can fill the same space at the same time. We cannot have a mind full of good thoughts and be pressured and pushed around by negativity—the positive thoughts will rule.

When Deanne learned of this marvelous reality called *displacement,* she began to recruit pleasant, positive thoughts. She had been having difficulty with some negative co-workers and was having a hard time concentrating. She began to imagine a pleasant atmosphere and good outcomes, and soon, like rocks filling a bucket, she was able to enjoy her work more and have patience with her co-workers. She also began to find the best in her husband—qualities that she hadn't paid attention to for a long spell.

So, it is true—*the only way to get rid of old, bad thoughts & habits is to actively recruit new, good ones.* Try it—you'll see.

September 20

Losers visualize the penalties of failure,
while winners visualize the rewards of success.

Rod Gilbert

Personally, I don't espouse the terms "winners" and "losers" because, well, NO ONE is a loser, and to call others winners means that *there must be losers*. Anyway, the spirit of the concept above is true, to me. What we visualize and hold true in our minds is what we eventually will become. Fr. Frank Burke put it this way..."What I tell myself I am I am in the process of becoming." How true!

You've heard of the rags to riches stories—the ones about the boy who dreamed he would become president—and did! Or the girl who saw herself as a CEO of a large corporation and worked her way up the ladder to be just that.

They say "it's all in your head"—and I believe this is true. It's also said that the human mind cannot distinguish between something vividly imagined and reality. If this is so, why aren't we all visualizing ourselves into success? Usually, lack of training. Visualizing is a science <u>and</u> an art. Most kids visualize with precision and confidence. Finger painting is the visual expression of an active mind.

But often we adults lose our ability to visualize because we have moved onto more "important" things. Or, many of us find ourselves using negative visualization—worry. If we only knew that "the mind never works without a picture," we would find ways to use our positive creative imagination to make our dreams come true.

Are you guilty of only using your analytical mind?
Can you see yourself using visualization to make <u>your</u> dreams come true?

257

September 21

Every problem carries a gift inside it.

Richard Bach

Bipolar Disorder—a chemical imbalance in the human brain that can cause dramatic mood fluctuations and brain malfunctions—is an illness that has been a part of my life for the past 30 years. It has been the catalyst for more havoc and unbalanced moods and confused thoughts than I care to write about. But it has brought many gifts.

Sensitivity and compassion are probably the most predominant gifts. I have been given the gift of being able to empathize and relate to most any person because of the suffering I have encountered with bipolar. Although I have not been chemically depressed for many years, I KNOW what it is like to be down and out, and to drag yourself around life from activity to activity with little energy and even less ambition.

I also know what it is like to be manic, and <u>too</u> <u>full</u> of life, not being able to stop my thoughts or curtail my energies. This sensitivity and compassion have come in handy as I counsel other people with mental illness challenges on a volunteer non-crisis phone line once a week. If you've been there, you can relate to someone who <u>is</u> there.

Another gift bipolar has placed in my lap is *creativity*. I often say to my wife, "I wonder how..." ...trying to figure out why the blades on a wind turbine are so huge, or why a highway is paved in one area and made of concrete in another. Sometimes TOO over-creative but always thinking. This is where my writing skills have come from...the ability to apply my imagination to the realities I see around me. What blessings bipolar has given me—I don't know who I'd be without them!

Yes, *every problem carries a gift inside it*...what gifts have <u>your</u> challenges provided?

September 22

My mom always used to say,
'Give me my flowers while I can smell them'

Cecelia

This request is all about *living in the moment*, and cherishing others while they are alive—not after they have passed on. A humble man here in Milwaukee was recently honored for his enormous contributions to the people of this great city. It was something we all deserve—to be celebrated while we are alive, not just after our coffin disappears into the ground. The event was a delight!

Why do we wait to tell others how great they are? Why do we shy away from blessing them with compliments and approbation for a job well done? Often, I think it's because we believe that it may "go to their head," and they may become conceited. But much more often, I believe it's because we are just not used to it.

Coming from a German background, it just wasn't the way of my ancestors to continually compliment and raise others up in appreciation. No offense to my predecessors, but I think this does a great disservice to mankind.

I once came up with an acronym of "NBA"...

we **N**eed to

Be

Appreciated

Not just as children, but as adults. I often shock the people I speak with on the phone who are giving me exceptional service by honestly saying, "You do a really good job, thanks!" The response is often one of surprise, but it is always favorable.

Do you go out of your way to make people feel good about themselves? Try it. It's easy to do, and you may be surprised at how soon it comes back to you.

Cecilia's mom had it right! *"Give me my flowers while I can smell them!"*

September 23

*We are expected to take our experiences and grow
from them—to move beyond the shame of them . . .
to celebrate what they have taught us.*

Each Day A New Beginning

Fr. Anthony de Mello, once said, "Enjoyable experiences are delightful. Painful experiences lead to growth." Have you ever re-entered some painful and discouraging moments, and chosen to learn a crucial lesson?

Fr. John Powell, wrote, "The only REAL mistake is the one from which you learn nothing"—a quote I have used in this book before because I believe his words are so life-changing. They certainly have changed mine. If we can re-imagine past struggles (and even failures) and vow to change our attitudes and actions, then we can take these "painful experiences" and convert them into learning experiences...and, at times, transcendent experiences.

I believe that a breakthrough can occur when we take personal ownership of our situations—outside (job, relationships) and inside (choices, feelings). It is this ownership that helps us reclaim responsibility and allow us to be creative and in-the-moment. Lives—ours and others'—can be changed when we take ownership, as we choose to grow, not hide, form painful experiences.

The gold mine is that once a past failure or painful experience has been transformed into a lesson-learned, it NEVER goes back into the *failure column* but joins with successes in the *winning column*. This magic can be yours when you act on "the only *real* mistake is the one from which you learn nothing." This can make a REAL positive difference in your life!

September 24

As important as hanging on is knowing when to let go.

Sherri de Witt

Many songs, spiritual and popular, promote hanging on—"Hold up, Hold out & Hold on"—one song repeats. But the counterpart is no less important—to know when to let go. Endurance is crucial, yet surrender and "giving over" (as opposed to giving in or giving up) can be just what the doctor ordered, at times.

The story is told of a young man hiking in the mountains, on a difficult trail, when he suddenly loses his footing and slides toward the edge of a cliff. Luckily he grabs onto a bush at the edge of the cliff—but finds himself dangling over a 10,000 foot drop. With no one around and barely clutching the bush, he yells, in desperation…"Is there anybody up there?" To his surprise a booming voice answers, "Yes, I'm here." The hiker yells, "What should I do?" The voice calls out, "Just let go of the bush and I will catch you."

The man thinks for a moment, then yells, "IS THERE ANYONE ELSE UP THERE?!"

Is there any area of *your* life when you need to have a little **faith** and risk letting go?

September 25

Everything can be taken from man but one thing:
the last of human freedoms—to choose one's attitude in any
given set of circumstances—to choose one's own way.

Viktor Frankyl

Frankyl realized this truth as the Nazi "scientists" performed ignoble experiments on his body during World War Two—he came to realize they could do whatever they wanted to his body, but they couldn't destroy HIM—the person that lived inside his body. The spiritual self, the soul, cannot be destroyed, as we value our dignity in ANY "given set of circumstances."

This realization can change a life around. When one understands that they're not controlled by others, they often realize they have a choice as to how they will meet & greet life.

Rosa Parks displayed this wonderfully. When she refused to give up her seat in a city bus in 1955, Montgomery, Alabama was turned upside down. Soon Dr. Martin Luther King, Jr., got involved, and the Civil Rights Movement was born. Rosa Parks had expressed her "last of human freedoms," and the world was changed forever!

This freedom entitles us to know a most essential truth—that we are self-motivated and independent beings. As one scholar noted, "We can do all things for the price of an effort," and the *effort* of being ourselves and taking the risks to step into the unknown are some of the most admirable qualities in the world!

September 26

If I have a care in the world I have a gift to bring.

musical duo, Indigo Girls

Is it true that those things that pique our interest often may be the very things over which we have influence? Sometimes yes, sometimes no. We may have an interest in a global issue such as famine, yet feel powerless to do anything about it.

But we can serve at a meal program or at a food pantry on a local level that CAN make a difference. Stevie did just so. He was unemployed and living in a shelter, but he decided to become a part of a meal service team at a local church. He became a trusted and integral component of the team—finding fulfillment and a great distraction from his difficult circumstances. Eventually he gained the confidence to get a good job and moved on with his life.

When we have an interest or "a care," we DO have a gift to give. We just need to be creative in finding a way to have influence and be willing to serve.

What "care in the world" could YOU act upon?

September 27

*Evermore, people today have the means
to live but no meaning to live for.*

Viktor Frankyl

There is certainly a difference between "means to live" and "meaning to live for." "Means" equals *livability*, while "meaning" is the *quality of life*. What is YOUR meaning of life? Have you ever thought about it before?

I have...and I have created a simple life purpose statement that goes:

**Think & Thank
Listen & Learn
Teach & Touch
Observe & Love
Gone & Go On**

These 16 words
abbreviate a life plan for me that helps me
focus on what's most important.

Another way I find meaning—and put it into action—is through my many acronyms. *CAIS* (Connectedness with the Authentic Inner Self), centers me on my individual gifts and aspirations...while I try to *FLIP* (Fully Living In the Present), focusing on the now moment.

Acronyms help me remember important concepts so I'm able to pull them up when I need them—what's the point of knowing things if you can never recall them when they're needed ?

I ask again…what is YOUR meaning of life?

September 28

> *You become successful the moment you start*
> *moving toward a worthwhile goal.*
>
> *unknown*

It isn't just achieving a goal that is important—it's all the steps we take to move in the direction of that goal.

A Chinese proverb reads: "The journey of 1,000 miles begins with a single step." The journey also continues with the 2nd, 3rd and 4th steps. And success starts with the direction we are facing and, hopefully, moving.

Janet had thought her only accomplishment would be getting her Masters in Education. But as she proceeded in her studies, she realized that *every step* along the path was leading her beyond the Masters program, as she discovered her love for working with children who had special needs. This realization was a success itself.

It was an enormously encouraging and gratifying moment when, after graduation, she landed a job at an urban grade school, working with autistic children. This clarified that every day she had worked to achieve the masters degree was leading to this moment!

Dr. Alan Zimmerman calls this "little victories"—this process of recognizing the small successes along the way. Janet's *little victories* of picking up on her passion throughout the period of receiving her masters degree paid off. She is now excelling in her work and finding happiness beyond any expectation.

September 29

Lord, let me talk less and say more.

unknown

Sometimes, the greatest gifts come in simple packaging. We don't need to be verbose to be understood. In fact, usually, the less we say, the better, as long as we're sincere and concise.

Meaning comes to us in many ways...sometimes it's merely a quote, other times a speech...or a book, magazine or newspaper. But whatever the exchange, it doesn't have to be complicated to be meaningful.

Winston Churchill once gave the briefest speech ever presented to a graduating class. He said, "**Never...never...never...never...never... never give up!**" He was met with a rousing ovation for his efforts!

How do YOU communicate with others? Do you try to impress with big words or do you rely on brevity and honesty through which to carry your message?

May that we can come to pray ..."Lord, let me talk less and say more."

September 30

"...you can sit and agonize 'til your
agony's the heaviest load..."

Indigo Girls

Experiencing self-pity? How long will you choose to sit on the dung heap? Self-pity is a grand illusion because the outcome is a vicious cycle of... apathy,

envy,
brooding,
and more self-pity...

> and the process
> continues...

In another great song, the Indigo Girls sing: "I gotta get up and get a hammer & a nail—learn how to use my hands...."THIS is the best prescription to counter the self-pity cycle—

ACTION!

> It is the cure for self-pity---
> ANY action! To do something
> productive is the answer. It may
> be sweeping a floor, stitching a quilt,
> playing golf or rollerblading...costing nothing
> but a sincere effort.

> If and when you start feeling
> the self-pity cycle coming on, just follow Arsenio Hall's
> declaration: "Let's Get Busy!!" or Nike's "Just do it!!" The
> negative cycle will most likely be defeated.

~ *October* ~

October 1

If you always think what you thought
you'll always get what you got.

Earnie Larsen

Earnie is a stand-out in the 12-Step Recovery field, which started with Alcoholics Anonymous and has branched out to include many other addictions and maladies.

Above, Earnie speaks a simple truth. He also describes it in his statement, "If nothing changes, nothing changes!"...meaning that our efforts must be positive, goal-oriented and include appropriate follow-through, or we will get nowhere. If we don't get creative and try new ways of overcoming difficulties, we can stay stuck.

Wasn't there once a definition of insanity going around that said: *Insanity is doing a non-productive, negative behavior over and over (the "same old/same old") and expecting different results each time?* We need to look at our options in a creative way.

One young gent decided to try beating his pattern of apathy in the morning by buying a cheap dart board that had 20 numbered "pie slices" outlined in green & red on its surface. Then he created a list of enjoyable activities—numbered one through 20—one for each area of the dart board. Before going to bed, he made a habit of throwing three darts at the board to see which activities he would get involved in when he awoke.

Sometimes the dart board led him to going for a morning walk, enjoying coffee and relaxing with the paper. Other days, the darts brought him to a completely different combination from the list, such as reciting his spiritual readings, getting involved in speech creation and watching the morning news.

Whatever the combination, it was an impetus for him to get up and going. It worked for him—throwing darts at night and having something specific to look forward to in the morning. He only needed the dart game for a month or so because this fun exercise changed the way he got up and became a huge motivator for the rest of his day!

Sometimes just a simple change can make a *big* difference.

October 2

By learning you will teach, by teaching you will learn.

Latin proverb

Have you had the opportunity to tutor or mentor a youth? It's an enriching experience. The old saying, "I learned more from him/her than they learned from me" is nearly always the case if you're open to being touched by a young person.

Ryan, a 14-year-old blind 8th grader I worked with as a special education teacher's aide a few years ago, taught me so much about life. His curiosity was ceaseless, always asking me about a sound he heard or commenting about the state of the weather as we walked from building to building.

I especially liked his sense of humor, always cracking jokes and actually laughing at *my* silly jokes. He had a light spirit and never felt sorry for himself because he was blind. Ryan's curiosity got me interested in what was going on around me, and he taught me how to enjoy the simple pleasures of life—warm sunshine, tasty food, pleasant conversation. The way he noticed details, I sometimes felt I was the one who was "blind." He was an amazing kid!

Fr. John Keller wrote, "A candle loses nothing by lighting another candle." Have you lit a youth's candle lately? He or she may just light yours.

October 3

*Of all the virtues we can learn, no trait is more useful,
more essential for survival, and more likely to improve the quality of life
than the ability to transform adversity into an enjoyable challenge.*

Mihaly Czikszentrihaly

The above quality is an important topic in Steven Scott's <u>Simple Steps
To Impossible Dreams</u>, where Scott writes about making criticism a friend.
How? By seeking the *usable truth* in a criticism so that you can improve
your life.

"*S.M.A.R.T. Criticism*" is my own version of Scott's process...

   S = consider the **Source**
   M = what was their **Motivation**?
   A = was there some **Accuracy** in the critique?
   R = **Respond** appropriately at the moment of the criticism
   T = seek any **Truth** in the criticism that can help you improve
       by exploring the "Accuracy" component above

The surprising thing is that by using this process, you can learn more
details on how to better your life and your skills than by avoiding or
stuffing the criticism away, never to be seen. It takes courage to do this
kind of work!

So your "best friends" may become these *golden nuggets of truth* that
can come from a critique which had initially stung. Remember, "the truth
shall set you free," and when you use *S.M.A.R.T. Criticism*, you can make
progress faster than you ever thought possible. Try it!

October 4

So often it happens that we live our lives in chains,
and we never even know we have the key.

The Eagles

Such is life in the heart of an unreflective person. It's been said that "the unaware life is not worth living," which points to the caveat that we better *know ourselves.* Sometimes we can feel trapped by habits or circumstances. Often it takes another person to help us bust out of a cage we've put ourselves into, and find new ways of succeeding. This means letting go of the old and "ringing in the new"—especially new attitudes.

A while back, I had a life-shifting experience while writing in my journal, and also writing this book. I had been having a very difficult time in a job as teacher's assistant, not getting respect and cooperation from the kids. But while writing and thinking, I suddenly realized that it was MY attitude that needed changing. **I** was not putting a full effort into my job—**I** was not being very proactive. So I vowed, at that moment, that I would double—even triple—my efforts and fully give myself to the job.

It changed my life, my expectations and my participation. It didn't change all of the bad behavior of the students, but it did make it possible for me to be a more effective teacher's assistant!

Since our attitudes rule our lives, we need to be open to whatever comes our way and keep a positive outlook—if at all possible. Then we can shrug off any chains of negative habits by using the key of *observant optimism,* a key we may not have *even* known we had. We <u>do</u> hold the key!

October 5

> *There's a difference between interest and commitment:*
> *When you're interested in doing something, you do*
> *it only when it's convenient. When you're committed*
> *to do something, you accept no excuses, only results.*
>
> Ken Blanchard

There's the story of the origin of the ham & egg breakfast: The hen made her case about how important she was...then the pig retorted, "Sure, you hens make a contribution (eggs), but we pigs—we make a *commitment* (ham)!"

Commitment takes goals, and goals reflection, and reflection enthusiasm, and enthusiasm a vision...what is *your* vision? And when will *you* follow through on fulfilling a purposeful commitment?

Henry David Thoreau once wrote, "It's not enough to be busy, so are ants; the question is: What are you busy *about*?"

Me? I reluctantly gave up a dream of becoming a grade school teacher, realizing it would be too stressful and too "busy-ing." As a man with bipolar disorder, I realized years ago that stress can be a precipitating factor in relapse. I have to watch it—stress-wise.

So, with the help of my best friend (my wife Sandra), I began to look at the possibilities of teaching through *writing and speaking*...I had been writing *this* book for over 6 months ...hmmm...what could I do with these skills? Sandra and I came up with 4-5 other possibilities and...I "switched dreams" from becoming a grade school teacher to a speaker/author on issues of respect and mental health. I'm now committed to public speaking and writing books—for youth *and* adults! THIS *is what I'm busy about*!

What are *you* busy about?

October 6

> *Living fully in the present—soaking up all*
> *the responses of the life we are immersed in for the moment—*
> *is the closest we can get to our Higher Power, our God.*

> *Each Day A New Beginning*

Years ago, I came up with the acronym "FLIP": Fully Living In the Present...which helps me—and hopefully those with whom I've shared it—to see NOW as the only moment we can live and act in. When one *FLIP's*, he or she recognizes the potential of the present moment and can then choose to live it out with confidence, competence and joy.

But, of the 40-50 acronyms I've created, my very first was "*NIATI*: Now Is All There Is"... which came to me on a gorgeous spring day in 1981. As I've contemplated *NIATI* over the years, I've found myself NOT living by this maxim at times. I'd be worrying about an upcoming event, or fretting about job responsibilities, or wasting time focusing on past negative events. It is when we don't recognize the preciousness of the moment that we tend to waste it by complaining, comparing and continually moping.

In contrast to this, in 1994, I volunteered at a summer school program in Minneapolis, Minnesota, where I worked with an awesome young teacher named Bree. She was **on fire** for teaching and got her students to be **on fire** for learning. She even led them each to create a book, totally written and illustrated by them. She was an inspiration and a true leader. And she was an excellent example of "*FLIPing!*"

Living in the moment is a highly **spiritual** way of acting. God is in the NOW—the ever-present NOW...God said, "I am," not "I was" or "I will be"...but "I AM!" Living this way, we can't help but *be a good example* to those around us! See if you can slip a little more *FLIP* into your day.

October 7

Life is an adventure to be lived, not a problem to be solved.

Deacon Ken Vernon

It's the focus we choose that makes the difference. We can choose to live pessimistically, which shuts down our opportunities and distances us from our resources. Or we can choose optimism which creates a bond between opportunity and reality, furthering our possibilities for success. Dr. Alan Zimmerman has a great definition for optimism: *Optimism means seeking the opportunity in **every** difficulty, while pessimism means spotting the difficulty in every opportunity!*

When we focus on our challenges as "adventures," this attitude of healthy risk-taking pervades the scene, and we become "seekers"...we seek the positive, taking on effortful ventures which can potentially lead to success.

Dr. Zimmerman tells the story of a woman in her sixties in Seattle, years ago, who—after working all day as a secretary—would go home, dress in some comfortable clothes and head to the "red light" district...the tough part of town. But she was a black belt in karate so she could take care of herself. There she would walk the streets and often get her purse stolen. When the thief would open the purse expecting to pilfer cash, all he/she would find was a note which read, "I feel <u>so</u> sorry for you—having to steal a purse from a little old lady...you must be in trouble...call me, or, better yet, come and see me..."—leaving her address and phone number! Consequently, many called or visited! She's been a driving force for reforming dozens of them.

Now THIS is optimism in action!

October 8

The purpose of life is to be a growing, contributing human being.

David McNally

The concept of contribution is an important one. We need to feel like we're contributing or our motivation can slide into despondency.

I have spent many years in the uniform of a custodian. Many may think that this is a demeaning and lowly job, but I beg to differ. Think about it…if you work in an office, what would it be like to not have your trash emptied for *2-3 weeks*? Or to have the bathrooms cleaned only once *every other month*? Suddenly the custodian would have visible worth.

Fact is, every legal, worthy job has qualities which make the workers indispensable! I remember the feeling of cleaning a building and knowing that I did something important and worthwhile with my day. I would hope that everyone could have that feeling at the end of a long workday.

The challenge is to find a type of work that you love *and* that gives you this feeling of contribution…have you found it yet? If you feel stuck, would you *consider* a change?

I have a friend who was working for a collection agency and decided to go back to school to get his teacher's license. It took two years of further schooling, but he achieved his goal. Then he got a job with his local church working with youth and as a substitute teacher in the local high school. His courageous measures to go back to school paid off in worthy employment. He left the collection agency for the opportunities to educate others—a more fitting and fulfilling contribution for him.

Is your contribution meaningful and fulfilling?
If not, are there steps for which you could make it so?

October 9

Wisdom comes by staying the beginner. Then we remain open to further learning...once on the path, we are all equals.

Touchstones

It's been said that "the expert's options are few. The beginner's options are endless." When we "stay the beginner," we are able to observe all that is going on in and around us. Even when we become seasoned professionals, humbly *remaining the beginner* allows us the opportunities to notice new possibilities among the many factors we encounter.

This also undercuts self-righteousness that many so-called experts flaunt. A humble person sees all people as equal and that we all have something positive to contribute.

I love talking to my brother-in-law, Tom, because, even though he's had many years as a college professor, and now many years as a dean of students, he never talks down to me. He explains complicated situations in simple and understandable ways. He's a great conversationalist because he doesn't act like the expert (even though *he usually is*).

Wisdom does come from remaining the beginner. What's one area you see yourself as a beginner? How about one area you can take on *the consciousness of a beginner*, even though you may be very skilled?

October 10

Enthusiasm is caught, not taught!

unknown

In the 2006 movie "Freedom Writers," a new English teacher entered a hostile, multi-racial classroom overcome by gang connections and racial segregation. For many weeks, the young white teacher, Miss G., could do little or nothing with them. Fights, scuffles and ugly banter enveloped the room.

Then one day, some of the Latino students were laughing as they passed around a drawing of a guy with huge lips, making fun of one of the black students. Miss G., grabbed it and became indignant at the meaning behind the cruel caricature. She was aghast at how far one group would go to prove its superiority.

She laid into them, saying, "You think YOUR gangs are tough?! I know a gang that took over countries!" Without using specific names, she described how Jews were downgraded by the Nazis, the "gang" drawing pictures of them with big noses, which were displayed in the newspapers. Then she mentioned the term "Holocaust"—*not one* student had heard of it—oh, except for one—the only white student in class.

When Miss G. told them of the details of the Holocaust, they became intrigued by the topic. They hadn't imagined any place being as bad as their tough, unruly neighborhood. Other people had suffered even worse than they.

The next day she came into class and proposed a little game. She cut the classroom in half with a long piece of red tape and asked them to step on one side of the line or the other based on the questions she asked. Easy questions at first, enough to bring a giggle and an easy movement for all to one side of the tape. Then the questions got harder:

"How many of you have lost a friend to gang violence?"

As the students shifted sides, they began to look around and notice that Latinos, Asians and blacks alike were on that side of the line. They saw a similarity.

"How many have lost two friends?" Students shifted. "Three?" More moved over to the others side of the line. "Four or more?" There were still a few left. "Now, please call out the names of those who have been lost. Feel free. Call them out. "Rachael...Devon ...Juan...Tai...David..." The names were heard for 20-30 seconds—then silence.

Something profound had happened. Their silly *red line game* had become a moment of bonding. Suddenly they had recognized similarities rather than differences. They had seen one another in the same struggle rather than in a struggle against one another. Something had changed.

Out of her own pocket, Miss G. mustered up the money to buy each student a copy of <u>The Diary of Anne Frank</u>, the memoir of a 14-year-old Jewish girl who hid from the Nazis during World War II. They related to it like no other book they had ever read. Eventually, they visited a Holocaust museum on a Saturday and enjoyed a dinner in a fancy hotel, accompanied by actual Holocaust survivors who told their tales of indignity and pain from being imprisoned in Nazi camps such as Auschwitz and Dachau. The teacher had struck a nerve, and the current carried the students along a yellow brick road of intrigue and discovery.

The process of learning to value one another—and LIFE—began to gain momentum. The students bonded and became good friends, crossing all racial lines. There was even some inter-racial dating—in a class that previously had no tolerance for racial differences. They had learned to *value the differences* instead of keeping up walls between them to keep the differences out.

The peak moment was when they each wrote to the woman who had actually helped hide Anne Frank and her family—and she came to their school as a welcomed guest. After one student said she was his hero, this wonderful lady stated that *THEY* were <u>her</u> heroes.

Their teacher had, once again, turned their interest into a memorable, touching, learning-event. She encouraged a transformation in the hearts and minds of these students who discovered meaning and purpose in their lives—lives that had been so bleak and discouraging.

To transform others—could this be the ultimate goal
of a great teacher? To take the risk of being transformed—
could this is the ultimate goal of a worthy student?

October 11

Either I was completely distracted or totally focused . . .
sometimes I don't think there's much of a difference!

Corsair

Jason was the kind of kid who was always staring off into a fantasy world of his choosing...rocket ships, valiant conquests in ancient lands, treks up rugged mountains. His distractions led to a pretty poor attention span, and his studies suffered. His 7th grade teacher was always calling his name to bring him back into reality.

But in science class, he was the star of the show. There, his imagination met practicality, and he thrived in this world of planets, places and people in white coats. It was only after a few months that his teacher began to realize his potential and bolster his enthusiasm.

Funny thing happened—Jason's excitement about science class began to spread into all his studies and, in a few months, the distractions became an intense ability to focus. He had broken out of his spell and was launched into the world of academia in a new way.

Jason is now a researcher for a large pharmaceutical company, delivering his focused attention to all his encounters—thanks to a teacher who saw his potential and acted upon it.

October 12

No one can out-perform their own self-image.

Earnie Larsen

Speaker Denis Waitley says, "The mind always moves toward its currently dominant thought." This shows us that we need to stay optimistic and open. We achieve what we imagine and practice. If we can't imagine doing something, we most likely won't be able to do it.

At age 11, I had been dragged beneath the water trying to learn how to water ski and had avoided water skiing like the plague until I faced my fear at age 14, and got up the first time! My self-image as NON-skier had shifted to "skier," never to go back.

After getting up on two, I envisioned myself skiing on one. Two weeks later, my image came true. I was skiing along quite contently on two skis when a big wave came up and dislodged my right ski. I found myself wobbling and swerving, but I stayed up! One ski! Then I saw myself *getting up* on one ski and by the end of the summer—up on one ski it was.

The next summer, at age 15, I took the gamble to imagine that I could learn how to "barefoot water ski"—yes, skiing with no ski at all. My skiing buddy had recently gone to Florida to attend a "waterskiing school" (hadn't known they had such a thing) and he gave me ideas and hints about how it worked. I listened, tested putting my right foot down into the water— while skiing—with the left foot still in the ski boot. In time, came to believe I could "barefoot." Two weeks later, with the right foot skidding across the water and leaning back as if I were sitting in a chair, I released my left foot from the boot and planted it in the rushing water! I was "barefootin'!"

This is where I learned that if you want something badly enough, and can imagine yourself doing it consistently, you CAN do it. Dr. David McClellen wrote, "You can do anything you can consistently think of as possible." At a fairly young age, I had *tasted and seen* this reality.

Learning to barefoot water ski gave me a confidence that has spread over numerous areas of my life. As Earnie Larsen says, "no one can out-perform their own self image," but when you image yourself as MORE, you can live up to it, then perceive yourself as MORE, and live up to that. An upward spiral of positive progression can emerge. It worked for me with barefoot water skiing!

Try it & see!

October 13

Nobody told me how hard and lonely change is.

Joan Gilbertson

Change needs to come from within. This can bring great loneliness if we don't allow anyone in with us. By sharing our struggles with another, we lighten the burden and give another a chance to show empathy. This allows God's grace to flow in our lives.

God knows and sees that we need companionship in order to live a healthy life, socially, emotionally, spiritually. This may mean marriage, or it may mean deep friendship, but to be healthy human beings, we need to share with *someone.*

On my shifts as a volunteer non-crisis mental health phone counselor, I have found the typical call to be from someone who is isolated and lonely. They often have few or no friends and very little contact with the outside world. It's as if their whole existence were like looking backwards through a set of binoculars—distant, out of focus, distorted. I've felt like a band aid on a gaping wound, at times, during these calls.

The saying goes, "We are as sick as we are secret"…which flies in the face of isolation. Who wouldn't agree that many of our best moments in life were times we shared with a friend? Meaningful conversation is not merely enjoyable but absolutely necessary. I sure hope I've offered bit of "meaningful conversation" to my callers on the non-crisis line.

Change will be "hard and lonely" if we try to do it by ourselves. Reach out—and you <u>will</u> find companionship and hope.

October 14

...(regarding the previous reading)...

in this life of mine
there is one thing I most want-
a loved one to be there, and here,
as the drama unfolds
this would be my greatest loss in life
if I were not to have become *me*
(the me I'm supposed to be)
because there was no interaction
no one to hear me in times of confusion and pain
or in times of joy and fulfillment
to help me see it, feel it, and pull it together
"I" would not *become* without this gentle,
firm confrontation and interaction
what a loss it would be not to have become me

(Corsair, 1996)

(years later)
having found a special person has
changed my life—a woman who really
sees who I am and brings the best out in me
a woman whom I cherish in so many ways—
emotionally, intellectually, spiritually,...just as
she cherishes and supports me...it was she who
brought out the writer in me when I met her many months
ago and I AM becoming the person I'm supposed to be
with her love and affection leading me on the path to fulfillment
I thank God for her companionship—yes—but also for her honesty,
her *peacefulness*, her courage and strength...she's wonderful! She
brings life to Life! I thank God I have one here with me
as the drama unfolds...

Corsair, 2007

(Sandra became my wife soon after)

October 15

Art is the elimination of the unnecessary.

Picasso

It's said that when Michelangelo created a sculpture he was trying to "free" the imprisoned figure from inside the block of marble.

He certainly did so with his statue "David." On a recent trip to Italy with our choir, I saw the 15-foot-high masterpiece which depicts the youthful David, holding his sling. The sculpture is so big that the right foot had to have supports to keep the statue from toppling. How Michelangelo could chip away at such a huge piece of marble and end up with a *David*, I will never know. I'm simply amazed!

Sculpting is probably the best example of Picasso's "eliminating the unnecessary," but we can all gain from this example by being concise when we speak and write, and frugal when we shop. This leaves us with the "necessary" that will express what we intend. Less is more, simple is better.

There's the story of a Japanese man who had a gift for teaching, and a yearning to serve his people. He wanted to get the Japanese Holy Scriptures translated into his native language, so he decided to begin giving public teachings for huge fees to raise the money to have the Scriptures translated. But just as he was approaching the money needed, a famine hit. He felt torn, between completing his project and helping the hungry. He finally decided to put all the money into purchasing rice to feed his people.

But his passion for translation was only fed by the event. Again he struck out to raise the money—this time he was older and wiser, but the money was hard to raise, although he had stepped up his speaking schedule. He spoke for years, and just as he was about to seek transcription of the Scriptures, an earthquake hit the land. Again—the dilemma: Transcribe or assist in providing aid in the tragic times. He struggled with his urge to fulfill his mission once again, but gave all the money to rebuild the surrounding communities.

As the years went by, now an old man, he decided to try one last time to raise the money for transcription. His wisdom and peacefulness attracted large groups of people to his teachings, but he could no longer charge the exorbitant fees. Still, he trudged on until, years later, he achieved his goal and was finally able to get the Scriptures translated into his native language.

Years after the man's death, his legend was passed on as the man who translated the Scriptures THREE times—once onto paper, and twice through his failed efforts and thoughtful generosity.

A simple man with a simple mission—who achieved simply amazing things. He eliminated the unnecessary and kept his vision alive. Do you have a focused vision like that?

October 16

A nice definition of an awakened person
is that this person no longer marches
to the drum of society—this person dances
to the tune of the music that
springs up from within.

Fr. Anthony de Mello

Fr. De Mello speaks of a common downfall in human nature—this need to "march to the drum of society." There is so much conformity in our society: Watching the same TV shows, going to the same old bars, grabbing on to sports teams as if they were gods. It's so refreshing when we find someone who has broken out of that mold!

There is a young woman in Minneapolis who fits this description quite well. At her suburban alternative school, she leads her classes in dynamic and informative discussions that seem to make the students gleam with self-confidence. Her style is more like that of a facilitator of discussion rather than a teacher of topics. It's fascinating to watch!

This Language Arts teacher is also a professional painter, producing wondrous canvases that are created in her artist's loft in Minneapolis, *and* she is an excellent writer. These talents are balanced with her drive to seek political office and her active participation in her neighborhood's progress and affairs.

> It is when we "dance to our music" that we
> find the best parts of us expressed.
> Here's a woman who has found it!

October 17

> *Leave your baggage behind—carry on your luggage.*
>
> *Dick Rice*

Luggage...baggage...what's the difference?

Emotional baggage is the stuff some carry around that gets them nowhere. It can be guilt over past mistakes, anger over past or present perceived injustices, or shame which can create the mirage that "I am the problem." Baggage has one universal quality—*mustiness*. It's the mildew of these negative emotions that stinks up the place. Some people tend to hold onto the past and cling to present negative perceptions. This gets them into more trouble than they will ever know.

Yet "luggage" is what we carry on the plane, train or ship which gets us going—the provisions, if you will, that make for safe, clean, comfortable travel through life. Luggage includes those positive, forward-looking attitudes and actions that make life pleasurable—and workable—as we move toward reaching our goals and fulfilling our dreams.

Baggage and luggage are polar opposites. We can either wither in a musty past <u>or</u> proclaim the present as a place for which to be thankful, moving towards a bright future. These are the extremes and there are plenty of hues in between, but I promote carrying the attitude of *luggage*. We all deserve to feel the freedom of spirit that this image presents.

Do you want to have old, dusty *baggage* deserted in some dark, dank basement, or do you carry on your *luggage* to destinations hopeful and exciting? The choice is yours.

October18

Our successes are less to be proud of than to be grateful for!

Corsair

Many people base their lives on the pride that they have succeeded at making the big buck or buying the big boat. But others take a more humble stance.

There is a generous woman in Milwaukee who retired from teaching years ago. She is the president of a charity that serves the poor in the central city. She spends hours a week lining up clients for her group to visit, two-by-two—giving vouchers for the basic essentials of life such as appliances and beds.

Her great-nephew and the charity—along with choir and a church group—keep her soooooo busy that *retirement* seems to be a ridiculous word to her. But she lives a very rich life, and for which she shows continual gratitude.

Here's a woman who proves, in her generous ways, that *successes are less to be proud of and everything to be grateful for.*

October 19

Everything can be taken from a man but one thing: The last of human freedoms - to choose one's attitude in any set of circumstances— to choose one's own way.

Viktor Frankyl

When we soberly think about it, Frankyl was right. No matter how much we may choose to believe that people or situations have power over us, we must—ultimately—make the decisions about what we will do and who we will become.

I had a math teacher in high school, Mr. B., who was always warning us about "the bottom line"—the fact that some day we must "pay the piper" and deal with how we made choices. If we worked hard, paid attention and tried our best, this *bottom line* would mean success, he promoted. But if we goofed around and took absolutely nothing seriously, our bottom line would catch up with us and possibly haunt us for the rest of our lives. Mr. B. has proved to be—like Frankyl—*right* also.

There's a difference, says author Stephen R. Covey, between getting a degree and paying the price to get an education. The first *can mean* sliding on by and studying only to pass tests, yet the latter means putting the effort and energy into really learning and connecting with the material. It's our choice in life what we will do, and with choices come taking responsibility to live with the consequences—good or bad.

Do you remember a choice that led you in a completely different direction? I do. It was my sophomore year in college, and I had been contemplating a switch in majors from construction management to mass communications. One afternoon, in a construction-oriented class, the head of the department was describing to us some way to do something that I saw as somewhat deceitful. So I asked the question, "Is this the way it's *supposed to be done*, or is this just the way that it's done?" I guess my professor took this as a challenge to his authority because he responded, "Mr. Melcher, this is NOT an ethics class!"

That sealed it—I was *outa there*! I soon changed my major to mass communications (journalism), and I have never turned back. But sometimes

I wonder if I would have had the impetus and the vision to move toward my inclination to write—which soon became my passion—if it were not for that unscholarly professor's comment.

Sometimes the choices are just made for us—in the heart—and we just need to follow through on them.

In what direction are *your* choices leading you?

October 20

> *I could choose to see this situation*
> *as a setback or a starting point.*
>
> *W Mitchell*

What's the most ridiculous thing you have ever done? Coming from a family where my mother once stole the principal's car, my personal pattern of silly behavior goes pretty far back. It's in my blood.

It's hard to decide which of my numerous follies was the most ridiculous—but they all seem to stem from unawareness and inattentiveness.

One of the most flagrant examples occurred on a Sunday afternoon in 1988, in a Target parking lot in St. Paul, Minnesota. I had passed a good parking spot in the lot, and, without looking, backed up my '78 Ford pickup to grab the spot. Suddenly, there was a huge SMASH as I backed into the front end of a big red Cadillac convertible! My bumper took out the front end of the Caddy, and *to add insult to injury*, the two vehicles became locked together! The anger from the owner, and the humiliation cast upon me made it one of the worst moments of my life.

A few years later, I came up with an idea (of course, it was an *acronym*) that was very soothing and refreshing. I heard someone say that our greatest joys can come from our greatest sorrows...a biblical thought, I think. And, I also heard that it is through our biggest struggles that we can make our greatest gains. Then, on came the acronym . . . "WCIL"...

*W*hat *C*an *I* *L*earn

I imagined that there was a little radio station—"WCIL"—always playing in my head, helping me see how to take folly and make the moment flourish. This "station" became a mindset, a habit of thought that has taken me away for the blame/shame game of "I'm just an idiot—look at the dumb thing I have done." *WCIL* has moved me into a compassionate and aware state of seeing that "we all make mistakes" so I can glean the lesson and move on.

The lesson from the red Cadillac was quite obvious, on the surface... *don't back up without looking—turn head over shoulder and LOOK!* And that's been my policy ever since. But many-a-time I have found myself "backing into the red Caddy" in social situations. The gaffes and goofs produced by my inattentive—often insensitive—states have caused pain and embarrassment to others, and myself.

It's through realizing the statement by Fr. John Powell that I receive instruction and comfort: *The only REAL mistake is the one from which we learn nothing!* This statement has been one of the most helpful in my life! At any moment, we can revisit a past mistake and learn our lessons—that we don't have to be caught in the shame and self-pity of past mistakes—but actually use them as our greatest allies! *WCIL* says, "Never do I have to revisit this error as a loss...it can become my strength. I can gain from my mistakes!" And so can you!

Since 1988, I haven't backed into another red Caddy, or anything else! And if I were to do so, it would just be another opportunity for a *WCIL* moment!

WCYL...What can you learn?

October 21

I don't claim to have all the answers—
I have THE answer . . . God!

Corsair

I remember going over to a friend's house when I was a kid, and we would say grace before a meal..."God is great, God is good, and we thank Him for our food." At another friend's house he would jokingly say, "Rub-a-dub-dub, thanks for the grub...YEEEAAA God!" as he slapped his hands over his head. It was these early expressions of gratitude for God's grace that were the underpinnings of my spiritual life.

Do you have such memories of how God has touched your life?

It was 9th grade when I went on my first retreat. I had only been away from my parents overnight a few times by that age—pretty sheltered, I know. Oh, I guess I had been away many times, but not for a specific *religious* purpose. What I gained was a camaraderie with many other young people and a new confidence that I was indeed loved by God.

Spirituality is now my main force. It has brought me through many dark corners of depression and out of the blinding lights of mania, as I have struggled with bipolar disorder. My *relationship* with God is the most important connection in my life, although I am not always the best at giving attention to and expressing my gratitude for God.

But I believe God understands my frailties and inconsistencies, for He made me, and knows me better than anyone. I hope *you* have a relationship with a Higher Power, and that this relationship is nurturing your spirit. It has made <u>all</u> the difference for me!

October 22

We either make ourselves miserable or we make
ourselves strong. The amount of work is the same.

Carlos Castaneda

We have a choice EACH day as to the attitude we will embrace for the day. We can be pessimistic and grouchy—we can be optimistic and affirming...either way, the energy expended is the same.

Have you ever had a boss who was negative and even possibly abusive? This type of person probably uses *more* energy and effort being this way than a boss who is understanding and positive. This "effort" exuded by Mr. or Ms. Bossy pushes negative energy onto everyone around 'em, and often intimidates and discourages others.

This was the nature of my very first boss...belligerent & bossy...and I've heard it said that your very first job may well set a pattern, a groove, for all your future jobs. Gotta admit, I can be very sensitive to humiliation, even in a current job 30 years later!

Still, Mr. Bossy has helped me to make choices away from negativity and ill-temperedness. So it's actually somewhat of a blessing that I had him to show me what NOT to do!

October 23

Good teaching is ¼ preparation and ¾ theatre.

Gail Godwin

On a recent trip to Italy with our gospel choir, we toured Rome with a marvelous Italian guide—Geno. In his 60s, Geno did much more than describe architecture. He described the politics, the religion and the artistic expressions of the various sites in the city, at the time when the edifices were constructed up until the present.

At one point someone asked him how long he had been a guide…24 years! He went on to tell us that his main role is not really as guide but as an *actor*. His dramatic and emotional descriptions of St. Peter's Basilica prompted me to ask him many questions. He informed us about how the architecture represented the religious ideas of the times…such as domes representing eternity and God, (circular), and elongated forms representing the oblong ways if humans—our imperfection.

Also, Geno showed us a geometric form on the floor of one church that was Arabic in origin and *symbolized* God. Hmm…Arabic in a Catholic church! Geno told us that it was against Arabic teachings to express the name of God, but—as he walked on this spiral pattern on the floor, he showed that in a few steps—in this circular design that swirled toward the middle—he could no longer get out…his walking in circles became the *symbol* representing eternity…God.

Fascinating and uplifting! But we would have missed most of it without our guide, Geno. Funny how we gained so much because we happened to have *him* as our guide…or should I say, *how God blessed us* with this superb guide—an actor par excellence! He made Rome come alive for us! Geno transformed teaching into theatre, and I will always be grateful for that. Have you had a similar experience?

October 24

Optimism means living a life of opportunity, not dread.

Corsair

My understanding is that much of dread comes from fear of the unknown. But by accepting that there will always be unknowns, we can reach toward our opportunities with confidence.

It's been said that optimism means "seeking the opportunity in every difficulty, while pessimism means spotting the difficulty in every opportunity"…these diametrically opposed views can motivate us or de-motivate us, depending on which we choose to see exhibited.

I once turned around a job as industrial janitor when *I took ownership* of my job and began noticing what needed to be done—and just doing it! No longer did I constantly have to be told what to do. I just saw what needed to be done and found ways to get the job done! I suddenly realized that my job was to make everything "look nice." So I gave myself a new title—"Aesthetic Engineer"—I went from pessimism to optimism that day—never to go back!

When we live a life of opportunity, we expand our abilities to be creative and productive, <u>and</u> we *avoid dread* by being active in our pursuit of worthy goals.

October 25

*Self-love, full of self-acceptance, is necessary before
we can give anything of lasting value to someone else.*

Each Day A New Beginning

The key that opens the door to happiness and success is self-love, which fosters self-confidence. What is self-love?

It's acceptance—of our past mistakes and our daring dreams. It's knowing we can come through tough times and experience happiness and even joy. It's acknowledging our deficiencies and raising high our proficiencies—keeping the latter always in view, as we learn more every day.

A 5th grader I once worked with, Randy, has an effervescent demeanor, and his excitement rolled off onto those around him. He was eager to take a reading test—not usually the most popular activity among students—and he aced it! He knew he was a great reader so he was excited to "show me his stuff." Randy had a strong self-confidence and seemed willing to help other students when they were struggling. He seemed to like who he was and who he was becoming.

Then one day, Randy became so upset, egged on by other students who were teasing him, that I had to take him out of class and walk around the school halls for 15 minutes while he fumed and stomped up and "grrrrred." I talked to him intermittently, trying to understand what had gone wrong. He could barely talk, he was so upset. After the "angry walk" and pounding feet, he settled down and rejoined his class. He had come out of a steep dive toward despair and seemed to progress from there. I was glad to have played an encouraging role for Randy that day—God's tool to calm a storm.

We all need this encouragement…are *you* ready and willing to give it to those around you who need it most?

October 26

> *We consider that each problem, each crisis, is our necessary*
> *preparation for moving another step down the road.*
>
> *Each Day A New Beginning*

So often lately I have felt the opposite of this - that my problems, past & present, were leading to more problems, and eventual failure and defeat.

But I had a breakthrough yesterday. I was on my daily walk with no Walkman headphones, so I had silence and solitude, and began to pray for guidance and insight about my recent lack of motivation. God came to me through a sight I see most every day—a stop sign! I looked at the red and white sign and saw something new and refreshing…wisdom came to me in the form of an acronym (wouldn't ya know):

*S*truggles
*T*ransforming into
*O*pportunities of
*P*romise

This was the insight—a new vision. No longer need I worry about the failures of my past as baggage or deficits…these very happenings can now be seen as assets toward empathy. The struggles I have had and am having are no longer to be avoided but analyzed for their potential helpfulness in relating to my struggles and sufferings and those of others.

Not every time, but often, when I look at a stop sign I see something more than a command to halt, but a teachable moment in which to reflect a bit about any struggles I can transform into opportunities of promise.

What simple visual reminders can you set up in your life to remember crucial key concepts, such as my *STOP* sign? They're fun to create, and a trigger like this can prove very helpful in the long run.

October 27

Watch what you say, but be sure to say what you believe.

Corsair

Dr. Martin Luther King, Jr., was one person in American history who took the risks to say what he believed. Starting with the Montgomery bus boycott in 1955, King began to speak about racism, discrimination and segregation in bold and dynamic ways.

Talk about pressure…he not only had the leading role in the Civil Rights Movement, with all its responsibilities but had to deal with death threats and jailing after jailing—protesting what he saw as unjust laws.

But King kept talking and writing and promoting the cause of freedom in the often-unjust American society at the time. He spoke for the masses who were affected by the systems that kept the races estranged and the white moderates silent.

I believe King was one of our greatest examples of how to stand up for what we believe and stay active, even in the face of hatred—and sometimes worse—indifference. He was assassinated when I was 6, so I didn't know much about him until I graduated from college in 1984 and took a volunteer job in a central city Milwaukee grade school. At this predominantly African American school, King was *their* hero, and quickly became *my* hero—a true man of word *and* deed!

October 28

Every mistake has the seed of greatness inside—
an opportunity to learn a lesson that would
otherwise not have been presented.

Corsair

The greatest thing about "learning our lessons" is that they can be pursued and captured at ANY time—whether 5 seconds after the mistake, 5 minutes, 5 hours, days, months, years—even <u>50</u> years! All it takes is the *"4 Rs of Gaining From Mistakes (GFM)"*...Revisit, Reframe, Redirect and Rejoice.

The first two "Rs" are done in the imagination, the last two in real life. First we need to have the courage to *Revisit* the mistake in our minds—to sketch out the details, the happenings, even the feelings that accompanied the mistake. For example, *I remember 30 years ago when I drove a forklift onto a muddy surface and, because a heavy forklift and greasy mud are not compatible, I got massively stuck! I felt like an idiot for attempting the maneuver.* These are the details.

So now I *Reframe* the error (in the present moment) by correcting it in my mind and successfully restructuring the situation—as I wish it had been done then. *"Hey, there's mud up there...I don't think the mud will hold the weight of this forklift. I'm going to find another way to my destination."* A little observation and common sense would have saved me from the embarrassing situation, so I reconstruct the successful outcome in my mind.

Third comes the *Redirecting.* This entails choosing to LEARN THE LESSONS that are presented and deciding to apply these lessons to life today. *"Man, I was so non-observant that day! I wasn't using common sense! So I'm going to keep my head up and really see what is going on in and around me today. I have gained common sense over the years, and I need to apply it every day. Like today—I'm going to be very aware of my computer cord so I don't trip over it and end up dashing my computer on the floor! This is an idea I can use EVERY day!"* There's the *Redirection.*

Now the fun part...we need to *Rejoice* that these first three "Rs" have brought us to a new place where we *never* have to go back and relive the "mistake" again. Our imagination and actions have overcome it.

This is how *the 4 Rs of Gaining From Mistakes* work. Try it and see if it can help you let go of a bit of guilt or shame that may be clogging your psyche. As you can see above, I just did it, and I'm on the *Rejoicing* end now. I can forget about muddy forklifts and live in the freedom of Gaining From Mistakes.

October 29

Finally, the true enabling factor for good is intensely held vision.

Beyond War, 1988

One person who had "intensely held vision" was (is) Jesus Christ. It's recorded in *The Holy Bible* that after He performed the miracle of *feeding the 5,000*, Jesus was to be marched away to be crowned king...earthly king. So He slipped away and up the mountain to be alone because He knew this wasn't *His time.* He had a vision of something much more powerful than becoming an "earthly king." He could have been merely a miracle worker, world-changer, lover of all and soon-to-be Savior—to been seated on an earthly throne. This would have been like a mighty lion becoming a microbe!

Yet His position was to become much more than just earthly king. His stance turned into something infinitely more majestic and powerful. Jesus had a Heavenly vision that couldn't have been lived out any other way! This is one of the attributes that I am most attracted to, in Him. He had such a focus—to be *servant-leader*—to LOVE, no matter what the conflict, hatred or "impossible" circumstance. He had confidence—yes... assurance—even more!

Can you think of people who model this powerful quality? Do YOU have an "intensely held vision" for your life?

October 30

*The universe responded to allow this kind of activity
to take place, and I'm totally grateful every day.*

*~ words of a teacher/potter from <u>Do What You
Like & the Money Will Follow</u>*

by Marsha Sinetar

Gratitude is crucial if we are to live a good Christian life—or a life of any religion—or of NO religion! So, I guess gratitude is important to & for <u>everyone</u>!

Fr. Anthony de Mello, once said, "There is no sweeter prayer than a grateful heart." This rings true for me...how about you? It's when I've misplaced my gratitude that I find myself listless and even depressed. If I'm unable to see the goodness all around me, to notice the blessings offered to me, I lose perspective and may become apathetic. Does this ring a bell for you?

Gratitude creates lift, not drag. It puts the focus on the power of Love and gives attention to God who is always ready to listen—up in the heavens, and deep within us.

When I get down and in the doldrums, I **focus on the good** and praise God for these blessings. This places me in a proper perspective, and in the presence of my God.

How does gratitude affect your life?

October 31

(a prayer for the times)

Oh Lord,
send me in a way You want to send me~
where to live and what to do
all is up to You~
it brings me, this life, no success
or fulfillment if it is not Your WAY, oh Lord
let Your Kingdom ride in me like
a horseman mounted tall on majestic steed
show me Your way
this way of blessing
this way of truth
let me honor You and feel
Your goodness inside me
often unaware as I am of my own
beating heart
glance at me, oh Lord
as I travel Your road
bless my steps as You step
inside my shoes and guide
my every step, my every thought
my every *every*
Lord Jesus,
help me know You in
Your constant efforts to win my soul
for the Kingdom
may You always rain in my heart~
a thunderstorm of faith and hope
as this kite of my life battles
with high, heavy weather and tugs
tremendously to keep an altitude of Love
help me rise above and keep flyin' high

Corsair

~ November ~

November 1

Want to know the most important question in the world?
You think it is, "Who is Jesus Christ?" Wrong.
You think it is, "Does God exist?" Wrong.
You think it is, "Is there life after death?" Wrong.
The great masters tell us the most important question is,
"Who am I?"

Fr. Anthony de Mello

How could this be? Sounds so selfish. But the realization of *WHO AM I* filters all we think and all we do.

There is a saying—"you are what you think about most"—and when you know yourself, you can act out of this true authenticity and fully be *yourself.* When a self-aware person meets a self-aware person, the self-acceptance is easily transformed into *other*-acceptance. Was it Socrates who said KNOW THYSELF? Whoever...it is our home base, our starting block, our place of residence.

In the movie *The Wiz*, the African American version of the Wizard of Oz, Dorothy is on a quest to discover herself. Glinda, the Good Witch of the South, reminds Dorothy..."*Home is knowing—knowing your heart, knowing your mind, knowing your courage—when we know ourselves, we're always home—anywhere!*" Quite a moving & influential statement! If "home is where the heart is," it can also be said that "the heart is where home is." Our dwelling place, spiritually, is in our own hearts and minds. So we need to have peace within ourselves first, in order to bring goodness to others.

Have you ever found yourself in a confusing or anger-filled situation where you just wondered who you really were, bringing out unfamiliar and unwelcomed thoughts, feelings and actions? Was it frightening? Bewildering? Figuring out who you really are and where you stand is crucial at these emotion-packed times. It was once said that "it is when tested that we discover our true character." We rarely "find ourselves" in the ordinary times.

Answering the question *"who am I?"* may just bring a valuable and insight-filled journey. Will you choose to embark on it?

November 2

*Faith is…the ability to carry on with our plans or to be true
to our work even though we feel discouraged or tired.*

Touchstones

Are our plans important to us? Are our goals worthy of us? If so, we will most likely be able to carry on in the face of discouragement.

Jim had a dream of becoming a college English teacher. He believed this was how he could best serve others. When study loads got heavy and his buoyant self began to drag on the bottom, he refocused on his dream which gave him a vision to follow and work toward. It took a few years of graduate level coursework, but he finally graduated and landed a job in the English department at a Midwestern state university—just what he was looking for!

Without the clear vision and the faith he had in himself, in his goal and in his God, he may have given up. Locked in on his goal and putting his faith in God, he used his time, talents and energy to pull him through.

Have you had times when your faith was challenged—and times when your faith has pulled you through? I have a friend who found out he had major depression. He took a job far from his friends and family and did not find his boss nor his work hospitable. Soon he became very depressed and began sleeping a lot to avoid his pain.

Finally he had to cut his losses, quit the job and come home. His faith had been rattled in the process of seeing himself go downhill. But as he regained his health, he related to me that one of the most important factors was his faith that God would pull him out of the mire of depression. He steadily became himself again, as the depression faded away, partly due to proper medications, a healthy diet and good sleep. Supported by family and friends, my buddy soon got a job and was on his way again.

Jesus often said, "Your faith has healed you"...this is the prominent factor in my friend's testimony, that indeed, his faith in God was the deciding factor in his recovery.

Can you name a time when YOUR faith was stretched? How did *you* make it through?

November 3

Anything that is rare is irreplaceable.

National Public Radio

Gold...why is it precious? Not just because it's beautiful or fashionable, but because it comes in a limited quantity. When King Midas came into contact with things, they turned into gold—actually devaluing gold because it became so prevalent.

Human life—each of us different, and special, and rare...we are all irreplaceable! So it's a crying shame to have starvation, wars, treatable diseases, hatred and racism that ruin so many lives. If we could see one another as precious, as God does, more people would be working to save others from suffering rather than causing it.

I read a spiritual reading today that spoke of "the image and likeness of God." This means that each and every person—no matter the defect or disability—is crafted after the likeness of God. How could this be? Here's a person with down syndrome—an image of God?

YES! Know why? Because to God, every human soul is the same. It doesn't matter what the intellectual or physical capacities one has, we are all the same to God. God sees the soul and knows each of us intimately. We are rare and irreplaceable. Copy that!

November 4

It's not what happens to you but what you do about it.

W Mitchell

For many years, I have played this little game inside my head... experience an annoyance or inconvenience and wonder whether I could handle it if I had to put up with it for the rest of my life. Like that itch in the middle of my back that I can never seem to scratch; or the summer cold that has me sneezing and wheezing as if it were mid-winter; or getting a flat tire on the way to an important appointment; or dealing with a major foot problem that plagues my every standing moment; or discovering I have an incurable disease that may afflict me for the rest of my life...and on and on and on.

Well, today at church I had an epiphany: I recalled a statement that "God will never give you more than you can handle." "Hmmm," I thought, "so all this time I'd been thinking about how I could put up with certain things and how I bet I could carry on with the inconveniences and annoyances being a part of my life...was this a waste of time?"

Then I thought of W Mitchell (above quote), who is now a global public speaker. This man had been in a motorcycle/tanker accident which left him badly burned and a small plane accident which left him a paraplegic. Even though, with a grafted and scarred face, he had the tenacity and courage to run for mayor in his small Colorado town on the motto of "NOT JUST ANOTHER PRETTY FACE!" And he won!!

Here's a guy who had much more than "inconveniences and annoyances" but life-threatening conditions, extreme pain and enormous struggles to overcome, and he "succeeded." He succeeded not only in becoming the mayor, but in overcoming the stares that were cast upon his burned face and body. He succeeded in powerfully coming back from great loss. And he succeeded in becoming an exquisite example for all of us of how to come back from adversity with poise, strength and a healthy sense of humor.

The "inconvenience game" is over for me. Now it's time to concentrate on the business of living in the now-moment, not worrying if "I can take it" in the future.

What about you? Do you see the value in this type of letting go? Do you have any "little mind games you play" that have over-stayed their welcome? I dare you to do as W Mitchell has done and look beyond the pain, the appearance and the "inconveniences" and

risk the moment!

You may just surprise yourself with previously unacknowledged strength and wisdom!

November 5

You've got to put the past behind you before you can move on.

Forrest Gump's mother (movie, Forrest Gump)

Oh how I struggle with this. Even though one of my favorite quotes is "*The only REAL mistake is the one from which you learn nothing*," (and the freedom this brings is enormous), I still struggle with memories of past failures.

Failures in relationships, at work, in my personal life...I struggle with the shame and guilt of having made many mistakes. Yet I do have hope...hope that I can learn my lessons of the past & let go of the negative memories.

Forrest Gump (in the movie by the same name) ran back & forth across America for three years—three years of *therapy*—running while putting his past where it belongs—in the past. I need to heed Forrest's mother's admonition, "You've got to put the past behind you before you can move on." This is crucial as I travel this road to a brighter future. How about you?

Letting go of our past and not clinging to it may just be one of the most important emotional, psychological and spiritual lessons we can receive. We may be molded by our past, but it doesn't mean we can't break that mold and strike out for something new and more productive. The old adage, "Let the spirit move you," may be exactly what we need to overcome old, bad, rusty habits of thought and emotion.

God help us break through our past imperfections
and discover who You really want us to be!

November 6

*The more you love and respect yourself, the more you'll be
attracted to people who will love and respect you.*

unknown

It all starts with loving and accepting ourselves. When we choose to respect and love ourselves, we make the biggest decision—a constant decision—that will affect every area of our lives.

I can remember a time in my life when I not only didn't love myself but loathed myself! I hated life and myself with a passion and never thought life would get any better. But my family and friends kept showing me how they valued me and how great I really was, which helped me out this dive-bomber state to a safe and restful place. Sometimes emotions, when unbalanced, can lie to us about our worth. Having bipolar disorder, a brain chemistry disorder which was at the base of this depressive bout, didn't help either.

But I can attest, for certain, that if you don't like yourself—much less love yourself—you will suffer. You will suffer some of the deepest pain known to mankind: Self-loathing, personal disillusionment and being devoid of self-confidence.

It's a "victorious circle"...when you love and respect yourself, you show the same to others, and receive the same back, which bolsters your self-confidence—and round & round it goes. Yet it's obvious that it all starts at home plate...the individual, the self...with both you, and me.

Where is your level of self-love? How can you strengthen it? Do you recognize your talents and gifts? If so, are you sharing them in service of others?

November 7

> "...you're not "OK"— you're not "_not_ OK"—you're YOU!
> Cut out all the "OK"   stuff & the "not OK" stuff—cut out all
> the judgments and observe, watch,...you'll make great
> discoveries—those discoveries will change you!"
>
> *Fr. Anthony de Mello*

A Jewish rabbi once stated that, if & when he went to Heaven, he would be asked one question...it wasn't, "Why were you not Moses?" or, "Why were you not Abraham?" but, "Why were you not YOU?"

There is only one person who can be *me*. Just as there is only one person who can be *you*. It almost sounds silly, doesn't it? But think about times when you acted like someone else. Sure—*fake it 'til you make it,* and all that—but choosing to be other than who you are is most probably a mistake. We may mimic others' qualities at times—following another's good example is a virtue. But, in the end, we need to just BE ourselves. That's where we find contentment and personhood.

It's been written that "being genuine is far more important than being great" (Touchstones). And it has also been written that "when we are unable to find tranquility within ourselves, it is useless to seek it elsewhere" (La Rochefoucauld). I can't say it any better.

Can you "*cut out all the judgments,*" as de Mello states, and truly see the giftedness and beauty in others and yourself? My hope is that you can.

November 8

*Emancipate yourself from mental slavery~
none but ourselves can free our mind.*

Bob Marley

Freedom begins in our hearts & minds. There is an old saying that goes: "Two men at night stare out from behind bars; one saw mud, the other stars."

Freedom is a state of mind. Even the captured and imprisoned can be free. Dr. Viktor Frankyl writes about the different ways people dealt with their captivity in the Nazi death camp, Auschwitz. Those who had something or someone to go back to after the war seemed to hold onto life with a tight grip. And those who had nothing to look forward to, who had lost the spark of life, died in a short amount of time. Age was no real factor—HOPE was!

What brings the spark into your life?

November 9

The 5 Basic Fears

1. rejection
2. failure
3. change
4. intimacy
5. **freedom**

(St. Michael Hospital
Milwaukee, Wisconsin)

One can understand fear of rejection, failure, change—even intimacy... but *freedom*? How could one be afraid of freedom? Well, having unlimited options is often more stress-producing than simply having one direction to go.

Look at Dorothy in the Wizard of Oz...when she was just ramblin' on down the yellow brick road, she had no worries. But when it came to a crossing, with 3 options, she didn't know what to do. She experienced *the fear of freedom*. The scarecrow had to point for her, then they went merrily down the road—the ONE path, easily and freely.

Yes, freedom can cause fear—"what if we make a mistake?" Or—"now I actually have to do something, to show some initiative"—the fear of having to put out effort.

Meeting this fear of freedom with appropriate action can bring strong and resilient confidence, and eventual success...as the song goes, "Don't be afraid of your freedom!"

November 10

Real difficulties can be overcome; it is only
the imaginary ones that are unconquerable.

Theodore N. Vail

What we put in our minds makes all the difference. "Garbage in, garbage out." AND good stuff in, good stuff out! Sometimes our imaginations can work against us, especially when we fill them with worry, doubt and envy. Such perils await those who stuff their heads with this garbage.

Unfruitful imaginings can slow our progress and even bring us to a halt if we get bogged down in worry. It was said well this way:

Most of my ills I have cured
And the most I have always survived
But the very worst ones I've endured
Are the ones that never arrived!

In the movie K-19, which is about a nuclear submarine that malfunctioned in numerous ways, the protagonist who engineered the sub fights his fear about what would happen to him if he went into the nuclear core to salvage the engine. He encountered struggles with real and imagined fears that tore him apart mentally. Finally, he had the courage to enter the containment area and make the necessary welds to save the sub. He overcame the latent fears and dealt with the practical ones. The sub came out of it with most of its crew alive and well.

Real difficulties can be attacked and solved; but worry and negative imaginings just waste our time and need to be set free. Do you have the courage to seek such freedom?

November 11

Injustice anywhere is a threat to justice everywhere.

Dr. Martin Luther King, Jr.

Dr. Martin Luther King, Jr., had great insights into social complexities, far beyond his initial role as a preacher. King could see problems more clearly than most. And he had the skills and confidence to charge problems like a bull, not shrivel like a bull weevil, like many would have.

I respect King highly not just for his speeches, letters and books, but for his having the courage and faith to become an instrument of peace who saw injustice and did whatever it took—jail-time, receiving death threats, overcoming enormous pressures—to follow his light within.

King represents peacemaking at its most influential and spiritual stages. I thank God for this true example of Christ's loving ways and hopeful gaze.

We SHALL overcome!

November 12

> *We are most often in the dark when we are most certain,*
> *and the most enlightened when we are most confused.*
>
> M. Scott Peck, author of *The Road Less Traveled*

Sometimes, to be totally certain comes from self-righteous insecurity. In 1984, I was totally sure that a song I was listening to was NOT George Benson (based on his previous works). I surprisingly found out later that it WAS Benson. This sparked a curiosity in me: "How come I was so certain and SO wrong?"

I thought long and hard and soon realized that I felt I needed to be *the expert* in order to find acceptance with my peers. I remember how my friend clammed up in quiet disgust after I insisted upon my point—that it was another artist singing, not Benson. That silence rang in my memory as I re-thought the incident many times, realizing how wrong I was. The main mistake was not that I said it wasn't Benson singing, but that I *pushed my way through* and socially alienated myself—even if for a moment—from my friend. This insistence on being the know-it-all seems to be a family trait I learned growing up and I have spent years & tears trying to restructure it. "You just have to KNOW. No questions—just know!"

Adolf Hitler is an example of a person who was seemingly "enlightened" and definitely brilliant. He created a war machine that nearly conquered the world, yet he was bathed in a confusion of morals and values that brought down the Third Reich, and all his dreams of power and honor.

Conversely, the morning that the first woman attempting to swim across the English channel reached fog bank, she stopped swimming. Her mates in the accompanying boat asked if she was too tired. "No, it's the fog. I can't see my way ahead." She gave up, only a few hundred yards from the English shore. Her disorientation and disillusionment brought her attempt to a halt.

Have you ever been in an upward spiral that was heading nowhere, or a downward spiral that was heading towards significance? As a person with bipolar disorder, my many manic rises have, at times, led to much insignificance, while my downward depressive bouts have often led to a greater of compassion and understanding.

Yet the mania has brought the gifts of energy and creativity, while depression has slammed me with morose thoughts and ugly, painful feelings. So I guess it goes both ways.

Indeed, we are all probably filled with contradictions. The trick is to take the good and leave the rest. What disparities in your life can you recognize—and do you have the insight and courage to *take the good and leave the rest?*

November 13

> *Success is having a positive expectancy of winning*
> *and taking every setback as temporary.*
>
> *Lou Tice*

In the movie *Clara's Heart*, Whoopi Goldberg plays a Jamaican nanny named Clara who encourages the teenage boy in the family to strive for his best. He begins the show with a losing attitude toward his skills swimming and gets humiliated in a swim challenge by some popular stud.

Clara is fiercely loyal to the boy even when he breaks a confidence. But when he mimics her Jamaican accent, her friends are so impressed that they "adopt" him as their own. This was a confidence the boy fiercely craved and gladly received.

The boy "finds himself" and his confidence sky-rockets when he challenges his "humiliator" to a rematch and is triumphant. He learns how to incorporate this positive expectancy into all aspects of his life.

Clara's influence is crucial. She gives him the most precious gift of all—the ability to see himself as good, competent and lovable. He also picks up on her lightheartedness and her hope that things will work out. This "positive expectancy" becomes his mode of operating as he charges toward a bright future.

Thank God for nannies!

November 14

> *The 3 hardest tasks in the world:*
>
> 1) *To return love for hate*
> 2) *To include the excluded*
> 3) *To say "I was wrong"*
>
> *Sydney Harris*

#1: God calls us to this unique challenge—Jesus
  being the example—raising a torch to light the path.
    If my Christian faith is to mean anything,
     it must include the calling to love and
      and not hate…to find the good in
       others, no matter what the
        circumstances.

#2: To love in a different way, by bringing in the
  un-welcomed, the excluded, the unpopular.
    We've all probably been there, out-of-
     bounds, left out, on the bench at one
      time or another…and
       what a feeling it is to be wel-
        comed in from the cold.
         These are moments we
          will probably never
           forget.

#3: Saying you made a mistake, admitting an
  offense is a grace in itself. This is humil-
    ity in action—become the path for
     others to stride over, then lifted
      up and given a higher place
       in the world of
        awareness
         and truth.

November 15

There is no sweeter prayer than a grateful heart.

Fr. Anthony de Mello

Gratitude

sun setting in cool April sky
but for the Grace of God go I
a day gone by and I hadn't thought
or noticed gifts given I had not sought

it hit me hard to serve a meal
to the disadvantaged, the poor—for real
and in their faces I saw myself
my hidden ghost upon a shelf

but when I closed the door to leave
God said to me "Do you not believe
these very people you served today
could have been you, or could be you someday?"

my throat tightened with a throbbing heart
as I realized I'd forgotten the most important part
of my faith, religion and spirituality
it is <u>gratitude</u> that needs to be most important to me

for it is God's Almighty plea
for us to know and come and see
that thankfulness is a grand virtue
as faith and hope and love are too

as I drove away in awe of God's Grace
with a simple message and a smile on my face
"too say 'thanks' as often as I say 'please'
and to see Him in the least of these"

Corsair

312

November 16

Always be smarter than the people who hire you.

Lena Horne

Employment is a grace—a gift. In the movie *Dave*, Kevin Kline plays Dave Kovak, a DC temp agency manager who was hired as a presidential look-alike when the real president had a stroke. Ironically, he becomes a "temp" at the Whitehouse.

Dave completely changes the tone of the administration. He decides to make it the job of "his" administration to get a job for anyone who wants one, an idea seen as naïve and unrealistic on Capitol Hill. But Dave truly believes in its importance, observing how a person looks like they're walking on a cloud the day they get a job—having seen this often at his temp agency. Dave makes the best of his time as president, showing an optimism, interest and youthfulness that the real president just didn't have.

Sure, be smarter than your boss—but also be thankful for the opportunity to serve others in WHATEVER context. And be proud of what you do and do it well.

As Dave proved, there is **dignity** in every legitimate job—whether shoe salesman, fast food worker or US President—don't ever forget that!

November 17

God gave us our relatives; thank God we choose our friends.

Ethel Waters

Some of our family members turn out to be cherished friends. One of my best friends is my oldest brother. He has been there for me through thick and thicker, and I love him as a brother <u>and</u> a friend.

Yet, we get to choose our friends, people with whom we share time and space, interests and activities. When I moved from Minneapolis to Milwaukee four years ago, I went for many months in my apartment alone. Oh yes, I had people in my life—church, choir, volunteer activities, work—yet only had two occasions where I spent time with others in my apartment! Two in a whole year! It was a lonely existence.

Then I met my girlfriend—well, actually, she wasn't my girlfriend when I met her—but she changed my life. Finally I had someone to talk to, do things with, just be with. This friendship has meant so much to me! Now Sandra is my wife.

I can hardly remember the past days of loneliness that swarmed over my life like wasps. I now have a best friend, a mate, a companion, an encourager with me every day....and someone I can show my love and affection to also. My closest friend has become my closest family.

Thank God for friends who bring us out, and love us just for who we are! And thank God for *best friends* who bring life to Life!

November 18

Success, fame, fortune—they're all illusions.
All there is that is real is the friendship that two can share.

Scarecrow, The Wiz

Ironically, this quote came from the mouth of Michael Jackson in the 1978 movie, *The Wiz*, before Jackson had taken away his African facial features with plastic surgery. Jackson gave a contradictory example of the above quote, as fame and fortune seemed to rule his life.

Yes, "fame & fortune" <u>are</u> illusions but not "success." We succeed every time we reach a worthy goal and set another one. We succeed every time we forgive another. We succeed every time we channel our anger into positive ways, not negative.

Imagine if success were an illusion. We would have nothing to strive for, no goals needed to motivate us. Many people in many cultures at many different times most likely saw that there was no way to succeed...the enslaved, the conquered, to lowly, the homeless. I see it as our charge to bring dignity to all people, no matter their stature or status in life. Success is only possible *if we see success as possible.* And any way we can bring others hope and enlightenment will open up the door—even a crack—for them to see the possibilities of finding fulfillment.

What ways can you bring hope to others—to increase
their chances of success?

November 19

*When you really, really understand where someone's
coming from, your most natural response is respect,
caring, empathy—not judgment.*

Dr. Alan Zimmerman

Fact is, we rarely know the states of those we encounter. Someone who acts rudely may just be having one of the worst days of the year, or even their life, because of a recent death of a loved one or some other circumstance. Or that angry woman in the grocery aisle may be steeped in fear and bewilderment over a letter from the IRS claiming she will soon be audited.

But when we have the opportunity to really listen to another and learn the particulars of a stressful or painful situation, it often becomes quite easy to be empathetic.

It's important to realize that we need to be caring and optimistic as much as possible because we most often will never know what's really happening in the mind and heart of another unless it's shared in a trusting environment. Our smile and good-natured-ness may just bring someone back from the edge of despair.

Just because someone seems pleasant and unbothered doesn't mean they aren't going through stressful or even life-altering events. The heart cannot be deciphered by a facial expression. Also, we will, most often, never know how we will affect those around us. Our actions may have positive effects that we will never know about.

My mom told me that someone at church whom she had never met came up to her and told her how much of an inspiration she was. My mom was shocked by the pronouncement, never seeing her faithful church attendance as being something to be praised. We never know when someone is watching us, so we need to be *a good example* as often as possible.

Wouldn't the world be a much better place if we ALL saw the value of being a good example to others?

November 20

We all need a hope-filled teacher at some time, to help us move on.

Corsair

How important is a teacher? A tutor? A mentor? In February of 1977, my hockey coach, Mr. Peterson, held me back on the ice to try one last time—on this final practice of the year—to teach me how *to take my man out of the play.* This was a key skill for a defenseman.

He came at me with the puck, faked to his left and there I was—standing still in the middle of the rink. Encouraging me now, he said, "Watch my stomach—I bet I won't go anywhere without it!" He came toward me a second time, faked right and sped left—and UGH! I missed him again!

Finally, he said the words that would change my hockey skills and my confidence forever: "Melch! Watch my stomach and NOTHING ELSE! Take my mid-section out of the play!" When he came at me fast, faked right, then left, and I fell for none of it. He cut right again and I forcefully took his stomach out of the play—and the rest of him with it! I had it! I **KNEW IT** now!

The next weekend, in our big game in Duluth, Minnesota, I did something that surprised everyone on the team, including me. An opponent came down the ice in a huff and I not only took him out of the play but launched him into the air with a hip check that came out of nowhere! My teammates stood up and cheered as I chased down the puck and continued play. What power a little hands-on teaching can have!

This was definitely one of the defining moments in my past that encouraged me to become a teacher and a tutor. My hockey coach had planted a seed in five minutes of extra instruction that will live on in all I do and affect all those I encounter as teacher. Bravo, Coach Peterson!

November 21

> *When you're going through hard times, it's like money*
> *in the bank . . . you learn humility, empathy and sensitivity.*
>
> *Paul Kolars*

Does suffering have a meaning in your life? My friend Paul seemed to have a handle on it. He told me of moments of struggle in his life at a critical time when I was choking down a life of seeming insignificance and stifling unemployment. His words were so significant that I chose to write them down and share them here.

His observation and encouragement has helped lead me on a mission to find out what "makes people tick." One of the lessons I have come to understand is that, yes, suffering CAN be a blessing—if we decide to find the benefits that the painful situations may be offering us.

Having bipolar disorder, *a hereditary chemical imbalance in the human brain that can cause dramatic mood fluctuations and thought distortions*, I have definitely had my *very up* and *very down* days, mixed in with plenty of joy <u>and</u> suffering. It's been said by Sydney Smith (a man who lost both hands in World War II) that, "It's not what you have lost that matters, but what you have left." Grand advice for anyone suffering from a disability! If we only focus on our losses, this is what we will bring about—more despair.

But by focusing on, and being grateful for, our gifts—even amid our despair—we will most likely bring about the good! Sounds so simple, but, in my view, it's true. Suffering has its benefits—"humility, empathy, sensitivity"—yet only if we take ownership of these redeeming qualities and move toward them.

November 22

"I hate idiotic technology!"

Corsair

My father had a new-fangled Lincoln Town Car in the 1980s that had "idiotic technology" which made one so "taken care of" that it went beyond the call of "luxury" and into stupidity.

First, the rear view mirror had a little motor to switch positions at night when its sensor detected a car coming close enough to create annoying glare.

Next, when its headlights had a sensor that detected when a car/truck was getting close enough for frontal glare problems, and the high beams would switch to low. We found out how stupid and even dangerous this function was when coming home one night in a downpour and the on-coming traffic's lights couldn't be detected, and the high beams wouldn't shut off—which blinded the on-coming traffic. Not good!

The final unneeded Lincoln technology was discovered one day while I was washing the car. I had been cleaning out the trunk and when I went to close it I heard a "clump," as if something had been shifted and was obstructing the closure. So I reached into the trunk with my right hand and the trunk closed down on my hand! The dumbest "luxury," a self-closing trunk! Luckily, I had the keys available and avoided an embarrassing and possibly damaging situation.

My question is—*are we so lazy these days* that technology needs to cater to such useless and frivolous uses of "technology"?

November 23

There is a purpose for our lives far grander and more significant than perhaps we might ever have considered.

David McNally

It's been mentioned before that Christopher Reeve was famous for his numerous portrayals of Superman in the 1980s. Little did he know that he would become a *Superman* of a different type in years to follow. In June of 1995, Reeve was injured in a horseback riding accident which left him paralyzed from the neck down.

Although in an electric wheelchair and intermittently breathing through a plastic air tube, Reeve and his wife Donna started a nonprofit organization to find a cure for spinal cord injuries. They had raised millions of dollars for research—efforts that have made great strides in finding solutions for this type of injury.

I saw Reeve at a speaker's convention in 1998 and of the seven speakers, he was the most sincere speaker and had the most worthwhile information. There were some pretty strong speakers who spoke that day—Zig Ziglar, Brian Tracy, Kirby Puckett—but Reeve showed them all up.

It amazed me how a man with such a grave disability could speak from the heart with such dignity and poise. I didn't see on that stage a man with a disability but a Superman still flying high. Reeve recently died because of complications with his disability but he lived as a man with a fulfilling purpose and inspired those who heard him to seek their ultimate purpose too.

November 24

> *My satisfaction with myself and my satisfaction*
> *with other people are directly proportional.*
>
> *Sue Atchley Ebaugh*

Have you ever tried to respect another when you're not respecting yourself? This was what it was like in junior high for me. I didn't know how to love or respect myself. It was a mess! And to love and respect others came slowly, as I was able to *discover myself* and see my goodness.

I remember in 9th grade making fun of a developmentally disabled boy in our school who wasn't present, but his neighbor was—the teacher whose class I was in. He brought me out on the hall and scolded me fiercely for my insensitivity. It seems I had had a need to cut down others in order to feel better. This shaming experience with the teacher made me much more sensitive—and eventually, compassionate.

Can you remember time when you were having a hard time seeing your brightness & loveliness and therefore couldn't give to others? I see it as a part of the human condition....we cannot GIVE what we do not have.

Ironically, I ended up working as a special education teacher's assistant for many years—tutoring students similar to the one I had teased so many years before. The compassion I had learned in 9th grade paid off in this job—many times over.

It's a multi-dimensional process of learning to love and respect ourselves, and learning our lessons along the way. It makes the whole world work better when we increase self-love and then are able to give it to others.

If it's a matter of accepting ourselves, in what way can you do so you can share more?

November 25

*You always have to look at yourself
and see what kind of compass you are.*

Loyce R.

These wise words from an acquaintance reminded me of a story:

A man in India was walking into a village one day when he spotted a Sinyahsee (kind of a spiritual wanderer who saw the sky as his roof, the forest as his walls and God as his protector...so he just wandered from village to village, as the breeze blows a dried leaf).

The man grew very excited upon seeing the Sinyahsee and ran up to him, calling out, "Give me the stone—give me the precious stone!"

"What are you talking about?" said the Sinyahsee.

"I had a dream last night," said the man, "and in it God Himself told me ...'you will see a Sinyahsee in the village tomorrow, and if he gives you the precious stone he has, you will be the richest man in the world!'...Do you have the stone?"

The Sinyahsee rummaged around in his satchel and pulled out a huge diamond— the biggest diamond in the world!

"Oh!! Will you give it to me?!" cried the man.

"Sure," said the Sinyahsee, "I found it in my travelings—I think in a forest somewhere." How great was the man's surprise and his joy!

Being the middle of the day, the Sinyahsee walked on and sat under a tree, to get out of the hot rays of the sun. The man, too, sat beneath a nearby tree to ponder his treasure. He thought for hours and hours. In time, his face changed from a glowing smile to a calm seriousness.

Then, as the sun was nearly setting, the man got up, slowly walked over to where the Sinyahsee was sitting, carefully handed the diamond back to the Sinyahsee and said:

*"Here...I don't want this diamond . . . but
could you give me the riches that make it so easy for you
to give this thing away?"*

November 26

Prayer is not about getting. It is being mindful
of the moment and perceiving the magic in the mundane.

unknown

Being mindful…experiencing the moment…it's been said that these are spiritual practices. Why? Possibly because the mind can be in so many other places than in the moment. It can be in a dreadful past, or a fearful future. It can be in a fantasy world or an over-serious mode that allows for no humor or even clear vision.

In 1981, I came up with an acronym that helps in discovering mindfulness. I was riding the campus bus down the hill my freshman year of college—as the newly forming spring leaves washed a light green hue through the windows of the bus. It was peaceful and calm; then suddenly I realized:

Now Is All There Is…NIATI!

It was as if a pretty little bird had landed on my shoulder and chirped a beautiful tune into my ear. I saw life in a new way! Over the years I've thought of NIATI hundreds of times. It helps me see reality in a peaceful and hopeful way. It can also be a motivator for putting in a fuller effort, even when *the now* seems mundane or packed with activity. When we live life *in the present,* we most often find a view point of opportunity and hope, leading to *joy.*

November 27

Don't envy anyone—you ARE the magic!

Leo Buscaglia

Isn't *envy* one of the seven deadly sins? If not, it's close to it. Envy wastes time that we could be using to discover our talents, improving them and putting them to use for good causes. Envy keeps us stuck, avoiding our natural gifts.

When Buscaglia says "You *are* the magic," this can often only come to light through self-reflection and quiet time. If we're always *bizzy bizzy*, we may never detect the gifts that God has given us.

One gift that I quietly discovered back in 1982 was that of creating **poetry**. I began writing poetry while in college—a sudden inspiration emerging on a cold, sleety late-winter day, sitting on the shuttle bus. I was moved to describe, on paper, this old athletic building that was being torn down on the old campus. I stared out the rain-wet window of the bus at the broken-down edifice…the long railing, the high smoke stack…it looked like an old ship, half-sunken, abandoned at sea. The words flowed into my journal as I described the seemingly mundane scene in a fresh and creative manner.

From that moment, I began describing my world—inner and outer—in poetic imagery. That moment of inspiration changed my life forever! From a humble, unexpected beginning, writing poetry has become one of my most cherished talents—a gift I can express in many forms and share in myriad ways. This was a serendipitous moment that I will never forget!

What was a moment of *serendipity*—unexpected joy or positive change—that you have experienced…a moment that showed you that "you ARE the magic"?

poet

what is it to be
poet
breeze flowing thru fingers
weeks and years of thoughts and feelings
found dancing descriptively in lines of black & white
where distilled emotion
and focused images
find home

poet

be poet
be who you truly are
far from scenes of
comparison and affirming glances
here—finding self
on the pages of the heart

poet

recognizing a soul breath
catching a butterfly then letting it fly free
exposed for all to see
yet only liberated thru
catching the wind

poet

finds the simple
and creates the important
where a mere observation
becomes an entire landscape
here life comes alive
and fledgling artist
becomes

poet

Corsair

November 28

Not the greatest guru can take one step for you—
you must take it yourself.

Fr. Anthony de Mello

This bit of simple wisdom makes seeking a psychologist less of a probability and listening to the inner-self more a priority. This wisdom IS inside us, if we would only take an "inner-look."

De Mello points out the reality that, in the end, we stand alone. We have to make up our own minds how we will respond to circumstances and deal with our own emotional reactions that arise in our lives.

We can do it! This reminds me of a song we sing in our gospel choir:

Yes you can
You can do anything if you try, just try
Yes you can
But you have to believe and rely on what you have inside
You can make it through your trials
For your trials will just make you strong
You can do anything—yes you can!

Yes, there may be time when we seek professional help—that's well & good. But in the end, we must take our own steps, make our own decisions and deal with the outcomes.

I restate this pithy statement, mentioned earlier; I call it "2 X 10":

"...IF IT IS TO BE, IT IS UP TO ME..."

Something to think about.

Rich Melcher

November 29

> *Peace is more than the absence of war—*
> *it's the connection between people.*
>
> *unknown*

Lasting peace only comes when we begin to value those with whom we have been at war. Look how the USA took on rebuilding Germany and Japan after World War II. It took *valuing the other* for the USA to make these commitments to reconstruct and to follow through. It was also probably pretty good business sense to do so, strengthening democracy and building peaceful relations with such key countries.

I have a priest friend, Tom, who always gives me the same greeting: "PEACE." In time I've come to realize the significance of this greeting. It is not just some pleasant platitude. He wishes for, and prays for, peace-in-me. You see, he has seen me in some of my worst of times, struggling with bipolar disorder. In fact, he was the one who brought me to the hospital for the first time, in 1986.

Tom also wishes and prays for peace in my relationships…that I am getting along with others in my church, at my job, in my community, in my family. I believe he sees peace in our world as the ultimate goal, which starts with each of us and diffuses to the community, the country, the world. Peace is possible, even in these days of terrorism, hatred and corruption. I thank God for a friend who continually reminds me of the importance of this thing we call PEACE.

November 30

...you make judgments in a purely human way;
I pass judgment on no one...

Jesus Christ (John 8:15)

Author and speaker Stephen R. Covey once said, "You cannot judge *and* understand at the same time." Wow! What an insight! Of all the helpful and enlightening words Covey has to offer in his <u>Seven Habits of Highly Effective People</u> series, this quote has stuck with me the most. It fits well with Jesus' words above.

What does it mean NOT to judge? I believe it involves going inside ourselves and realizing "*WAGS*" = **W**e've **A**ll **G**ot *Something*...some blemish, some deficiency, some ailment that makes us feel "less than." It is these moments of *less-than-ness* that we need acceptance the most. And as we see that we're all in the same boat, we will most likely not be judgmental toward others.

I will never forget how my mother supported and loved me through some very tough times...through my first depression and many manic bouts. When we receive unconditional love from another, we *always* remember it. Jesus' proclamation that *He passes judgment on no one* is so freeing and encouraging! His example is one I truly try to follow. And I've got plenty of kind and loving people to emulate, so that when I find myself judging others, I have many places to turn for guidance.

Is there someone you model, in this realm of non-judging?
If not, do you value it enough to find a mentor in this area?

~ December ~

December 1

What we do not remember we are destined to relive.

unknown

If we forgive, must we forget? Not necessarily. If we just accept what another does, having forgiven them—totally forgetting the event or offense—we may set ourselves up for more disappointment, even abuse, down the road.

Forgiveness is one of the greatest spiritual *and* social gifts we can give to others. This may sound kind of harsh, but I believe that it doesn't mean we just wash the precipitating event from our memory—we cleanse it and draw the emotion from it. If it does come to mind, it has no power to hurt the other, or ourselves.

There is also something I call *"spiritual amends"*...here, in situations when I will most likely never see the other person again, (because of their death or my lack of knowledge of where they might be), I pray for a cleansing of the relationship in the presence of God by imagining I am with the person and asking for their forgiveness. Or, if the tables are turned, I image them asking for my forgiveness.

This spiritual bridge-building allows me to pray for the other, and whatever conflict or disappointments may have been present. I may have hurt them—they may have hurt me—it doesn't matter. I just offer it up in prayer and praise God who offers me His Presence and Grace.

I do remember when I have been forgiven, and when I have forgiven another. Forgiveness is such a blessing, a true gift from God.

December 2

*Those who suffered the most in their lives
seem to have the most to offer.*

Al Gore

Former Vice President Al Gore said this after his son was nearly killed in a severe accident years ago. He must have come to this wisdom as he and his wife, Tipper, waited and hoped and prayed those long days and nights, anticipating their son's recovery.

Suffering is the great equalizer. It brings us all down to humility and vulnerability. Yet, as Fr. Anthony de Mello stated, "We can be in pain and suffer, and we can be in pain and *not* suffer." He distinguishes between the two by saying that suffering is *being bothered* by our pain.

We may have all met people who are dying from cancer, or some other life-threatening illness, and who have shown such incredible courage, a positive presence and a steady light- heartedness. These are folk who are *not* falling prey to their pain—and are not "suffering," but coping with the pain—even rising above it.

How will you choose to deal with pain? By making it everyone's problem, or by dealing with it constructively?

December 3

Get so mad there's no stoppin' you!

George W. Stevenson, III, Milwaukee, WI

In the movie *Anger Management*, actor Adam Sandler plays a mild-mannered advertising agent who is found to have a ton of well-suppressed anger.

Actor Jack Nicholson plays a non-traditional psychologist who is out to uncover Sandler's hidden anger and help him recognize and express it. Nicholson even goes to the extent of dating Sandler's girlfriend to get him riled up! Sandler finally loses it and ends up professing his love for his girlfriend in front of a Yankee Stadium crowd—breaking through his anger problem by expressing how angry he was with Nicholson. A job well done by the renegade psychologist!

Yes, hidden anger can be toxic. Some families "don't do anger." Growing up with eight brothers and sisters, we rarely did. Anger was taboo, seemingly nonexistent—on the surface, that is. But it was there, just getting swung beneath the surface, where, as Stephen R. Covey said, it just "comes out in uglier ways."

Personally, I remember exploding on my brother because he couldn't make it to my wedding. Passive-aggressive anger was at work as I spewed angry words at him like a flowing fountain. I've had to work hard to get my hidden anger under control—and when something's hidden, it's pretty hard to get a grasp of. But it's possible.

Anger needs to be expressed, not merely in an explosion of molten-lava-language, but in more appropriate ways. It's been said that anger is "a response to perceived injustice" and that "it's not good or bad, it just IS." But when expressed the wrong way, it can be a relationship-crippler. Thankfully, my brother accepted my apology and we are back on good terms!

How do you deal with YOUR anger? Do you stuff it or find positive ways to express it?

December 4

> *Former Minnesota Vikings football coach*
> *Dennis Green's mother once told him,*
> *'If you're expecting a promotion, you better*
> *have your bags packed right then.'*

Sometimes we speak too quickly. Sometimes we get ourselves in too deep. Jimmy, who was working toward an education degree at a

Midwestern college, took a job as a camp counselor, thinking it would be a breeze and tons of fun.

This was a camp for youth with disabilities and Jimmy found himself in a much more different situation than he had expected. The campers were friendly enough, but Jimmy did more lifting and "pottying" than he had ever foreseen. His educational studies had not prepared him for the long hours and hot, muggy summer weather... and it had not prepared him for the sleep-deprived nights catering to campers' needs.

Jimmy learned huge lessons at the camp...that the greatest "education" comes on the job, and that joy comes from meeting others' needs effectively. Jimmy left summer camp with many more tools in his grab bag and ample gratitude for his wake-up opportunities.

December 5

The readiness is all.

William Shakespeare

Jane didn't think she was ready. She had researched, written outlines, set goals and practiced for the most important interview of her life. The job promotion wasn't going to just jump in front of her like some startled deer in the headlights. This was her chance to move from the #3 position to the top position, and she was going to be prepared!

A friend who assisted in the preparation finally told her that she was probably much more prepared for the crucial interview than any of the competing candidates. Also, that she was most likely the most qualified and seasoned for the job. Relax.

Jane decided to have one final sweep of her materials, then planned a day of rest, at the suggestion of her friend—the day before the interview. The next morning, she was prepared and rested, ready for whatever the interviewers would challenge her with. The interview went superbly, although it seemed to go so quickly that she wondered a bit if she had emphasized all of her main points and her outstanding strengths. Yet she left the interview with satisfaction and with her head held high.

The panel took its time to get back to her but out of 10 final candidates, she was chosen for the #2 position, moving her up one notch—yet not exactly what she wanted. But she was satisfied with the progress and soon saw the blessings and even advantages of getting the new position.

Part of her success was to let go of the reins the day before the interview and relax, peacefully. Sometimes part of the readiness needs a bit of rest and relaxation, in the midst of rigorous preparation.

December 6

In concert with God's spirit, no problem or task can be greater than our combined abilities to handle it.

Each Day A New Beginning

Do *you* believe in this? Could you believe this? If yes, then you probably possess the thing called FAITH. Faith is...believing in God and God's ability to influence our lives. When we believe that no task is too great, we believe in *our own* abilities too, and that we are competent, loving individuals.

In 1989, God gave me insight that *"I can, I will and I am,"* which has become a positive mantra in my spiritual life. It's a way to abbreviate and punctuate the existence of God's grace in every part of my existence.

"I can" comes from the Bible proclamation, "I can do all things through Christ who strengthens me," words that have found permanence in my mind, heart & soul. This CAN DO helps me in times of self-doubt or weakness, reminding me that God's grace is ever-present. CAN DO is faith in action and allows spirituality to arise in thought and emotion quickly, easily, effectively.

In the mid-1980s, in Milwaukee, Wisconsin there was a guy they called the *THE CAN DO MAN*. Reverend Gerald was the choir director and civic leader who led the *Unity in the Community Choir*, a group of 100 African American youth, except for one—I was the lone white member. He brought these inner-city kids in from the surrounding neighborhoods to sing each Monday night. Then we traveled all over the region spreading the word of God through song. It was a marvelous group, led by an inspirational leader!

I thank Jesus for these inspirations that come to us when we have faith that He can affect our lives positively, at any moment we choose to let Him in. What little inspirations has God given you lately? Do you bring them into consciousness and into your life?

December 7

Say your thing and get out of here—if they profit,
that's fine . . . and if they don't, too bad!

Fr. Anthony de Mello

To be teacher is to often not know how you have really affected another. One teacher said, "The only thing bad about teaching is you may only find out the results 20 years later." Quite a delayed reaction, huh? Maybe not a profession for immediate gratification. Personally, I happen to believe that *any* lesson offered and taken in is a huge success and brings great satisfaction to the giver!

It's up to God how people will actually benefit from our attempts to teach. I was once told, in my job at a copy shop, "Rich—you're a good teacher!" I could have received no higher compliment. My ability to patiently instruct customers how to use the machines was living evidence that I have been given the skill of teaching...especially one-on-one. I thank God for that skill.

The movie *Mr. Holland's Opus* tells the story of a music teacher who ends up feeling unappreciated after 30 years of teaching. The music department had been cut from the curriculum, and he was forced to retire. While he was cleaning out his office, his wife and son called him down to the auditorium where he was greeted by hundreds of former students, parents and other teachers and civic leaders—cheering him on.

The highlight was when the governor of the state made a surprise entrance. She happened to be one of his former students—the lead clarinetist from his first year of teaching. She was his first success story back then, and obviously his biggest success story at the present time.

The kicker was that a curtain opened up revealing an orchestra comprised of his former students, and the governor sat down in her place as first clarinet. He was motioned to come before them and lead the orchestra. They began to play his very own opus—a piece of music he had worked on all those years! There wasn't a dry eye in the place. He turned out to be the favorite teacher in the high school after all.

God gives us the grace to assist others in most any aspect of life...do we take the time to *instruct*, or do we hurriedly just do it for others to get it over with? How does the saying go? "Give a person a fish, you feed 'em for a day—teach 'em to fish, you feed 'em for a lifetime."

We're ALL teachers—do you *decide* to teach?

December 8

The purpose of life is to be a growing, contributing human being.

David McNally

How do you contribute? With your talents? Your loving actions? Your financial contributions? We all contribute somehow. The trick is to find a way to give back and be fulfilled in the process.

Mother Teresa is one of the best examples of someone who had purpose in her life. She lifted up the suffering and dying in Calcutta, India for nearly 50 years. She started the order of the Sisters of Charity with eight former students—an order that has grown into the hundreds. People say that just being in her presence was a spiritual experience. She traveled the world spreading the love of Jesus Christ and championing the cause of the poor and destitute.

This is not to say that she didn't have her own suffering times. It was found after her death in 1997 that Mother Teresa went through long stretches of time—even years—when she experienced "the dark night of the soul." These times were filled with depressed thoughts and feelings, struggles with her purpose and meaning of life, and difficulty with continuing her arduous work—serving the indigent in the gargantuan city of Calcutta.

But by the grace of God, she never stopped growing in her spirituality—even in those tough times. "Helping one by one by one," as she put it, she and her sisters assisted tens of thousands, healing their wounds and sometimes comforting them and bringing them to God with their boundless love at their time of death. The Sisters of Charity still work diligently in Calcutta and other parts of the world today—all due to one woman who knew her vocation and followed her purpose in life.

December 9

I think a pessimist is someone who
gets stuck in a mistake, and stays there.

Charlie F.

Many people experience this stuck feeling when they make a mistake. The trick is to learn from it and leave it in the past and go on…not always the easiest thing to do. Sometimes it takes years to learn a lesson from a mistake.

I can attest to this. The first day at my first *real* job, my new boss yelled at me incessantly for incorrectly operating a forklift—a machine I had never used. This year, 32 years later, I realized I had numerous options and unrecognized responsibility in the matter. All I had to do was admit that *I had no clue* how to operate the fork lift and the onus to *educate* would have fallen on him! Of course it was his responsibility, as supervisor, to make sure I was trained to operate the machine in the first place.

But my immature response was to "get back on the horse" after each improper gear shift or incorrectly pushed lever, as I tried to figure out how to run the unfamiliar machine. My inability to ask questions had put me in a vulnerable spot, and my new boss took advantage of the situation.

I have told that story over and over in the past 32, years but this year I saw MY error, MY prideful attempt to make it look like I was no fool. I finally admitted MY blunder and inability to be assertive and use common sense. It only took 32 years. Lesson learned!

December 10

> *...if you would be a man, speak what you think to-day*
> *in words as hard as cannon-balls, and to-morrow*
> *speak what to-morrow thinks in hasrd words again,*
> *though it contradicts everything you said to-day.*
>
> *Ralph Waldo Emerson*

Words I had spinning around in my head until last night when I picked up Emerson's <u>Self-Reliance</u> and re-discovered them. This marvelous book, copyright 1900, had sat on my shelf for many years, holding a truth that I sorely needed to hear.

Do you change your mind a lot? My creativity is based on shifting from one idea to the next better idea, and I had been benignly made to think that this was a problem. It's called "editing." My style is to seek the BEST solution, not to stick with something that has proved to be inferior or outdated. The above quote confirmed my stance and gave me a new sense of myself as a creative artist.

To flow from one idea to the next based on new information received is, to me, THE WAY to function. Oh yes, I perform many perfunctory acts such as how I balance my check book or how I drive my car. But the joy of true creativity can, in my belief, only be acted upon from flexibility—not just functionality.

I have been working on an *interpersonal integrity philosophy* for a year and a half, changing it slightly over 75 times, until, now, I have it in a simple 10-concept form that is pithy and powerful. But it took hundreds of hours to get my *"Authentic Living Code"* to where it is...an impossible task were it not for the essence of Emerson's wisdom above!

Thank God for those ideas that roll around inside our heads, influencing us toward the good, in search of the better—eventually discovering the best!

December 11

"Remember people, brevity is good!"

Minnesota high school English teacher

My friend Larry recently gave me the above quote after he asked me to write a personal character testimony about himself for a cooking school he is attending. "Nothing long" said my friend, but with some people it's hard to keep comments of their excellence short. He's a fantastic guy who exudes many wonderful attributes...compassion, enthusiastic, a real "people person." It was a bit tricky, but I kept it to 3/4-page. *Brevity is good.*

And as I wrote my new book *Discerning Bipolar Grace*, a memoir about my struggles and triumphs with bipolar disorder, I edited it six times—all the way through. It turned out to be 140 pages long—much shorter than the original text. Therefore, it is succinct and somewhat pithy...a testament to the Minnesota teacher's observation that *brevity is good!*

Miss Milly, an 85-year-old African American woman was bed-ridden when her favorite politician Hubert Humphrey died. She watched the entire funeral, noting that Billy Graham's eulogy "breathed the spirit right into those people. But then he spoke so long that he breathed the spirit right *out* of those people!" At 85, Miss Milly surely knew that b*revity is good.*

Being long-winded can definitely be a deficit, so I will close this reading because—*brevity is good.*

December 12

I didn't have anything to do, so I didn't do anything.

unknown

Apathy is not a path you want to take very often. It builds up, like plaque on the teeth, until *"nothing"* is the norm.

Sydney Smith said, "Don't do nothing because you can only do a little—do what you can!" This incremental style of reaching success is crucial to those who "don't have anything to do." This "Do What You Can" attitude comes from being observant and optimistic even in the face of boredom and apathy—leading the way to productivity and effective living.

A Chinese proverb reads, "The journey of 1,000 miles begins with a single step"...a crucial step in thought and action for anyone dwelling in apathetic ways. That first step leads to another first step, and another, and another—until we can see a trail of success behind us. Then we can view the path ahead and plot, plan and anticipate future successes.

Timothy Robbins plays Andy Duphresne in the movie *Shawshank Redemption.* He is suffering from the boredom and stagnant routine of prison life, and cries out to a friend in desperation, "*You've got to get busy livin', or get busy dyin'!*" He had just been released from "the hole" after two months of solitary confinement, and was at a crossroads—whether he wanted to go on or give it up. He *does* make a decision. I decides to follow through on a reak-out that he has planned for 10 years. And he succeeds! This innocent man finally found his freedom.

In what ways are YOU "gettin' busy livin'?" How can you
bring more excitement and passion into your life?

December 13

*The successful person appreciates the fact that failures
are nothing more than a state of the mind, (an attitude).
This person believes that the way to react to failure is not
with fear, but with curiosity... 'Why did the mistake happen?'*

Dynamics of Personal Motivation

Oh, if I would have learned this in adolescence! So many painful moments could have been avoided. Guess I need to learn it now. I was 16 and trying to be cool, so I decided to drive my two-wheel drive truck up this muddy path. I got so stuck that it took two 4-wheel-drive trucks an hour to get me unstuck! It was a mess that could have been avoided with a little foresight and common sense.

But I continued my antics for another two years, getting the truck stuck on a frozen lake and driving dangerously in my Mom's little yellow Volkswagen. It took me until I had to start paying for the up-keep of the car for me to learn the lesson that a car was not for kicks, but for transportation.

Looking back, I see now my motivation—to be popular, to be liked. But one needn't act a fool in order to be liked. Expressiveness and being conversational work much better. This is where my curious mind has led me to—seeing a young man who was *driven* to get attention. And I keep that at a distance these days. Being a loving, generous man will get me all the attention I need. There are always lessons to learn.

December 14

You just can't take a lion and throw 'em in a cage
and expect 'em to be thankful for the shelter that you gave!

The Badlies

Expectations—unspoken, sunken—can be dangerous enemies in time. Expectations have a long half-life. They don't die easily. Do you have any suppressed expectations that have come back to haunt you? We probably all do, if we put our minds to thinkin' about it.

I had expected to find fulfillment in a previous love relationship yet my ideas and preferences were kept deep inside, buried and often forgotten. Our relationship had been *built on the sands* of non-confrontation and hidden views and needs, on my part—and, now that I think about it, on her end too. Personally, I was unable—or, maybe unwilling—to share my feelings and opinions openly. I had learned early in the relationship that to criticize or even admonish her was not acceptable. This killed about ½ of my nerve endings, and consequently ½ of our possibilities for intimacy because much intimacy comes from *working through* disagreements and conflicts. We avoided critiquing or correcting one another—a very unrealistic, strangling and contorted way to live.

It ultimately ended in our permanent separation, and we both had to start at base one. Yes, these unheard and unspoken opinions and preferences can be killers. To express ourselves may take courage and effort, but this is better in the end than to suffer the daggers of self-suffocation caused by an unexpressed inner-life, or the pain and hollowness of a broken relationship.

I'm learning how to more fully express myself in a new relationship. It's difficult, at times, but THIS house is being *built on the rock* of honest sharing. I'm not hiding my preferences and opinions—nor is she. This makes for an intimacy I have never experienced before—and I love it!

December 15

What happens when you are affirmed is that you receive the
gift of yourself from another person…you receive it,
accept it, possess it, and now you possess yourself, and
no one can disturb you anymore.

Dr. Conrad Baars

What is meant by "no one can disturb you any more"? Well, when you know yourself & possess yourself, you have a clear sense of yourself and your inner-beauty, which brings serenity—which can pull you through most any hard time.

In the meditation book, *Touchstones*, it reads, "Serenity develops, not by eliminating life's difficulties, but by having a reliable relationship with our Higher Power in the midst of it all." It is a very spiritual process, this journey of self-discovery & becoming our true selves.

Having a close relationship with our version of a Higher Power—be it God, or Jesus, or Allah, or Nature—is an important part of the process also. Serenity comes through faith that we are OK & lovable just as we are, and in faith that we have loved ones who believe in our potential and progress. Encouragement, from others and our Higher Power, is crucial to our psycho/socio-emotional and spiritual health…and even our survival.

December 16

It's who you are—that's your power!
Be yourself and let the world take notice.

Fame (the movie)

My wife Sandra and I recently began teaching a creative writing course to urban grade schoolers. It uses a 7-point philosophy that focuses around character development and classroom coherence. The class uses an acronym I came up with 4 years ago…RROCKSS, which stands for:

<u>R</u>espect
<u>R</u>esponsibility
<u>O</u>bservation
<u>C</u>ooperation
<u>K</u>nowledge
<u>S</u>afety
<u>S</u>ervice

With this structure, we got kids writing about themselves and what they saw around them. It has turned out to be a marvelous adventure for Sandra and me. As a part of the program, we chose to have our students recite a short reading before each session to motivate them...

*You have
the power in you
to make your dreams
come true!
Use the power!
Share the power!
<u>BE</u> the power!!*

They memorized it immediately and began repeating it back to us at the next session. In them we saw the world opening up, as they wrote in their journals. We saw the power in them take wing and decided to publish their best writings in a packet for them to share with family and friends. They LOVED it!

As we develop this program, we will always remember this first class and how they shared themselves so freely with us. These young students showed <u>us</u> that they could BE THE POWER!

December 17

*Do not compare yourself to others, for you
are a unique and wonderful creation. Make your
own beautiful footprints in the snow.*

Barbara Kimball

Think about those footprints in the snow . . . how brief, how delicate, how short-lived and transient—easily trampled by another, lost in the sun's influence, melting in springtime warmth. But such is the nature, most often, of our actions and ways here on earth—short-lived, *yet significant…* much more than a snowy stomp on winter white.

Comparison often keeps us from acting and from recognizing the good that is within us. When we give in to comparison, we find ourselves downgraded, pressured and in an unnatural posture. This hides our goodness, lost in an unhealthy use of our observation skills.

"Becoming *authentic*" is a term used to describe the process of valuing our uniqueness and proactively seeking ways to express this *authenticity*. It may be through art, or dance, or writing or sports—through any creative venture…but I see becoming authentic as one of the main components in creating a diverse and vibrant *spiritual* life.

We are unique, like those snowflakes, not-a-one alike—unique, yes, *just like everyone else*! And therefore valuable, like gold or precious jewels— valued in our beauty, our rare brilliance, and our priceless-ness. So, no need to compare—"Compare brings despair"—no need to put ourselves down… we ARE unique and wonderful creations!

December 18

Faith is . . . the ability to carry on with our plans, or to be true to our work, even though we feel discouraged or tired.

Touchstones

Just imagine for a moment what Mother Teresa of Calcutta came in contact with every day. She worked with the poorest of poor, in a squalid, hot environment with the dying and destitute in India.

Mother Teresa was once asked if she was succeeding in serving this population in sprawling Calcutta...she answered, "I am not called to be successful—I am called to be *faithful*."

"Called to be faithful"—a call to believe in that which we cannot see or even, at times, sense. Yet it is this call that we are ever-needing and being brought back to...to believe in the God of our understanding, above our fears, above our memories, above our emotions. Faith transcends all of these pervading influences and offers us direction and peace—when we seek it earnestly.

Mother Teresa was certainly true to her call, caring for India's underprivileged...and she carried on in faith, even in sight of suffering and death. She gave us all an amazing **example** of how to live the Christian life.

December 19

Love your enemies and pray for those who persecute you.

Jesus Christ, Holy Bible

Talk about a high order! But Jesus even did this as He hung in agony on the cross. He forgave His persecutors for torturing and humiliating Him, for meeting a man of peace with violence and scorn.

It's such a temptation to curse those whom we see as persecutors—our adversaries. It's not uncommon, although quite childish, to strike back or throw hate stares, gossip about or shun those who intimidate us. But these are the exact situations Jesus was talking about—a time to look beyond the bad behavior and plant *seeds*, not weeds.

Jesus had a unique way of ushering in peace and even tranquility—by giving the other a break and letting the displeasing circumstances slide. I remember the story of Jesus inviting himself to dine with the Pharisee, Zacchaeus, and by giving Zacchaeus the chance to be close to Him, Zacchaeus made sweeping changes in his life.

I bet Jesus prayed often for the Pharisees who gave Him such a hard time. In doing so, we too, like Jesus, can honor others and help them benefit spiritually by praying for their well-being—praying that they be released from whatever is causing them to act negatively toward us and others.

It's pretty obvious that Jesus' WAY was not the common way of acting. But He had His reasons—the main one being...bringing forth The Kingdom of God through His loving and patient gestures. And His uncommon influence lives on today, 2000 years later, as we struggle to *do His will*.

December 20

To live without hope is to cease to live.

Dostoyevski

Have you ever been there—hopeless, truly hopeless? You'd know it if you had...a future so dark and gloomy that the present becomes nearly unbearable.

Imagine a passenger train at night, with no headlamp, proceeding ever so slowly, inch by inch, wondering if there is any track laid before it... *snailing* slowly in fear that it will soon reach the end of the tracks and slide off, rolling down a steep embankment to its doom.

We have to have a future in order to have a *now*. If you find yourself stuck, like the inching train, please reach out for help. There IS hope—there is *always* hope! You may just need a lamp to show you the way, in order to start speeding down the track again.

In my most hopeless of times, struggling with bipolar highs and lows, there was always a shaft of light streaming into my dark and lonely corner. Hope came in 1990 when I started a job with a mental health organization that provided dignified work, housing and a community of people in the same boat. I stayed with them for 8 years, and honed many of my skills and abilities while gaining interpersonally and *intra*-personally.

Don't give up hope, even if you have but a pin-hole of light with which to see. Hope multiplies quickly, when cultivated. To live WITH hope is to live abundantly.

December 21

> *I'm beginning to suspect that I cannot even know*
> *my soul except as I disclose it. I suspect that I will*
> *know myself 'for real' at the exact moment that I have*
> *succeeded in making it known through my*
> *disclosures to another person.*
>
> *Sidney Jourard*

To discover someone through *a meeting of hearts, minds and souls* is a holistic way of loving another. In truly sharing the self, as in the manner depicted in the quote, we *find ourselves* in the process. Those who seek this heart/mind/soul connection often discover happiness in the interaction:

The HEART ~
sharing feelings & dreams, the inner story of emotion
and passion…creates a bond so strong and rich and beautiful;
then often comes tenderness and empathy.

The MIND ~
sharing ideas, stories, impressions and information helps
two people get to know what each is about as thinker and
knower...discussing books and movies and the day's events
can bring a camaraderie that is not easily shaken.

The SOUL ~
this is the deepest gift, sharing the most tender self,
the spiritual side...sharing the soul—this "one unit of God"
placed in us by our Creator—enlivens us by encouraging
and exploring this deeper self...sometimes honored by a glance,
a poem, a touch. The soul is effervescent in the presence of one
who truly understands and accepts its uniqueness and worth.

"Heart/Mind/Soul love" is eternal, yet difficult to find. But the journey
to discover this love is well worth the search!

December 22

*There is more in us than we know. If we can be made
to see it, perhaps for the rest of our lives, we
will be unwilling to settle for less.*

Kurt Keuhn, founder of Outward Bound

Do you know who you are? Almost sounds like a ridiculous question. But, do you know how you can tell? Not by moments of smooth sailing, but in times of rough waters.

When is the last time you were in a crisis? In a quandary? Possibly a car accident, experiencing the death of a parent, or watching a child struggle in school—it is most often not by the fun and great and easy times that we develop character, but by the difficult times. A wise person once said that tough times are like money in the bank, bringing empathy and sensitivity that wouldn't have developed otherwise.

347

Rich Melcher

A young man named Terry Fox, who had lost a leg due to cancer, decided to run across his native Canada to raise money for cancer research. He ran a marathon a day for many months—using a prosthesis (an artificial leg), and raised millions of dollars for this worthy cause! His contribution was outweighed only by his courage and fortitude.

> Struggles CAN be transformed into opportunities of promise
> when we have faith that *God can make a way.*

December 23

> *It's not what happens to us that affects our behavior...*
> *it's our interpretation of what happens to us.*
>
> *Stephen R. Covey*

One night, during a thunderstorm, the prize horse of a man in a small village ran away. It broke down its stall and pranced off into the countryside. Villagers came rushing to console him saying "What a misfortune! This is terrible!" The man responded, "Maybe so, maybe not."

Days later the horse came running back into town followed by 21 wild horses. The villagers exhorted, "What a stroke of great fortune!" The man responded, "Maybe so, maybe not." Then, the man's son tried to ride one of the wild horses, fell off and broke his leg. The villagers retorted, "What bad luck!" The man replied, "Maybe so, maybe not."

The next week the army came to the small village taking every able-bodied young man to fight in a current campaign—the man's son couldn't go on account of his broken leg. The villagers sounded out, "What a blessing!" The man repled, "Maybe so, maybe not."

And the story could go on & on...it is all in how we look at a situation that makes the difference. This man chose a neutral stance which saved him from a ton of emotional upheaval. What way do you chose to look at "problems"?

December 24

Don't let the past remind us of what we are not now.

Crosby, Stills & Nash

Self-depreciation is a killer attitude. When we put ourselves down for past failures, and make those past moments a part of our current reality, we do ourselves a great disservice.

In the movie *Forrest Gump*, Forrest says, "Mama said, '...you gotta put the past behind you before you can move on.'" Sound advice for any human being who wants to live a life of healthy peacefulness.

It is the making-the-negative-past-into-the-NOW that often gets people in trouble. It doesn't take a psychologist to see how detrimental regurgitating past failures can be to a person. It's OK to realize how failures can help us learn, but once we've learned our lessons, it's time to cut the rope and set them free—like snipping a kite string and allowing the flailing kite to drift from view.

These words of Crosby, Stills & Nash ring true: *Don't let the past remind us of what we are not now!*

December 25

You shall love the Lord, your God, with all your heart,
with all your soul, with all your mind and with all
your strength...and your neighbor as yourself.

Jesus Christ, Holy Bible (Mark 12)

What does it mean to love the Lord? To love God? Are we loving some nebulous majesty, some hidden cheer leader, some lofty cloud of all knowing?

Rich Melcher

I often see God as *mystery and paradox.* God is so huge *and* so minute. God is all loving, while being everything *and* nothingness all at once. God is ultra personal while resting in our unconscious, often un-noticed.

The life of Jesus Christ is what brings God "down-to-earth" for me. He *SHOWED* us how to live out the above Bible quote—His words of challenge and promise bring us a game plan for life. And with *His example,* we have many of the answers of how to live our lives.

For me, this is one of the most important readings in the <u>Holy Bible</u> because it lays out a challenge that is reachable and inspirational—in fact, it was recited at my wedding. I chose it. I thank You, Jesus, for Your powerful words, stories & acts that have changed the lives of so many, so deeply, so fully.

December 26

The work of the individual still remains the spark that moves mankind forward.

Igor Sikorsky

Imagine being jailed for 27 years, many of those years toiling in hard labor, never knowing if you'd get out, working the quarries, cracking rock, but still having hope . . .

This was the past of one Nelson Mandela who made it through all those years of pain and stress as a political prisoner in South Africa... and coming out of that horror to lead his people to victory, defeating apartheid! Out of the ugliness of prison, Mandela became the South African president, where he served for many years.

Although none of us can do it alone, it still takes personal motivation and discipline to get things done. Mandela is a quintessential example of how one individual can make a huge difference in the lives of others. He proved the fact that "the work of the individual still remains the spark" that moves the WORLD forward!

December 27

*Too often we're too quick to criticize
and too late to praise.*

Tom Schumann

It was five years ago, as I sat back to listen to the critique of my speech in the public speaking club with which I had been a member for two years. I was expecting *some* praise of how I had taken on a difficult topic—bipolar disorder. I was expecting a number of suggestions about how I could improve my approach also. I was expecting a complimentary connection.

What I got was much different. The "critique," which was to last no more than 2-3 minutes, went on for six! And <u>none</u> of it good. She didn't like my style, or how I fiddled with my ring, or my voice modulation or how I expressed myself, or...in her view, there was NOTHING of value in this speech, which took a lot of courage to give—if nothing else.

This was one of my last meetings with the group. Although I didn't really realize it until much later, I left because of how insulted and humiliated I felt by her criticisms. It was like a slap in the face and a kick in the pants all at once, and the fact that she offered no encouragement shocked me—and it went against all club guidelines. I found out later that the reason she "lost it" in her evaluation was because of the subject matter—she just wasn't used to having someone speak so up-front about mental illness. All I have to say about that is GET OVER IT!

That incident taught me the danger of a bad critique and the value of a good one. What a grand responsibility we have in our critiques of others, not to devastate them if they perform poorly but to encourage them in every way we can.

Recently my wife and I gave a creative writing class for grade schoolers in which we had the students write about various important topics. A few of them couldn't even write a sentence, but they had good printing. So in their comments for the week, they got a big "GOOD PRINTING" at the bottom of the page. What were we to do, react like the speech evaluator and throw the baby out with the bathwater?

It's so important to be an affirming person, to lift others up rather than drag them down. I love this quote by Dr. Conrad Baars:

> *What happens when you are affirmed is that you receive the gift*
> *of yourself from another person...you receive it, accept it, possess it—*
> *and now you possess yourself—and no one can disturb you anymore.*

What better way to treat others than to constantly be looking to bring out their best selves. At least, this is the respect and dignity I want to be offered by those around me. How about you?

December 28

> *As manager, you don't have to be 'high on your horse,'*
> *but you have to be <u>on</u> your horse.*
>
> *Corsair*

A friend recently spoke to me about a situation as a manager where she needed to express to a manager who reported to her that his workers needed to have more structure. This meant that the manager would have to show more leadership...and this "leadership" could cause him to be liked less by his workers.

Part of being a leader means making those tough calls, and leading people in ways they may not want to be led, at first. We can probably all remember a time in our careers when we were critiqued and *encouraged* to change aspects of our activities and habits on the job.

But managers often need to follow through on creating a workable climate where everyone is treated fairly and consistently. Remember, you don't have to be *high on your horse*—arrogant, critical and forceful—but you have to be *ON* the horse, as leader and director, fording the stream & leading the way.

December 29

You can't judge <u>and</u> understand at the same time.

Stephen R. Covey

Think about it! Name ONE TIME in your life when you were judging <u>and</u> understanding simultaneously. It seems virtually impossible—oil & water.

We've all probably had times when we've felt judged, picked on or down-graded. At these moments we were probably not feeling understood or valued.

Conversely, when we've been understood and encouraged, judging most likely was nonexistent—or, at least, set aside for the time being. We all have the need for acceptance and affirmation that provide the foundation for our social and *intra*personal lives. Judgment by others only impairs, rather than <u>re</u>pairs...casts down, rather than rescuing the cast-away. And we're ALL the cast-away, on a lonely island of brokenness, at one time or another—waiting for someone to recognize our woes and bring us to safety, or recognize our talents and bring out the best in us.

Next time you feel yourself ready to judge another, try countering with understanding instead, and see what happens. You may just discover the freedom and peace of affirming another and bringing the surprise of joy to the other's heart.

December 30

Life's most persistent and urgent question is, 'What are you doing for others?'

Dr. Martin Luther King, Jr.

In Dr. King's "I Have a Dream" speech, presented in August of 1963, during the March on Washington, King speaks of the **"fierce urgency of** now." This push toward immediate action on the part of the poor and disenfranchised seems to have been the cornerstone of King's philosophy of love in action. Whenever he could, King lived out this *urgency* in word and deed to further the Civil Rights Movement in any way possible.

In his now famous "Letter from a Birmingham Jail," King again reinforced why people of color couldn't wait—why the Movement couldn't wait—especially when "wait" really meant "never" and "forget it." King explained in this letter that the Movement must go on despite the foot-dragging by the white moderates and the hateful ways of many Southerners who backed segregation whole-heartedly.

Now it's the 2010s and the question is still fresh—"What are YOU doing for others?" You don't have to be a Dr. King to make a difference. As King once said, you just "need a heart full of love" to serve. Where can you begin to make a difference today?

In what area of your life do you experience the *"fierce urgency of now?"*

December 31

the journey has been long
and the path winding -
when the brilliant orange sun goes down
this feeling of incompleteness
veils the splendid scene
and the search
for contentment and purpose
goes on

stumbling upon the rocks
of despair and frustration
tears hide in the channels
of a deeper mind
where all is symbol and emotion

there is peace
no matter the chaos of daily life -
there is a serene meandering stream
which flows deep within
    quenching the thirst of a longing
    unexplained
        to live more fully
        to be authentic
        to be fully alive

        Corsair